With the Stroke

of a Pen

THOMAS DUNNE BOOKS

ST. MARTIN'S PRESS  NEW YORK

With the Stroke of a Pen

A STORY OF AMBITION, GREED,
INFIDELITY, AND THE MURDER OF
FRENCH PUBLISHER

Robert Denoël

A. Louise Staman

THOMAS DUNNE BOOKS.

An imprint of St. Martin's Press.

WITH THE STROKE OF A PEN. Copyright © 2002 by A. Louise Staman. All rights reserved. Printed in the United States of America. No part of this book may be used or reproduced in any manner whatsoever without written permission except in the case of brief quotations embodied in critical articles or reviews. For information, address St. Martin's Press, 175 Fifth Avenue, New York, N.Y. 10010.

www.stmartins.com

Design by Kathryn Parise

LIBRARY OF CONGRESS CATALOGING-IN-PUBLICATION DATA
Staman, A. Louise.
  With the stroke of a pen : a story of ambition, greed, infidelity, and the murder of French publisher Robert Denoël / A. Louise Staman.— 1st ed.
      p.   cm.
  Includes bibliographical references (p. 335) and index (p. 345).
  ISBN 0-312-27213-8
  1. Denoël, Robert.   2. Publishers and publishing—France—Paris— Biography.   3. Denoël (Firm)—History.   4. Publishers and publishing—France—Paris—History—20th century.   I. Title.

Z310.6.P37 S73   2002
070.5'092—dc21
[B]
                                                        2002023173

First Edition: November 2002

10 9 8 7 6 5 4 3 2 1

To Mike

for his unfailing support,
his technical expertise . . .
for everything

Contents

Introduction

During the turbulent period between the World Wars, Robert Denoël left his native Belgium, founded his own Paris publishing house,
and then proceeded to launch some of the most innovative and significant writers of the twentieth century, changing forever the face
of modern literature. At first glance, this famous and distinguished
man seems an unlikely murder victim. He took little interest in politics, intrigue, or anything outside the realm of publishing. His goal
was simply to become the foremost publisher in France. And he
nearly succeeded. Famous novelists published under the rubric of
Les Editions Denoël include Louis Aragon, Elsa Triolet, Jean Genet,
Nathalie Sarraute, Charles Braibant, Paul Vialar, René Laporte, and,
of course, the famous and infamous Louis-Ferdinand Céline, whose
innovative style has influenced such disparate international writers as
Jean-Paul Sartre, Henry Miller, and Kurt Vonnegut. Along with
Marcel Proust, Céline is considered to be one of the foremost writers
of twentieth-century France, and arguably of Europe.

In addition to novels, Denoël published important essays, art
books, and poetry. With his Three Masks collection, he presented

significant theatrical pieces, including works by Roger Vitrac and Antonin Artaud, whose ideas have profoundly influenced contemporary theater. As one of the first French publishers to recognize the significance of psychology (still in its infancy in the 1930s), Denoël also created a Psychological Library, which published and popularized works by Freud, Otto Rank, René Allendy, and other leading psychologists and psychiatrists of the time. Often serving as the only reader for his publishing house, Robert Denoël stood at the cusp of the new, the daring, winning a plethora of literary prizes, constantly working, passionate, eager to expand—and nearly always finding himself without the necessary funds for his ambitious projects. Who would wish to murder this man—or pay to have him murdered?

There were always two sides to Robert Denoël. The dark genius, Céline, may have described his publisher best when he cynically called him "a zebra," a man who played both sides of an issue. Even a cursory look at Denoël's life reveals a great many zebra characteristics, some of which go well beyond Céline's pejorative definition. A man of honor and integrity, Denoël was repeatedly accused of cheating and theft. He was at one time condemned and pursued by the Nazis (for publishing patriotic French works), by Vichy (for publishing anti-Vichy books), and by liberated France (for pandering to the Nazis). A man of principle who kept his word, he dealt on the black market and sometimes broke the law. Deeply loyal to his friends, he had powerful, dangerous enemies. Loving peace and privacy, he was the subject of sensational court trials.

Denoël's meteoric rise in publishing in the 1930s coincided with a global economic depression resulting in bankruptcy for many of his rivals. He was an ardent and admitted opportunist, always seeking more money and new ways to expand. Yet he would have done anything to publish a literary masterpiece, even if that work cost him a fortune and never made any money in return. He was himself a literary genius—famous, loved, and hated. He died as he lived—running, making deals, passionate, and always fighting for his company, Les Editions Denoël. Even as he lay dying, shot in the back, his hands were outstretched, curiously pointing in opposite directions.

Nearly every Paris newspaper carried the headlines of his murder on an allegedly deserted Paris street the night of 2 December 1945. They dutifully reported the official police version of the events of that night: "He was on his way to the theater when the car he was driving got a flat tire. He was shot while trying to repair that tire. There was another person with him in the car that night." The murder was officially listed as "a random crime of violence." And even today this version of events still stands—the murder remains officially unsolved.

Yet none of the newspapers let the story go at that. All of them implied that there was much more to this murder than the simple, straightforward police version would suggest. These newspapers, along with later scholars of the period, concluded instead that Robert Denoël died "under very mysterious circumstances." In fact, it is hard to find any account of the murder of Robert Denoël, even today, that does not contain the words "mystery," "mysterious circumstances," "mysterious aspects," or "unexplained."

My work began because I had access to the wonderful library facilities of the University of Michigan and decided to help a colleague in South Carolina, Dr. Harry E. Stewart, to fill out some of his Paris archival research on Robert Denoël. Ultimately, our collaboration resulted in an unpublished academic book on the murder of this publisher. As a teacher/researcher with two graduate degrees pertaining to contemporary France, I was naturally attracted to the life and ultimately the death of this "mysterious" publisher. And for me his story did not end with that first book. No, there had to be more. Locating materials from France, Belgium, and the United States, I continued the project alone, having no idea what incredible puzzle pieces still remained. What began for me as a single thread soon became an intricate, ever-expanding weaving that finally presented itself as a giant detailed tapestry of enormous proportions and impact reaching into the highest levels of French power, courts, and government. And even now, decades after the murder and safely on another continent, some of what I found is chilling still—and quite contemporary.

After concluding the research, I decided to tell Denoël's story in a different, more creative way than an academic work would allow. Research builds upon itself, multiplying like a cell, one name leading to another, going to a house, a place of work, a friend, family, growing larger and larger until a picture is formed, a life uncovered. For many researchers that picture remains in the mind, growing and changing as new bits of information are added, almost like a movie. I have occasionally placed myself within this work as an actual observer, thereby allowing the reader to "see" the scenes that the research suggests. Unfortunately, at the time of the Denoël murder, a theft also occurred. Nearly all of Denoël's private papers also "mysteriously" disappeared. Therefore, although the historical facts regarding Robert Denoël are true as presented in this work, I have sometimes used poetic license, added dialogue, and attempted to fill in certain gaps in order to develop and enliven some of the more sketchy research materials relating to the incredible life and death of this man. Most of these scenes are obvious, particularly since actual events and dialogue are cited in extensive endnotes. Let's begin this story then with the victim, Robert Denoël.

With the Stroke of a Pen

Prologue

On 2 December 1945, the last day of his life, the two of them arrived at her elegant Paris home at about 6:45 P.M. He was driving her car, a shiny black Peugeot 302. He stopped the car in the drive, and silently they entered the house and took off their coats. She rang for the maid, Mademoiselle Sidonie Zupaneck, and told her that they would like to have supper. After a few minutes, Sidonie served the soup, a consommé brunoise, in the dining room, followed by a cold ham braised in Madeira and a salade aixoise. Both ate rapidly, looking down, with little conversation. Neither wanted the dessert Sidonie had prepared for them. Following their meal, he finished his wine and smoked a cigarette, while she excused herself to freshen up and change into evening attire. At about 7:45 he got up from the table and went to the phone in the library, calling a business colleague. They had a long conversation, lasting more than twenty minutes. When he hung up, she was still not ready. He went to the hall mirror, straightened his elegant burgundy tie, adjusted his blue pin-striped suit and vest, and combed his hair. Then he took out his wallet, looked into it, and verified its contents: twelve thousand francs (more than six thousand dollars). When he heard the sounds of her high heels descending the staircase, he went to the closet, took out her black mink coat, and helped her on with it. While she adjusted her matching mink hat in that same hall mirror, he put on his own overcoat. The maid watched them as they left the house. Then she looked up at the grandfather clock. It was exactly 8:30.

Both seemed determined, tense, that night. They walked to the Peugeot, and he opened the door for her, then quickly walked to the driver's side, adjusted his overcoat, and got in. The maid could still see them from the window. The woman in the fur smiled briefly at him, then looked straight ahead, serious, as he started the engine and backed out of the drive. Quickly he turned the car into the street, and they roared off into that cold, rainy Paris night. Traffic was very light. They did not take a direct route. Instead, they went by (or very near) his publishing house. At 8:50 they stopped the car at a deserted area on the boulevard des Invalides, close to the corner of the rue de Grenelle. They both got out of the car. He had about twenty-six minutes left to live.

There were no witnesses.

All of the money in his wallet remained untouched.

Part 1

How to Found a Publishing House—

With No Assets, No Money,

No Contacts, and No Experience

1

Locating the Victim

Robert Denoël was assassinated . . . on 2 December [1945] under very mysterious circumstances that have never been explained.

Pierre-Edmond Robert, French historian

What happened to the woman who was with him the night of his murder? They ate supper together, and she got into the car with him that evening. "There were no witnesses to the murder." That's what all the newspapers said. Where was she when someone shot him in the back? Headline stories of the crime compounded my confusion. *Le Monde (The World)* reported that Robert Denoël, one of the foremost publishers in France, was accompanied that night by another publisher, a Monsieur Bonnat-Montchrétien. *Ce Soir (This Evening)* claimed that Denoël was with *"une amie,"* but tactfully avoided giving her name. *La Libération* was more forthcoming. Although it at first stated simply that Denoël and his female friend were together that night, buried near the end of the article was her name: Jean Voilier. I did not know then that it was not even her real name and wondered why she was called Jean (meaning John in French).

It took me weeks to sort things out. In the end all three newspapers were partially right. The night of his murder, Robert Denoël was with another publisher—not a man, but a woman. And although she was not named Bonnat-Montchrétien, she owned a publishing house called Domat-Montchrestien. In addition, she was a writer, a novelist who used the pseudonym Jean Voilier. I had already decided she was a researcher's nightmare. Who was she?

I realized it was best not to start with the elusive Jean Voilier, or even with the murder, but instead to begin with the man, the victim, Robert Denoël. He was my only real lead. He may even have known his assailants—or at least why someone wanted him dead. Although a successful biography requires meticulous, rigorous research, sometimes luck and timing are also essential. In this case both were crucial. While I was nosing into the details of this murdered publisher, the French government, always gravely and rightly uncomfortable about some of its twentieth-century history, decided to release some documents that had been sealed for decades. Among these archival hostages was a large box containing more than one thousand loose papers, some handwritten, others typed unevenly on ancient typewriters. That entire box had only one subject: Robert Denoël. The French released it without fanfare or even public announcement. I was among the first to peer into its contents. Without that box, this story could not be told.

It was months before I discovered those papers. When I began this project, all that I knew about Robert Denoël was that he was a Belgian who had come to Paris in 1926, where he published great writers—and was mysteriously murdered. I decided to look briefly at his childhood and youth, then begin the process of putting together the motives and leads, starting in 1925, one year before his arrival in France. That should be early enough, I reasoned. Then I hoped to trace him, carefully, painstakingly, along with any suspects I happened upon, month by month and, as the murder approached, week by week and, if possible, day by day. I never imagined that the large box, so recently freed from its archival restraints, would allow me to trace his murder minute by minute.

I began by locating a one-paragraph biography of Denoël in one of those huge French biographical dictionaries that listed everybody important or even semi-important in France in the 1930s. According to that work he was living in Liège, Belgium, in 1925. My first impression, when I turned my attention to that city, was of smoke. Histories of the town, even Belgian guidebooks promoting tourism in the 1920s, could not avoid mentioning it. Liège shrouded itself in the smoke of its factories and blast furnaces. Dark, sooty fumes billowed into a sky that was already often cloudy, rainy, foggy—cold. One guidebook even suggested that the smoke of Liège might be a blessing. "It spares the visitor the view of unsightly factories." Mists rising from the Meuse and other nearby rivers combined with Liège's industrial smoke, veiling the city in a dark, noxious fog. Strip mining, iron, and steel formed the heart of Liège, located in eastern Belgium, not far from the German border—in fact, not nearly far enough.

Robert Denoël grew up in the almost perpetual gloom and soot of this industrial city. He played in the streets, climbed the hills surrounding Liège and looked down at the Meuse, watching it quickly change from a stately, slowly curving river lined with linden trees and ivy into a smelly, dark industrial waste deposit, filled with coal barges. Within the city itself, those graceful old linden trees abruptly gave way to gently curving railroad tracks, puffing smokestacks, and rows of dark brick factories. As dirty and used as it was, the Meuse provided the only clear path through the center city, hemmed in by hills.

Sometimes at night young Robert would climb to the top of a point in the local Park of Birds. There he could look down and see almost all of Liège, not lit by gaslight or electricity, but alive with the fires of blast furnaces and factory chimneys. Flames licking out of the darkness reminded Robert of dragons, locked together in mortal battle, spewing fire from their gaping mouths. He watched these fires, transfixed. They were beautiful, horrible, fascinating to this young, imaginative boy. These industrial flames, some of which soared into the sky, earned the town its nickname, the Burning City.

Robert Lucien Denoël could not remember very much about the time before he came to live in the Burning City. Although he was born near Brussels (Uccle) on 9 November 1902, the sixth child of Lucien and Jeanne (née Déome) Denoël, he moved to Liège at the age of six when his father became a professor at the University of

Liège, then located on the shore of the Meuse river (it was later relocated). Robert would become one of the older members of this enormous household. In all, Lucien and Jeanne had fifteen children.

Row upon row of drab stone houses dusted with layers of soot replaced the great historic edifices that once marked Liège. Robert lived in one of those gray stone homes. Considered a magnificent town in the Middle Ages, this one-time European jewel had long ago lost its luster, primarily because of too many wars, annexations, foreign occupations, civil unrest, pillage, massacres, atrocities, and fire. Liège had experienced Burgundian, Spanish, Austrian, German, French, Dutch, and even a brief period of English rule. My antique guidebook noted Liège's dark river, coal barges, and surrounding countryside dotted by mine shafts, then cheerily stated, "One can also take a boat ride to see the sights of Liège." Or better yet, I thought, one might just use that boat to leave.

It was in the Burning City that Robert developed a liking for reading—perhaps to escape the noise and confusion of a family of seventeen, or as a refuge from the industrial pollution and dreary climate of his new city. Except for a period in a boarding school at Turnhout where, at his father's insistence, he learned Flemish, he remained in Liège from 1908 until 1926. From 1910 to 1919, he attended the Collège Saint-Servais, run by the Jesuits. An average student, he seemed gifted in nothing in particular, preferring reading by himself to class work. He developed the practice of reading one volume per day, a habit that he would continue as an adult. No apparent reasons for his murder in that childhood, I confirmed.

If reading had served as an escape from the commotion of his large family and the dreariness of his town, he soon had another reason to flee reality: the outbreak of World War I. The German soldiers came when he was eleven. Ignoring Belgium's proclaimed neutrality, they attacked Liège primarily from the east, but also with troops from the north and south, on 4 August 1914. On that day the ferocious defense of the Belgians prevented the German takeover of Liège. But the Belgian soldiers were hopelessly outnumbered. On 6 August 1914 the Germans entered the Burning City, taking control of its precious coal and steel. Once again Liège was occupied by foreign troops.

For nearly two weeks there was an eerie quiet in the town. Although university classes had been suspended, Robert's father, Lucien, soon grew restless. On 20 August, against his wife's adamant protests, he decided to return to his office at the university to retrieve some of his research. "If I don't get it now, God knows what could happen to it," he told her. And so in the late afternoon of 20 August, Lucien climbed the winding old oak steps up three flights to his office. And there, seated at his desk amid all of his papers, he lost track of time. Only the orange flickers from the dark window caused him to pause. Quickly he shoved the last of his papers into his briefcase, stood up, and went to the window. There he saw orange everywhere. All of the houses and buildings surrounding the university were in flames, even those across the river. He was at the center of a ring of fire. The Burning City—ablaze. "My God!" he said. Illuminated by the fire, Belgian citizens and German soldiers ran everywhere. From his window Lucien watched the Germans grab some of these people—not Belgian soldiers, civilians—men, women, even children. They lined them all up. Lucien quickly counted—sixteen, there were sixteen of them, all in a row, hands in the air, their backs to him. He watched in frozen horror as one by one the Germans methodically shot them all. He could hear screaming. Lucien dropped his briefcase and backed away from the window.

By dawn the University of Liège was all that remained standing, surrounded by smoking debris. In the early morning light, Lucien quietly took his bulging briefcase and slipped out a small back door. As he entered his modest home, his wife burst into tears and rushed to greet him, along with all of his children.

There was an official version, of course, for the happenings of the night of 20 August—quite different from what Lucien witnessed. The local newspaper announced that German soldiers had been fired upon. Of course, they had to return fire. Furthermore, the citizens of Liège could count on even more severe retaliation if they tried anything else contrary to German rule. The night of 20 August would simply serve as an example. "The Germans have annexed our news-paper," Lucien said to himself as he read the article.

Classes at the university soon resumed, and Lucien went back to his job—under German guidelines, of course. "Papa, do you collaborate with the Germans?" young Robert once asked.

His father's neck reddened, that blue vein on his forehead protruded. He looked severely at his son and replied, "What I do is teach! I hate the Germans and what they have done to this town. Plunderers, murderers, liars! I teach, I do my job, I mind my own business," he said. Lucien Denoël quietly taught throughout the entire occupation, keeping his home, feeding his family, and making sure that everyone in his large household stayed alive. Was that collaboration?

I knew that Robert would live under German occupation again in his life—the second time as a publisher during World War II. Being under German wartime control twice had to influence his life, I reasoned. Liège remained controlled by German soldiers during World War I until the armistice, signed on 11 November 1918, two days after Robert's sixteenth birthday. By that time much of the city had been weakened, pillaged, damaged, destroyed, or consumed. As it had done so many times in the past, it would rebuild.

Robert retreated from the horrors of war and occupation, not just by reading, but by writing as well. He even took a pseudonym and became Jacques Cormier, writer. Curious to know if *cormier* had a French meaning, I looked it up and found that this word means "European fruit tree, a sorb, or service tree." Interesting, I thought. He chose as his nom de plume something that puts down roots and produces fruit. Under this pseudonym (and sometimes others), he began to write short novels and stories. By 1921 he had published some of his work in *La Gazette de Liège*, to which Georges Simenon (also from Liège) contributed.

I sifted through the facts of his youth—searching for possible hints, factors that might contribute to understanding his life in Paris. Humdrum, ordinary—two years of military service, medical service at Anvers, unenthusiastic military man, then a university student where his father worked, studying philosophy and letters. Apparently, he entertained thoughts of law school or politics. Or was it his father who had such goals for him? I came across brief records of a big fight between father and son when Robert was nineteen, with yelling, threats, and slamming doors. It ended when Robert packed his bags, stormed out of the house, and went to Paris. History has recorded only one sentence of that argument, shouted by his father: "You can't make a living reading fiction!" Later, as a publisher, Robert was fond of quoting that line. After a few weeks father and son reconciled, and Robert returned.

While Lucien pointed to law and politics, his son read literature. As Lucien espoused the virtues of a career in medicine, Robert and two of his friends, Gilles Anthelme and Georges Thialet, established their own literary review: *To Create (Créer)*. Subsisting modestly from subscriptions, this work was published in six volumes. In 1925 it became part of the larger and more established *Sélection*.

With his own review, young Denoël came alive. He was everywhere, interested in everything, easy to work with, filled with significant ideas and suggestions. His blue eyes shone with excitement. He was enthusiastic, hardworking, friendly, quick to laugh (even at himself), and optimistic. More than anything else, it may have been his gregarious nature and love of literature that prevented the maturation of his own career in the more solitary field of writing.

In fact, writing seemed to be what Robert Denoël (alias, Jacques Cormier) put off until last in his busy life in Liège. One could often find him late at night slouched at a table, pen in hand, looking as if his back hurt him—writing. The brief paragraphs that I managed to locate concerning his early life announced that Denoël had wanted to be a writer, had longed to be one, in fact, but just wasn't good enough. And so, allegedly, this failed would-be writer turned to thoughts of publishing as a second-best way to keep his hand in the literary field. That was the official version. But in the case of Denoël, it soon became apparent that there were many "official versions" of his life that were simply inaccurate.

A close examination of his early works revealed that these allegedly "not very interesting" stories were actually well written, funny, engrossing. He filled his pages with young-man ideas, obsessions, desires, manipulations, adventures, even parents sometimes appearing at just the wrong time. Sex, love, lovers, conquest, rejection, yearning, experiments, these formed the framework of his stories. For example, in one scene the narrator tries to seduce his girlfriend, Diane, at the cinema. He tells us, self-importantly, that he knows what he is doing, that he is an experienced and accomplished lover, but as he is explaining himself to the reader, the man and woman next to him are making mad, passionate love, while his own girlfriend simply stares at the screen. Since up to this point all words have failed, he decides to take action: "I must cry now," he tells himself. At first he rejects the idea, "but it rebounds into my face like a rubber ball." Yes, yes, he envisions the scene: "I present myself with hot tears next to a completely surprised Diane. I watch her cover me with kisses and consolations." And then, of course, he envisions lovemaking.

The narrator then set about with objective and premeditated scientific accuracy to produce tears. Mentally rifling through his old physiology books, he realized he had to stimulate the lachrymal gland to get the desired result. "With trembling hands, nearly surreal, I seized my right eyelid between the thumb and the index finger: with a brutal movement, I turned it over." Not only did this action produce a tear in the right eye, but in the left one as well. "I leaned over and the full fruit of my labor dripped onto Diane's neck."

"She shivered with surprise." Then she grasped his head and held it against her breast. "She held me nervously and I felt her lips touch my hair; I remained there a long time, one ear partially crushed in her hand, the other wounded by the brooch on her dress." Then, to his utter astonishment, she didn't cover him with kisses or try to console him. She started to cry, too. In fact, she was soon sobbing. And the impact this action had on her would-be lover? "Ah, to flee, to disappear, to see myself annihilated!"

Our hero spends the rest of the story trying to decide whether to explain to Diane that it was all simply a ruse, or to continue with his little game. He chooses the latter, telling her, "Diane, I have not cried since the death of my grandmother." In the end, all possible schemes exhausted with no conquest at all, the young man asks hopefully, "You will meet me again next Tuesday?" "Oui," she responds.

Writing, literature, journals, books, and women—his adult life in Liège was filled with them all. In 1925 he changed pseudonyms (causing me great confusion at first). Instead of Cormier, he became Robert Marin, *marin* meaning "sailor" in French. As his new name implied, he was clearly ready to "sail on," to leave the smoke, industry, and provincialism of the Burning City and seek adventure.

Also in 1925 Robert's general interest in women became quite specific. He fell in love. He first saw her at the theater in Liège. One of his friends introduced them during the intermission. For the rest of the play, Robert did not watch the actors, but stared instead at the beautiful woman he had just met, sitting two rows down and a few seats to his left. He noted with pleasure her full enjoyment of the play, her keen interest and excitement. At the end of the performance, she rose spontaneously and vigorously applauded—and he rose, too. She couldn't have known then that he was applauding her. He was enchanted as she stepped out into the aisle to leave, then turned her head, looked directly at him, and shyly smiled. Her name was Cécile Brusson.

"So what is he like?" Cécile's girlfriend asked her the following day as they shopped for new clothes in Liège.

"I don't know, really. I just met him," Cécile replied coyly, taking down a soft mauve dress from the rack and examining it.

"Well, at least you could tell me what he looks like," her friend responded. "Is he handsome?"

Cécile paused and smiled, enjoying the moment. Then she said, "His eyes are blue, so penetrating." Looking back at the dress, she added, "His eyes seem kind, intelligent."

"And that's all you saw? His eyes?"

"No, silly." Cécile laughed. "Let's see. He is tall, slender, with dark wavy hair."

"Just your type!"

"And he wears glasses. They frame his blue eyes and make them stand out even more."

"I think glasses make men look unathletic," her friend replied.

Cécile sniffed, then responded, "I think he looks very distinguished with them. And he likes the theater. Since I plan to become an actress, that's very important to me, you know." Cécile said nothing for several moments, playing with the ruffles around the scoop neck of that mauve dress. Then she turned to her friend and slowly smiled. "There's something else, too."

"What? Tell me!"

"Well . . ." she waited a few more seconds, for dramatic effect. Then she blurted, "This morning he asked me to dinner on Saturday night."

There would be many dinners, concerts, plays. In fact, the old dirty town took on a new and special beauty for them both. Writing to Cécile many years later, describing their time together in Liège, Robert stated, "In that dead city where we lived, you represented, you were for me beauty, charm, originality, too. You even pleased me by your exuberance, your ardor, by all the forces of love that existed in you." Cécile was different from most of the women that Robert knew—she was exotic, mysterious, dramatic. She had been raised in South Africa, and her stories of that vast wild land amazed him.

They did everything together. One particularly warm night they climbed to the top of the Park of Birds above the smoke of the city, settled themselves on a park bench, and looked at the stars. The everchanging fires below them spewed and gasped, occasionally lighting up the smiles they gave each other in the darkness. They talked together of their dreams. He told her that he intended to go to Paris and become the most important publisher in France. "I shall discover great new writers, with new ideas. I shall publish them all," he said as he softly kissed her.

"Do you know who you are kissing?" she asked him, importantly. "You are kissing the new Sarah Bernhardt, the most famous actress in France . . . no, not just France, in all of Europe, in all the world!" She threw her hands out expansively and leaned back on their bench looking up at the stars. Then she hesitated before adding, "married to the most important publisher in all of Paris." He had already asked her to marry him. She had not responded immediately, enjoying her lover's suspense. Now, alone together with stars above them and fires roaring below, she gave him her answer.

They began to make plans together. "I will go to Paris first," he told her. "Then when I am settled and making some money, I will send for you."

He would leave the Burning City in October 1926. But first he had so much to do. One of his first duties was to write another article for that review he had worked on, *Sélection*. It was entitled "Vers Louis Aragon." *Vers* in this case means "toward, in the direction of." It was written in a lyrical style that contained an almost contagious enthusiasm. He described his profound joy in reading his first book by Aragon, *Anicet*. For Denoël, that book was like meeting Aragon himself through "an intermediary." He described Aragon's ideas, his style, his thoughts, as a great gift to him, providing a deep, rich renewal within his own spirit.

He ended his article very personally:

No one can speak for Louis Aragon, except himself. I know that . . . And now I publish these pages, without joy, but without anguish. Many will read this who do not really know me. Without doubt, during their reading, they will discover the imprint of my hand (bare, drawn with simple lines). Have them search here for my name and my destiny.

I read his words several times, realizing that here was Robert Denoël's good-bye to *Sélection*, to Belgium, to his old life. Enjoying his enthusiasm, his reverence for Aragon, for great writers and fine literature, I smiled after reading his words, for I knew what he could not possibly have dreamed when he wrote his farewell. One day in the not too distant future Robert Denoël would not only meet Louis Aragon, he would become his publisher.

He took a train from Liège to Paris on 15 October 1926. His entire enormous family, plus his fiancée and some of his friends, went to the station to see him off. Other passengers must have thought this serious young man with his huge entourage was someone truly important. It was a long and tearful parting.

At his side stood Cécile, clutching his hand. "Will you still love me when you are a famous publisher?" she asked him.

"Only if you will still love me when you are a famous actress," he responded.

Cécile smiled through her tears and hugged him tightly. "Send for me soon."

"As soon as I can scrape together enough money, I will," he promised. He could now see in the distance the smoke from the engine of the train that would take him to his new life, to Paris.

I followed the route of his train through southeastern Belgium and then through areas in northern France that still had not recovered from the bombing and devastation of World War I. Germany had taken special aim at the area north of Paris, rich in natural resources, mining, and industry. Denoël had only to look out his compartment window to see the awful remnants of war, the same war that he had experienced as a boy during the German occupation of Liège. But Robert was not thinking of the war, of Belgium or the past. He could think of only one thing: Paris. Now he would actually live and work there, become famous perhaps in the City of Light, the city of dreams.

Paris in 1926 has been described as a wild, mad, frenetic, endless party, where creative innovation and foolishness, genius and lunacy, happily thrived. This city served as a magnet for the entrepreneur and artist, the immigrant and expatriate. Rich in history, culture, and opportunity, Paris had one other major attraction for the foreigner: it was relatively cheap. The French exchange rate often favored immigrants, who found in Paris new job prospects, amazing entertainment, and cultural opportunities, along with inexpensive food and housing.

Paris needed those immigrants. The Great War, the War to End

All Wars, the war that historians would later refer to as World War I (impossible then to believe that such a war could have a sequel) had decimated France's population, particularly its young men. France was rebuilding; workers were needed, even immigrants, to fill the vacancy of all those Frenchmen killed in battle. With a population less than one-third of that of the United States, France had lost more than 1,300,000 young men in the Great War. Deaths of American soldiers in that same war totaled about 116,000.

France no longer wanted to remember and weep for what had happened. By 1926 its future seemed as bright as Coty's lipstick. Everything was changing. Even older women bobbed their hair and raised their hemlines in salute to this new era. In Parisian bars, clubs, and bistros, the sultry tango, *le jazz hot*, the frenetic Charleston brought men and women off their seats and silenced conversation. Surrealism and art deco, cinema and that dashing Rudolph Valentino, sex and Freud, all took precedence over dreary talks of politics or the tirades of that little German Fascist with the toothbrush mustache. The mood was set by jazz that seemed propelled by cigarette smoke.

One can argue that in the period between the two World Wars, the flowering of American and even British literature may have taken place on French soil. Ernest Hemingway, F. Scott Fitzgerald, Sinclair Lewis, Archibald MacLeish, John Dos Passos, William Seabrook, and later Henry Miller all spent time in that most colorful, eccentric quarter known as Montparnasse. American and British women too participated in this artistic panoply, including, among others, Gertrude Stein, Peggy Guggenheim, Nancy Cunard, Lady Duff Twysden, Sylvia Beach, Alice B. Toklas, Zelda Fitzgerald, and Isadora Duncan. As a result of the Russian Revolution, artists from that country also sought refuge and freedom in Paris. It is not surprising that Robert Denoël, connoisseur of French, English, and Russian literature, would be so excited on a train bound for the cultural and intellectual center of Europe—perhaps of the world.

In the fall of 1926, at the age of twenty-four, Robert Denoël arrived in Paris. He would be murdered there in the fall of 1945, nineteen years later—not a long time to build a publishing empire rivaling that of Gaston Gallimard, foremost publisher in France. Aside from his meager savings and a very small monetary gift from his parents, he didn't have any money, and apparently he had no important and wealthy friends, people who might have been able to provide financial backing for his project. He was a fool to think he could found a publishing house without any money, contacts, or prospects. I became almost as curious to know how he had managed to establish his publishing house without any funds as I was to know who murdered him and why.

Before World War I, the French were notorious for fiscal conservatism. Always suspicious of banks, they frequently stashed money beneath floorboards, stitched it into petticoats, or buried it under the cabbages. Saving was considered to be a paramount virtue. Following World War I, however, money safely hiding under growing vegetables began to lose its value. Inflation sniffed out all hiding places, even banks, attacking every conscientious money saver with a new kind of robbery—a slow and steady theft by percentages. The only way to stop this financial drain was to take the money out and invest it. Even long-shot investments provided more satisfaction than watching money, so carefully saved and hoarded, lose its value. Investing in Robert Denoël, with no assets, no contacts, and virtually no experience in publishing, may have been one of the longest shots in France.

Robert did have a friend in Paris: Georges Houyoux, who was also Belgian. Georges had come to Paris two years before his friend and had purchased a bookstore specializing in old, rare, and luxury editions. "If you do come to Paris," Georges had told Robert, "you can work for me." Like Robert, Georges wanted to become a great Parisian publisher. Both men dreamed of being at the cutting edge of literature, specializing in the new, the avant-garde, surrealism, and possibly even the outrageous.

So Robert began his publishing career in Paris working on commission as a salesman in the bookstore at 34, rue Sainte-Anne.

Friendly, intelligent, and energetic, he soon met and impressed important patrons. He was likable, well versed in literature, and eager to please. With his first paychecks he bought new clothes—a fairly expensive Parisian suit, trousers, shirts, and one pair of good Italian shoes. He exchanged his Belgian haircut for a Paris trim, wearing his wavy dark hair slightly longer, combed back without a part. He listened carefully to the nuances of the Paris accent, watching Parisian lips in conversation. Mimicking their speech and gestures before a mirror, he tried to lose the more guttural and heavy French of his native Liège. He was determined to look, feel, act, and be Parisian.

Not far from the Montparnasse railroad station, he rented a one-room dump, a fifth-story walk-up with a single window facing an alley—bathroom down the hall. Complete with two wooden chairs—one green, one dirty yellow—a small sagging iron bed, and a wobbly square table, the apartment, even in late October, held in its damp chill the vague smell of soiled sheets and old sweat. The price, however, suited Robert's budget, and the sparse furnishings satisfied his needs. Besides, he intended to spend his time elsewhere. With a job and all of Paris to explore, he would use his apartment for sleep, and as little of that as possible.

When he wasn't working in the bookstore, reading, or writing letters to Cécile, he explored the wonderful city where he intended to found his publishing empire. Montparnasse, that Left Bank magnet for artists, students, writers, philosophers, raving drunks, and sober lunatics, particularly fascinated him. Only a few days after his arrival in Paris, Robert set out to visit that magic quarter at night. He walked alone, silently, briskly down the narrow streets, slowing occasionally to glance into shop windows. Long before he even approached the heart of Montparnasse, he saw its red glow in the night sky, not unlike the light of the industrial fires he used to see from Liège's Park of Birds. Montparnasse had decked itself out like a giant gaudy whorehouse with lights in every window. Then he heard its thumping sounds—rhythmic, exciting. Coming closer, he caught the wail of a trumpet. People were everywhere—French, Asian, African,

American—wearing robes, tuxedos, long gowns, turbans, short skirts, kimonos, slippers, boots. They mixed freely in kaleidoscopic colors on the streets and sidewalks, speaking every language.

At first Robert simply walked and stared. Then he began to take notice of the nightclubs, *les boîtes de nuit,* with strains of jazz floating out the doors. He stood for some time in front of one small nightclub. It looked uninviting, painted black except for brightly colored silhouettes of cowboys and Indians. A small sign above the door read le Jockey. "Pardon," he muttered as a prostitute bumped into him.

A pink feather boa framed her heavily painted face. She smiled invitingly at him. "You want a good time? Come with me," she said, reaching toward him. He ignored her, unable to take his eyes off the crowd entering le Jockey, while she sauntered down the street.

Robert noticed that while people were constantly going in, no one was coming out. As he moved toward the entrance, he heard music, "The Saint Louis Blues," muffled by voices, laughter. He entered into nearly total darkness, then saw a staircase descending into a sort of basement. Immediately the scent of cigarette smoke, mixed with heavy sweat and rum, cloyed his nostrils. Slowly, he followed the line of people to the brighter lights coming from the lower floor.

Now he could see that the walls and ceilings of this place were plastered with posters, hung every which way. Graffiti, salacious poems, limericks, and American slang framed the posters and decorated all empty spaces. Halfway down the stairs, he saw a small, narrow dance floor surrounded by tables and chairs, densely packed with undulating, twisting dancers, moving almost as a whole within their tiny confines. They reminded Robert of a giant intricate machine at work.

Then he spotted a young woman. She was fairly tall and slim. Her glazed eyes were heavily outlined in black; her lips were thickly spread with bright purple lipstick, almost iridescent. Her closely cropped black hair lay like a swim cap against her head, with one small spit curl on her forehead. In her hair she wore a large lavender ostrich feather. At one point Robert could see that she was wearing purple high heels with straps that coiled snakelike around her ankles and up her calves. Between her feet and her feather, she wore absolutely nothing. She was expressionless, a simple cog in that sweating, writhing dancing machine, her bare breasts keeping time to the music. No one but Robert seemed even to notice.

"Well, at least her outfit matched," Georges joked back at the bookstore upon hearing Robert's account of his experience at le Jockey.

Robert smiled, but he was silent, pensive. In that whole mass of people are my writers, he thought. But how do I find them? He said nothing, busily straightening the books at the front of the store. I was wondering the same thing myself. How could he ever locate the writers he needed in that huge crowd in Montparnasse? And Robert always failed to take into account the fact that he didn't have the money to publish anything in the first place. How was he going to pull it all off?

His destiny changed less than one month later when a middle-aged woman entered Georges's bookstore. I had read about her in several books. She was an artist whose works have not survived, a writer whose books were long forgotten, and one of the leaders of an artistic movement that is no longer remembered. But she herself is renowned, described by several famous artists and writers not for her art or writing, but for something else. I read with great interest the description of her first encounter with Robert Denoël, on 6 November 1926. Wearing an open gray coat that revealed a blue cotton dress colorfully and tastefully decorated with an intricate batik design, she came through the door with a purpose. Her dark hair, streaked with gray, was tightly drawn back in a bun; her face had wrinkles made from smiling; her gray-green eyes were kind and penetrating. Quickly, she made her way to the back of the left-hand side of the store and bent over a small collection of old music books. It was clear to Robert that she had been in this shop before.

"Bonjour, Madame," he said, smiling. "Can I help you find anything?"

She looked up, stared silently into his eyes for a moment, then said, "Georges told me he might have some more old music books today, but I don't see them."

"Music books? Why yes, I believe he purchased some at an auction yesterday. They're still in the back. I can check for you. Are you looking for anything in particular?" he said, already moving toward the storeroom.

"Sea chanteys," she called after him.

He turned. "What?"

"Sea chanteys, you know, songs of the sea. I collect them."

Just then Georges walked into the shop. "Bonjour, Irène. You're just the person I wanted to see. I found two books yesterday that you might like. Just a minute and I'll get them." He returned with the books, then added, "I see you've met our new salesman, Robert Denoël. Robert, this is Irène Champigny, one of our most famous neighbors. She owns the Gallery Sainte-Anne across the street."

As they shook hands and exchanged greetings, she looked into Robert's eyes again for several moments. "She's got you pegged, Robert." Georges laughed. "She's got the gift."

"The gift?" Robert asked. Georges ignored him, obviously delighted by Irène's presence and happily showing her the books he had just purchased.

After some consideration, she announced, "I'll take them both." Right before she left, she turned again and looked brightly at Robert for a few moments, smiled, then turned and walked out of the shop. Robert had a strange sensation, as if he already knew her, had always known her, had met her a thousand years before.

"Is she an artist?" he asked Georges after she had left.

"Well, you might say that," murmured Georges, busily putting away more of his books. "She works a lot in batik and lives with a painter—Christian Caillard. Maybe you've seen some of his works. But that's not what she's known for."

"Well, what *is* she known for?" Robert asked.

"As I said, she's got the gift. She's clairvoyant. She's famous all over France."

"So she's a fortune-teller," Robert replied.

"It doesn't work like that. She doesn't take any money for her gift—lives off the proceeds from her gallery. But people come from miles around just to talk with her and get her advice. She's uncanny, really."

Robert was fascinated. A few days later Irène entered the bookstore again. This time she marched directly over to Robert and said, "If it's all right with Georges, how would you like to come work for me at the Gallery Sainte-Anne?"

She hadn't asked him anything about his experience, his training, his knowledge of art. And almost as quickly, Robert responded, "I would like that very much." And so it was settled.

By December 1926, Robert was working as a salesman, organizing paintings, and presenting expositions at the Gallery Sainte-Anne, located at 39, rue Sainte-Anne. Robert would soon learn that he didn't have to find his new writers among the hordes of revelers thronging Montparnasse. He made his first contacts on the rue Sainte-Anne. They came to see the artwork at Irène Champigny's gallery. Or sometimes they simply came to see Irène.

Artists, writers, and journalists strolled leisurely through the gallery, visiting with Irène and meeting and talking with Robert Denoël. One day not long after Robert had started his new job at the gallery, the door opened, and Irène immediately stopped cataloging a series of sketches done by Maurice Loutreuil. She stood up and smiled, then quickly walked over to the gallery entrance. Standing in the doorway was a small older man, impeccably dressed, wearing a monocle. He was thin, wiry, wrinkled, professorial. His large mustache, once black, was now mostly gray, as was his sparse hair. He had a long nose, and in one of his overly large hands he carried an elegant cane. Although he was far from handsome, his large, penetrating, beautiful blue eyes gave him a dramatic and distinguished look.

"Bonjour, Monsieur Valéry," Irène said. "How nice of you to visit our little gallery! Can I be of service to you in any way?"

"Ah, Madame Champigny," he said, taking her hand and smiling. "I have heard so much about your new exposition, I had to come see it myself. The artists in your School of the St. Gervais Meadow are starting to make a name for themselves, I see."

They walked slowly together, engaged in lengthy and quiet conversation. Robert, who was hanging paintings in an alcove, quietly watched them. "So that's the famous Paul Valéry," he mused to himself. As they approached him, Irène warmly introduced her new young Belgian salesman to the most famous poet in France. When they shook hands and exchanged greetings, Robert noticed a cloud briefly come across Irène's face. For a moment her eyes were wide, startled. Quickly she caught herself and resumed her friendly conversation. Then just as suddenly as he had appeared, Paul Valéry exited the gallery with a brief and courteous exchange of good-byes and thank-yous.

"I didn't realize you knew Monsieur Teste himself," Robert told Irène after Valéry had left. People often referred to Valéry as Monsieur Teste, one of his poetic personages who was devoted entirely to thinking, the abstract, and knowledge.

"Oh, I don't know him well," she replied. "He has come in here two or three times before, likes to look at our works, and to engage in a little conversation, that's all."

That was not all, as Irène apparently knew from her clairvoyance, and I would later learn. I had already found a diary that stated that Jean Voilier (whoever she was) was linked to Paul Valéry. So this celebrated poet (age fifty-five), and Robert Denoël, a nearly penniless salesman in an art gallery (age twenty-four), were both somehow connected to this same woman. It was time to go after her, and since I had found no hint that Robert even knew her in 1926, I decided to research Paul Valéry, more famous today than my publisher, and therefore, I thought, much easier to trace.

2

Finding That Woman

I consider that women who are authors, lawyers, and politicians are monsters.

Pierre-Auguste Renoir

*T*here were 277 books by or about Paul Valéry in the University of Michigan library. Over the next few weeks, I checked them all, searching for basic information on him, but really looking for his . . . what should I call her? His friend, maybe his mistress? I would soon learn that the "accepted" description of this mystery woman was that she was his *égérie*—his "muse"—that is, if scholars chose to mention her at all. Most Valérian scholars skipped her entirely. And if they did mention her, they used her pseudonym, Jean Voilier. As for Valéry himself, while it was clear from his writings that he was madly in love with someone, the wily old poet refused to disclose her name. Instead, in his *Notebooks (Cahiers)* he referred to his lover by using various nicknames, sometimes even numbers. I imagined a great love story written this way: "233 entered the room, embraced and kissed me." Valéry always did love secrets.

Then one Valéry scholar mentioned in a footnote that Jean Voilier had once been married to Pierre Frondaie. But who was he? I imagined a dentist. I looked in all of the usual places—old records, references—but got nowhere. On a whim I decided to find out if this man had ever written anything. With my computer I checked the holdings of the University of Michigan, practically in my backyard, and stared dumbfounded as title after title appeared. Novels, plays, and even a short statement about his most important work, *l'Homme à l'Hispano*, written in 1925. Frondaie may not be remembered today, but he was certainly famous in the 1920s.

The title of his most celebrated work confused me. Just what exactly could "l'Homme à l'Hispano" be? I knew the French words; "The man with the Hispanic." I just didn't know what they signified— in French or in English. A title? A nickname? I ordered the book from Michigan's Buhr annex, a storage building for little-used works, waited the obligatory twenty-four hours, then quickly leafed through it. And there, on page three, was a picture of a fantastic automobile: the Hispano-Suiza. Now I realized what the title meant: "The Man with the Hispano-Suiza."

I spent the next few hours immersed in the study of vintage cars. The Hispano-Suiza was the French equivalent of the Rolls-Royce. Its name literally meant "Hispanic and Swiss," because the first model had been created by a Swiss engineer, and one of the very first customers and promoters of the car had been King Alfonso XIII, of Spain. It was said that the Hispano-Suiza's excellent body and four-wheel braking system made the Rolls-Royce Silver Ghost, which had only a rear-wheel braking system, seem out-of-date. It was a royal car, owned by millionaires and blue bloods throughout Europe. Looking at Frondaie's book, it became obvious to me that Pierre Frondaie adored the car and wrote about it in his novel almost as endearingly as a man would write about his lover. In fact, Frondaie owned just such a car, and he was even nicknamed "the Man with the Hispano-Suiza." The true hero of his most famous novel may have been the automobile itself, whisking lovers, the rich, the important, the beautiful, to the Riviera and other exotic locations with ease and hitherto unimagined opulence. In 1925 there was arguably no greater luxury, speed, comfort, or engineering advancement than the Hispano-Suiza. What better setting for romance and intrigue than in the interior of this wonderful automobile, swiftly moving from one posh place to another? It is no wonder that the novel, the automobile, and Pierre Frondaie were a hit in Paris. Nearly everyone in France had read his book and admired his car.

Although I still did not know her real name, some scholars did confirm what I already suspected: Paul Valéry was in love with Jean Voilier. His passion for her began in the mid-1920s and lasted apparently unabated until the end of his life two decades later. Several writers even noted that when Valéry was separated from her, he seemed old and ordinary. Yet when she was with him, he magically rejuvenated, looking and acting younger, and once again talking of new creativity and writing projects that without her lay dormant. But Jean Voilier had married Pierre Frondaie at about the same time that Valéry fell in love with her. He had to have seen them together in that most distinctive automobile.

I sat in a large overstuffed chair, with my enormous black cat, Rupert, placidly sprawled on my lap. Absently petting Rupert, I shut my eyes and pieced together all the information I had accumulated. I pictured Paul Valéry exit Champigny's gallery right after meeting Robert Denoël. Somehow on the sidewalk he looked older than he had at the gallery . . . even older than his fifty-five years. I knew from my reading that he had health problems. His stomach often bothered him; he coughed a lot, was sometimes wracked by coughing fits. His teeth were rotting, brown from cigarettes. He had bad breath. His thin face sagged, lined by wrinkles. What hair he had was nearly white. He walked slowly, with a slight slouch, using his elegant cane to help him.

Suddenly, he looked down the street, stared briefly in surprise, then immediately straightened, assumed a lofty stance, and started walking in a much faster, younger fashion. Turtlelike, his neck grew out of his coat collar; his chin, formerly aimed toward the sidewalk, now rose, starting to point upward. He continued to walk, increasing his speed and improving his posture with each passing second. It was as if he had just shed his old-man skin, replaced it with something almost dashing. I looked down the street, trying to figure out what had caused Valéry's transformation. An automobile was approaching.

It was the car I had been reading about, the Hispano-Suiza. Although there were lots of cars in Paris at that time, most of them were black and not particularly distinctive. The body of this automobile was bright canary yellow, with shiny black fenders and a chamois-colored convertible top. The car had five silver-spoked wheels—the fifth, a spare, was mounted as an ornament in front of the running board on the passenger's side. The hood was sleek and very long, clearly housing an enormous engine. Everyone on the street, except Paul Valéry, stopped to look at the approach of this fabulous automobile. There were soft murmurs, long stares, even a few gaping mouths. One man on the street, with a beautiful woman on his arm, briefly pointed toward the car as it passed. "Look, it's l'Homme à l'Hispano, himself!" he said to her. And she smiled, nodding and admiring that car. Driving the car, Frondaie wore goggles and a cap. Beside him sat a woman, but I couldn't make out her face. It was not until the car was nearly out of sight that Valéry turned around to watch it disappear in the distance. Then he took up again his old-man skin and walk, slouching, using his cane. His face seemed sad.

I smiled to myself as my cat slowly raised his head to peer at me with half-shut green eyes. My research subjects were coming to life in my mind, making my work so much more interesting and vivid. They lived and moved not as I desired, but as their histories demanded. And right now I wanted to see more of the man behind those goggles, Pierre Frondaie, and that woman seated next to him in his marvelous car.

I searched journals, microfilm, histories, old encyclopedias, biographical sketches, diaries—doggedly hunting for leads regarding the life of this man. Then on my third long day of looking at the microfilm of French newspapers from the 1920s, I spotted him. I had set the microfilm reader at a fairly fast forward and was almost mesmerized by the endlessly moving words and pictures, when all of a sudden, Frondaie sped past me in that same automobile. I lurched forward in my chair and stopped the machine. I set the microfilm reader to a much slower speed and pressed the rewind. And Pierre Frondaie slowly backed up his car until he was once again in my view.

He was driving down the Champs-Elysées on the crisp fall afternoon of 7 October 1925. Apparently oblivious to the admiring stares he received from all sides, he was streaking through traffic when suddenly a car veered in front of him. He screeched to an immediate stop, stuck his fist out the window, and gestured wildly at the other driver. At that moment, a newspaper photographer snapped his picture. I imagined a deep, commanding voice bellowing at the other confused driver. I knew where he was going. I had recognized the date, had already seen it on one of his playbills. He was headed for 19, rue de Bondy, the address of the Théâtre de la Renaissance. In only a few hours this theater would be filled with dignitaries, ready for the premiere of Frondaie's new play, *La Menace.*

Armed with the playbill, the play itself, grand detailed descriptions and pictures of the events of that evening (found in a booklet called *La Petite Illustration),* several newspaper reviews, journals, and society pages of the time, I mentally followed him through the doors of the Théâtre de la Renaissance and entered into his life that day. He gingerly jumped out of the car and walked swiftly to the door. He was not dressed in a normal black topcoat, like most Frenchmen of the time. Instead, he wore a long black cape (which looked quite expensive) and carried a beautiful cane ornately decorated in gold. As he approached the door, he flipped the cape with his hand, revealing its crimson satin lining. Upon his arrival, there was a flurry of activity around him.

"Did Marcel rehang the lights for the second act yet?" he asked as he strode across the stage. "Have they improved on the timing of the scene change in that last act? Two minutes, that's all they should need," he boomed to a man standing in the wings. "And how's Cora's voice?" he asked in the direction of a woman, who was frantically sewing sequins onto a gown. "She shouldn't be talking to anyone before curtain. Understand?" he announced to no one in particular.

Frondaie quickly slipped off his cape, revealing elegant attire. He was wearing a long double-breasted light gray suit coat, which resembled a smoking jacket, with a darker vest with beautiful gold buttons, white shirt, and silk tie beneath. I soon discovered why he was dressed up so many hours before the opening. He had a newspaper interview, and a photographer would be taking pictures. I watched as the photographer, a small, thin man with a large blond mustache, set the stage for the photographs. He placed a striped silk chair in front of an enormous abstract painting, then had Frondaie assume various positions, sitting in the chair, then sitting on the arm of the chair with his beautiful cane across his knee, his face first looking straight ahead, then off to one side. He took many pictures in spite of Frondaie's increasing restlessness, and gave me a good opportunity to look at this man up close. Frondaie was robust, athletic, yet sensual with big soft brown eyes, large well-defined lips, muscular shoulders, and a very oval bald head. He was handsome, strong, commanding. "Enough, enough," Frondaie said, waving his hands and getting up from the chair. "If you don't have your picture by now, you never will," he muttered as he strode off. "I must speak with Cora now."

Cora was Frondaie's leading lady, Cora Laparcerie, a celebrated French actress in 1925. I would soon learn that nearly every French actress aspired to be in a Frondaie play, for, unlike most playwrights, Frondaie usually made the heroine, and not the hero, his play's true centerpiece. Lovely, delicate, palpitating, often in grave danger, feverish, tender, romantic, and frequently finding herself in larger-than-life situations, a Frondaie heroine was often the role of a lifetime for an aspiring actress.

Frondaie tapped on Cora's dressing room. "*Entrez,*" a soft feminine voice said from within.

She was sitting in a chaise longue, studying her lines. A pink hand-knitted blanket lay across her lap.

"Cora, how are you feeling, my dear?" Frondaie asked solicitously. "Are you taking care of those sniffles?" He bent over her, kissed her cheek, and patted her shoulder.

"I'm feeling fine, Pierre. Much better. I'll be ready," she assured him. "In fact, I can't wait until tonight."

Neither could I. And I was not disappointed. The house was packed, sparkling with dignitaries and socialites. As the curtain rose, revealing the heroine, fragile and beautiful, standing alone amid a sumptuous set, the audience also rose as one in an ovation to the celebrated Cora Laparcerie. She was perfect for the part. Reviewers later pronounced her performance "tender, nuanced, passionate." The play was a hit.

Of course the gala party following the performance was a veritable Who's Who of Parisian notables. I searched names, faces, some of whom I knew about, others who met their death with only brief snippets of their existence on earth left behind in literary journals or gossip columns. And I listened.

"Frondaie has done it again," said a portly gentleman with an enormous diamond ring on his pinky. "He certainly knows how to arouse the passions of an audience. I must say he kept my interest."

"I wonder why he made one of his characters a Fascist—certainly a fringe element, don't you think?" asked a thin older woman with short stylish gray hair and a beautiful silver-and-pink crêpe de chine dress.

"Did you hear about his fight with the surrealists? He even issued his own manifesto. Said the surrealists could never make a good play without a strong plot and plenty of action. I hear André Breton is furious about it," said a younger man with dark hair, a quick smile, and flashing brown eyes.

"But I must say he has a point," responded the tall man next to him, busily straightening his cravat. He accepted a glass of champagne offered by a waiter with a large tray of glasses sparkling with bubbles, took a sip, then continued, "All that surrealistic dialogue and standing around on stage puts me to sleep. I don't like to watch an actor do nothing on stage."

I moved slowly through the gathering, looking at faces, listening to sentences, searching. I edged closer to Pierre Frondaie, who was surrounded by a large group of well-wishers. He was involved in an apparently serious conversation with an elegant man with gray hair and matching goatee, and again Frondaie was making broad gestures with his hands. Then I saw her. She was dressed in an exquisite shimmering black velvet floor-length gown, with long sleeves, a high Empire waist, and a low V neck. Two bands of velvet rose from her waist and crossed over her shoulders to form one piece in the back—making a small cape that tapered to a V just behind her knees. Three long silver tassels rhythmically swung from the bottom of the cape as she walked. Just above her waist on the front of the gown she wore an exquisite, large square diamond pin. Her light brown hair was severely drawn back into a chignon, revealing diamond earrings that matched her pin. She was elegant, beautiful, patrician, with a high forehead, a long straight nose, and large piercing blue eyes.

When Frondaie saw her, he seemed to light up, excused himself from the gentleman with the goatee, and quickly moved toward her, his hands outstretched. She took both of his hands in hers and smiled. She had long delicate fingers, artistic, I thought. I could hear him introduce her to the man beside him, saying *"ma femme"* (my wife). Good! Good! This lovely woman must be the one I was looking for, Frondaie's wife! Then he spoke her name, "Madeleine." Madeleine Frondaie—she must be the one who was with Denoël that night . . . but she wasn't. I soon learned that she wasn't even a writer. She was an artist, a sculptress, and she had never used the name Jean Voilier. Damn, wrong wife!

I decided to follow both Valéry and Frondaie, at least as much as I could. Because he is still so famous today, I could often follow Valéry's daily activities, taken from some of his calendars and appointment books, and note the people with him. But that stubborn Valéry had certain rendezvous with only the time and place duly noted. It was clear that he would do almost anything to keep his private life out of the hands of future researchers. I only caught a glimpse of him once, seated with a woman in the private back room of an elegant Paris restaurant. Candles and small mirrors with elaborate gold frames were everywhere, reflected in the white china and sparkling through the crystal. Valéry's eyes shone; he was animated; they had champagne. The handsome woman seated with him was decades younger than he, beautifully dressed in a green velvet gown with a large scoop neck, attentively listening. She placed her hand on the table, and the smiling Valéry put his own large hand over it.

As for Frondaie, after weeks of research, I caught a glimpse of him with this same woman. They were on a balcony of a quaint hotel in the south of France. Flowers spiced the warm twilight air. Frondaie's large brown eyes were soft with emotion. He took her into his arms, and they danced slowly in the last light of a purple sunset. Both men seemed entranced by her. Who was she?

I wasn't getting very far. But what could I expect? They called her "darling," "dearest," "my sweet." They wouldn't address her by her full name in such romantic situations. I decided to try to follow her.

Paris—enormous, swarming with immigrants and expatriates, alive, moving, exciting. Parisian records—confusing, bureaucratic, sometimes confounding or illegible, and very, very male. I knew that my chances of finding a woman whose real name I still didn't know were slim. Perhaps someone knew of her novels. I wrote some letters to Parisian officials and publishing houses. Several weeks later I received polite bureaucratic responses informing me that my requests could not be answered unless I had more information. I did not bother to point out to those bureaucrats that if I had had more information, I would not have written those letters. Finally, in desperation, I returned to one brief statement I had found in some old documents. It seems that this woman was also connected to another man. Apparently everyone who was anyone knew him. His name was Maurice Garçon. Well, I didn't have any other leads. I decided to try to find out who this Garçon was.

That's the amazing thing about research. One never knows when that tightly closed kernel of the briefest information will unfold like a flower. For me, Maurice Garçon turned out to be that yielding fruit pointing to pathways I had not yet considered. To my astonishment, the Michigan library abounded in information on Maurice Garçon, a lawyer who, while not yet famous in 1925, would defend some of the most important people in France against charges of collaboration following the Nazi Occupation. Better still, Garçon was himself a writer. Eleven of his books rested in the Buhr annex, waiting to be rifled.

Garçon's own writings led me to his modest legal office in 1925. Using his books and descriptions, I mentally entered his office and glanced around, seeing several diligent young lawyers seated at small desks. Walking to the back of the room, I spotted her, the woman who had been with Frondaie and Valéry—the only woman who also had one of those small desks. Since there was no identification on her desk, I glanced at her papers. On top of the papers in her out box was a letter. I took a deep breath, then looked at the signature. It was signed, "Jeanne Loviton, avocate." She was a lawyer, then! The woman who was with Robert Denoël the night he was murdered was working in the law office of Maurice Garçon in 1925.

I wanted that sudden moment of discovery, that joy and excitement, to last forever. I wanted to reach out and grasp her, shake her hand, ask her to look up so that I could examine her face. Her name was Jeanne Loviton! Now, at last, I had something to go on. If only I had looked more closely that day. If only I had known more then, I would have found in that office not just one lawyer who would be with Denoël the night of his murder—but two.

Almost immediately I came upon another bit of information. It was only a short poem. It was trite, really, hardly a poem for future generations, but a very significant name appeared in the verse: Jeanne Loviton. The author praised this "lady lawyer," who (according to the poet) conquered everything. He concluded the poem by comparing her "eloquence" to "a rose." And the author of this seemingly schoolboyish poem? Paul Valéry. So now I knew that in 1925 Pierre Frondaie was with his artist wife, Madeleine. And the mysterious Jeanne Loviton was working in the law office of Maurice Garçon, receiving love poems from famed poet Paul Valéry and accepting rides in Hispano-Suizas.

I remembered Valéry's poetry from college, required reading for any advanced French student. The verses I had seen were almost crystalline in their purity and sharpness, never comparing lady lawyers to eloquent roses. I also knew that sometimes he spent hours, days, even months seeking *le mot juste,* the exact word, phrase, or image. And his most famous poems, at least those assigned by my college teachers, were definitely not about women or romantic love. In fact, Paul Valéry had a reputation for misogyny.

Jeanne Loviton was twenty-one in 1925, Valéry was thirty-two years her senior. Furthermore, he had a wife, children, and (like most Frenchmen of the time) a mistress. His most important works had already been published; his fame was established. In fact, in November 1925 he would receive what was possibly the most prestigious award of all: election into the Académie française. He would take the seat left vacant by the death of Anatole France the previous year. As a result of this election, Valéry was given the honored title, The Official Poet of France.

So two men courted Jeanne Loviton (and possibly more—I picked up faded whispers that she had an affair with her boss, Maurice Garçon). Both Pierre Frondaie and Paul Valéry were clearly entranced by her. Such different suitors! Valéry was influential, respected, revered. He was a brilliant conversationalist, sought after by nearly every prominent person and salon in Paris. All doors were opened to him. He could intelligently discuss nearly any topic. As for gossip, snobbery, and sarcasm, Valéry knew no equal, spicing his discussions with pointed witticisms. Certainly Jeanne Loviton could see her own stature increased by this important lover.

But then there was Pierre Frondaie, famous playwright and novelist, far younger, fitter, and better looking than Valéry. He, too, had considerable fame and power and could help Jeanne gain influence and prestige. And he had that beautiful Hispano-Suiza and seemed himself so commanding, so powerful.

Frondaie loved women—perhaps too much. Valéry, on the other hand, viewed women not just as inferior, but occasionally as reprehensible. He even mocked them, sometimes to their faces. Newspapers of the time abounded with stories of Valéry and his misogyny. For example, in August 1927 there appeared in one literary journal an account of an unnamed female novelist of considerable talent who met Valéry and highly praised his work. "Really," the poet responded, with a flip of his monocle. "You understand them then?" Turning to his male companion, he said, "And who told you that women aren't intelligent?" The woman was not amused.

For Valéry, women were useful only if they satisfied his personal needs or served to increase his prestige and status in life. His wife, for example, not only provided him with heirs and meekly carried out his every wish, but increased his renown by her ancestry. She was related to Manet, and to Valéry's literary idol, Stéphane Mallarmé. Their marriage not only gave the Valéry family a more impressive past, but served as a link to the artistic world for Valéry, providing him with important contacts.

Valéry's mistress at the time, Catherine Pozzi, had considerable talent and creativity. She tirelessly helped her lover with his multi-volume *Notebooks* and other books, cataloging, critiquing, and providing valuable suggestions. While graciously accepting all of her help, he failed to acknowledge it in any way. In his mind, she simply served as a "resonator" for his thoughts. "One day," Pozzi said, "I asked Paul Valéry to read and critique one of my essays, *De Libertate*."

He took the book from her, saying, "I promise to read this just as soon as I can find the time."

"Several weeks later he returned the essay to me without comment. I was disappointed by his lack of interest." At about the same time Valéry was writing about Edgar Allan Poe. Pozzi continued, "Imagine my surprise when I read his work. There were all of my ideas that he had discovered in *my work*. He stole my ideas and claimed them as his own. When I confronted him about it, he simply ignored me."

Valéry also used the women in the literary salons for his own aggrandizement. He clearly enjoyed salon life and was skillful at ingratiating himself into upper-class society, always careful to remain the center of attention. He made money that way; he was often asked to write a preface to an important book, or make a commentary about a certain subject. He preferred the salon of Madame Catherine Muhlfield, whom his mistress detested. Pozzi called her "Muhlpilate" or "la Tordue" (meaning deformed or twisted one), referring to

Madame Muhlfield's hip deformity. But in spite of Pozzi's protestations, Valéry assiduously curried Madame Muhlfield's favor. And he was amply rewarded. Apparently, it was she who pulled the strings to secure his election to the Académie française. As one wry observer, André Billy, put it, "How did she [Madame Muhlfield] get Valéry elected to the Académie? We are not privy to the secrets of the gods, but there is no doubt that it was she who got him elected."

"I am a man of action," stated Frondaie.

"I am a man of reflection," stated Valéry.

"I love women," said Frondaie.

"I dislike them, unless, of course, they can be of use to my career," said Valéry.

Both Frondaie and Valéry spent considerable time reflecting upon romantic love, but their conclusions there, too, were almost diametrically opposed. For Valéry, the emotional state of "being in love" was something to avoid at all costs. Love was not unlike a serious disease or unfortunate fate, hindering all productive activity: mathematics, science, pure thought, aesthetics. "For Valéry love is not a choice, but a painful destiny to which he courageously submits."

For Frondaie, romantic love was the goal, the centerpiece of life. "It's what makes life worthwhile. In all of its various shadings, romantic love is what I write about, think about, and seek in my life." To be in love was not some horrible trick of fate to be endured, as Valéry had claimed. Far from it. "Romantic love is precious, unique, rare; it gives life meaning," said Frondaie.

As for salon life, it wasn't suited to the temperamental and solitary Frondaie. He sometimes frightened and angered people with his remarks, his passion, and his temper. No, men like Frondaie seldom did well in the literary salon. He did not like its greenhouse atmosphere. He preferred travel, adventure, and his glorious automobile to the gossip, flattery, and social rituals of the salon. If Valéry best exemplified the literary salon hero, Frondaie might be the one best suited to start a riot. He was famous for his ability to "whip up with nonchalance the worst passions of an assembly."

Yet both men, however different, wanted Jeanne Loviton. Both offered her reflected fame and influence. But Frondaie simply had more to offer—marriage, relative youth, good looks, action—and one other thing, something that Paul Valéry never had and which Jeanne prized more than anything else: wealth. Pierre Frondaie was not only famous, he was rich. And so on 24 May 1927, only about four months after his divorce from Madeleine, Frondaie married Jeanne Loviton at the Mairie de Saint Raphaël. Jeanne Loviton was in fact the lawyer who handled Frondaie's divorce. She would become Frondaie's third wife. Her boss, the lawyer Maurice Garçon, served as one of the witnesses.

Now I knew who was with Robert Denoël in the car the night he was murdered: Jeanne Louise Anne Elisabeth Loviton (nom de plume, Jean Voilier), born in Paris on 1 April 1903. (I would later discover that in her signed police deposition the 3 of her birth year was carefully doctored with black pen to become an 8, thus shaving five years from her age.) She was the daughter of Fernand Loviton, who founded the small publishing house Domat-Montchrestien, specializing in legal and judicial publications. She was well educated, a lawyer. And in 1927 she became Madame Frondaie. Now that I knew who accompanied Denoël that fateful night, I was content to return to the rue Sainte-Anne to see what the victim was doing.

3

Starting Out . . . Starting Up

These are not books, lumps of lifeless paper, but minds
alive on the shelves.

Gilbert Highet

At the Gallery Sainte-Anne, Robert Denoël was happily at work. His
friendship with Irène Champigny had clearly blossomed. She introduced him to her artistic circle of friends, and they welcomed him.
In addition to his keen intellect and energy, he soon displayed another talent essential to Irène's business: he could sell. Customers
liked the boyish charm of the good-looking Robert Denoël. They
listened to him, often happily carrying out of the gallery some treasure that had been carefully pointed out by this disarming young
man.

Robert felt at home with Irène's friends, but most of all, he liked
the clairvoyant and fascinating Irène Champigny herself. He called
her simply "Champigny," explaining, "Even some of her friends
don't know the first name of this extraordinary woman. They simply
say 'Champigny,' as one would say Réjane, Goethe or Citroën." Denoël discovered that she was a writer who really didn't have the time
or inclination to write, preferring the active life, conversation, and
that strange propensity toward divination that she naturally had. He
later said of her, "If she wanted, she could write twenty juicy, aching

novels drawn from that marvelous reality so many talented writers breathlessly try to imitate."

Her instincts, her gift, her natural leaning toward the occult intrigued him. "She can read faces. I don't think she reads hands, but has an infallible ability to read handwriting. Several lines and a signature and there is enough for her to size up an individual, to paint the most detailed, correct, and precise moral and physical portrait of that person." It was through his "Champigny" that he learned the elements of graphology. He made a mental note to himself to sort out and publish a special series on psychology, the supernatural, and the occult (not clearly separated or defined at the time) when he was an important publisher. And, in fact, he did.

One day Irène strode into the gallery, accompanied by a well-dressed middle-aged woman. They went directly to Robert, who was seated at a table in the back of the gallery, working on a new exposition. "Robert, I want you to meet my friend, Anne-Marie Blanche," Irène said. "She has been looking for someone like you for some time."

Puzzled, Robert stood and took Anne-Marie's hand. *"Enchanté, Madame."* Anne-Marie smiled. Thanks to Irène and her glowing description of her new employee, Robert was going to be Anne-Marie's long-shot investment in those dizzying times of inflation.

Immediately, she invited him to lunch at a nearby café. Over a fine *daube de boeuf à la bourguignonne* (beef stew), she told him of her plans. "I'm looking for a partner, really," she said. "At 60, avenue de la Bourdonnais, there is a small antique business, called Chez Mitsou. I'm going to buy it. Irène tells me you might be just the right person to run it for me."

Robert put down his fork in surprise. He sat silently for a moment. She continued, "I don't want to be bothered with the day-to-day running of the shop, and I don't care exactly how you run it, or even what you sell, really, just as long as you make some money for both of us." The wonderful meal before him vanished, replaced by possibilities. She added, "I would expect you to put up some of the money, but mostly I want you to run it as if it were entirely your own." The restaurant vanished, along with the street, the quarter—almost all of Paris vanished for Robert Denoël as he mentally pictured the potential of this offer. The only thing he could see at that point was 60, avenue de la Bourdonnais. Back in her gallery, Irène Champigny, sitting alone at her desk, smiled.

There were more discussions, of course, plans, contracts, excitement. As it turned out, Anne-Marie put up nearly all of the money for their partnership—Robert borrowed from his friends the small portion he needed. And then, in January 1928, Chez Mitsou was theirs. By March Denoël had transformed it into a unique and inviting shop, part antique store, part bookstore, part art gallery. Even then he had a fourth part in mind. In the tiny space that still remained, he planned to found his publishing house.

They renamed the shop Les Trois Magots, obviously a takeoff on Les Deux Magots, the popular restaurant frequented by many artists, but also more than that. *Magot* in French has multiple meanings, all of which somehow suited the unusual flavor of this little shop. Its first meaning is "a pile of money" or "a reserved cache of money" (implying hidden treasure?). It also refers to a Barbary ape, or a figurine from Asia (allusions to the exotic). The name and the shop itself soon attracted the curious and customers alike.

In the basement Robert displayed the works of famous writers, including those of Jean Cocteau and even Paul Valéry. It was called an "astonishing boutique" with lampshades and bric-a-brac on one side and all kinds of books on the other. It was an instant hit. It was also a trap, set by an enterprising young would-be publisher. If he couldn't separate the writers he wanted from the throngs of people swarming through Montparnasse each night, he would bring them, individually, to him to see his amazing shop.

One morning a distinguished-looking man, aged fifty, with deep blue eyes, a balding Nordic head, and soldier-straight posture, once described as "a reformed eagle," entered Les Trois Magots. The trap was sprung. When Robert shook hands with the visitor, he noticed the roughness, worker's hands—or those of an artisan or artist. And when he spoke, Robert detected that distinctive and unmistakable

Belgian accent, exactly the same as his own. He would soon learn that they were both born in the same town. His name was Jean de Bosschère, and at the time, he was already famous—at least in certain artistic and literary circles.

Sometimes the professions of writer, poet, illustrator, artist, and philosopher overlap. A writer, for example, might illustrate his own work, or demonstrate his philosophy in his fiction. With Jean de Bosschère, this overlapping was more far-reaching. Although he sometimes illustrated the works of others, and produced paintings and sculpture that stood alone, much of his work was a profound synthesis of prose, poetry, art, and philosophy, so intermingled that it was nearly impossible to extricate one from the other. In fact, much of Jean de Bosschère's personal life was a reflection of this fusion.

The two Belgians liked each other instantly. Before he left the shop, Jean asked Robert to visit him the following evening at what he (and all his friends) called his "avenue de Corbéra perch" or sometimes "the Corbéra roost." Robert happily accepted, curious to know why Jean had referred to his apartment as a roost or perch. He would soon find out. Arriving at the avenue de Corbéra, he located the apartment house and discovered that Jean lived on the seventh floor. Taking the creaking elevator up the seven flights, Robert thought perhaps its high location was why it was called a perch. (When he left, he would learn that this strange elevator only brought people up; one had to walk back down.) He knocked at the door.

After a moment, Jean opened the door to his new Belgian friend. Robert stared, amazed. There were birds, books, beautiful plants, and flowers everywhere. Canaries, finches, parrots—some caged, others spreading their exotic, colorful wings as they flew freely around the apartment. Everywhere Robert looked there were treasures— paintings, easels, jewels, and beautiful rare books on high shelves surrounding a comfortable reading corner. Jean and Robert sat in that corner and talked well into the morning, drinking fine wine, laughing, and examining some of the magnificent books that Jean had written and/or illustrated. I read several works about the genius of Jean de Bosschère and began to understand the rapport Robert and

Jean almost immediately shared. Both men were deeply attracted to books, fine books, well written, well made. As his biographer said of him, "You see the real Bosschère, perhaps when he begins taking down his books, one by one—many of them rare editions, association copies, with highly personal inscriptions, etc.—and starts caressing their bindings."

Jean became deeply interested in Robert's dreams of becoming a publisher. That night Jean de Bosschère and Robert Denoël hatched a wonderful scheme that pleased them both. Jean had shown him one of the many works that he had illustrated while living in England: *The Golden Ass of Lucius Apuleius*, published in London by John Lane in 1923. "It's beautiful, amazing!" said Robert. Then he hesitated a few moments, admiring the book. "Too bad it's not written in French so this country could better appreciate it," Robert said, almost to himself. Jean sat silently, head down, a hint of a smile on his face. Bold, excited, Robert continued, "Would you allow me to publish a French version of this wonderful book?"

Jean responded almost immediately. "If my English publisher, John Lane, agrees, I don't see why not. But you have to get his permission first."

And Robert Denoël did manage to get John Lane's permission— I'm not sure how. Perhaps he thought the publicity of a new French version might engender enough interest in England to sell more English copies. For whatever reason, Robert Denoël had permission both from Lane and Bosschère to publish his first book. But how? He didn't have any money; he didn't have any experience; he didn't have any equipment; he didn't have any backing; he didn't have anything at all—except, of course, permission.

I wandered back to the library and started collecting any book I could find about French publishing from 1914 to 1928. Soon I realized the devastating impact that World War I had inflicted upon European publishing. In fact, with paper and other supplies practically nonexistent, and transportation nearly impossible, publishing had almost ceased in France during the Great War. Even after the war, paper was controlled primarily by the English and Americans, who greatly increased its cost; transportation continued to be a nightmare; and new labor laws along with continuing inflation made publishing, at least for established French publishers, very expensive and daunting. There were no publishing houses in France in the early 1920s that were not in some sort of financial difficulty or crisis. In fact, several previously successful French publishers simply closed their doors during World War I—permanently.

Although significant publishers still remained, most notably Bernard Grasset and Gaston Gallimard, the Great War left room for tiny publishing enterprises, even one-man operations, to open in garages, sheds—even possibly in a combination antique shop/bookstore/art gallery. Expense was minimal, and usually the author paid the costs. The publishing entrepreneur would find a manuscript he liked and print it himself on a hand-operated printing press he might either own or rent, or have it printed at a nominal cost. Usually only a few copies were printed at first, just to test the market. Then the so-called publisher personally carried his books to bookstores to try to sell them, and to try to have them prominently displayed. Advertising was either nonexistent or minimal. Sometimes these publishers sent free copies to important people, journals, and newspapers, hoping for recommendations. These small-time fly-by-night "publishing houses" operated all over France in the 1920s, but particularly in Paris, often opening and closing with little notice. In addition to books, many of them published journals, or short magazines, which came and went, sometimes with only one or two issues. I would soon learn that Robert Denoël started his own publishing business in just this fashion.

There were two significant differences between Denoël's first enterprise and those of most other would-be publishers at the time. First, Robert was a perfectionist, as was his author. And second, his very first author was celebrated and experienced. I wondered how Robert had convinced Jean to allow him to publish that first work. I would soon discover the answer. To write, illustrate, and then actually make a book was ultimately a part of Jean de Bosschère's philosophy, his fusion. Before, he may have written and/or illustrated various works, but he had nothing to do with the actual publication. Jean wanted to use his own fingers to produce the entire work from start to finish. He loved the manual crafts, and at that time (at least for Robert Denoël) publishing, too, was manual. As Bosschère's biographer put it, "This is the Bosschère who regrets that he hasn't a printing-press in his town studio—though where, one wonders, would he put it?—and that he cannot print and bind, as well as write and illustrate his own works." With Robert Denoël, at last, Jean de Bosschère could truly make a book. Oh yes, the money. Robert could not ask this notable man for money to publish his work. Instead, he borrowed it from Irène Champigny's companion, the artist Christian Caillard.

And so the two Belgians worked together, laughing, thinking, suggesting, their hands stained with printer's ink, each one contributing with critical eye and painstaking effort. The result was remarkable. *The Golden Ass of Lucius Apuleius* was transformed into *l'Ane d'or d'Apulée*. Jean contributed sixty engravings and color designs to the project. It was finished in July 1928, less than two years after Denoël's arrival in Paris. And the "great publishing house" that offered this precious work? It was published under the rubric of Les Trois Magots, of course.

Jean and Robert made only 130 copies of this book. It was elegant, wonderful, expensive. Robert featured it prominently in his own shop and took copies by taxi to other rare and artistic bookstores around the city. The striking book soon caught the attention and admiration of several artists, intellectuals, and bibliophiles. Even the famed book collector Léon Bartou bought the book, admired and recommended it. Robert was able to repay Caillard with the proceeds—and even have a bit left over for his next big venture. I already knew that throughout his publishing career, Robert Denoël would sometimes turn from literature to art, or to that rare combination of art and literature that Jean de Bosschère so loved, to publish beautiful, rich, magnificent, artistic books. Perhaps the passion of his Belgian friend infused this publisher as well. And now thanks to Jean de Bosschère, Robert Denoël really was a publisher, of one great book.

I located many Jean de Bosschère books and illustrations in the graduate library. His illustrations were bold, fanciful, unique. I was attracted by his imagination and use of color. His prose and poetry were rich and inventive. I could see why Robert Denoël was drawn to this multitalented, eccentric man.

In spite of the excitement and activity of Robert's shop and the publication of his first book, he had not forgotten the exotic and lovely woman he had left in Belgium. He had written her often, telling her of the exciting events in his life, confiding in her, sharing his plans and dreams. And she had answered his letters passionately, encouraging him. By the fall of 1928 he had saved enough money to send for Cécile Brusson. Excited, he met her at the train station. So many people exited the train before her that Robert began to worry. Then he saw her and moved quickly forward, taking her hand as she descended the train and pulling her into his arms. He swung her around, hugging and kissing her. They had a small simple wedding on 2 October 1928. By that time Robert had located a nicer apartment, much nearer Les Trois Magots.

"I shall not just be your wife," she announced to Robert. "I want to be an actress."

"You will always be my leading lady, Madame Denoël. And you will always have first billing," he responded, taking her hand, bowing theatrically, and kissing it.

She smiled back at him. "Where do they give their auditions?" she asked.

"They are always giving auditions," he said as he nuzzled her neck. "Antonin knows everything about that, and about auditions for silent films, too. You can ask him tomorrow." Antonin was not yet famous then. He was an artist, writer, actor, and poet, whom Robert had also recently published, at the author's expense.

"But let's not worry about auditions right now," Robert continued. There's plenty of time," he said as he scooped her up and carried her to their bed. "Let's practice our own love scenes now," he whispered, kissing her gently.

With a new husband, an apartment to put in order, Robert's friends to meet, and an exciting new city to explore, Cécile postponed those auditions for a while. After all, she had plenty of time for that after she became more accustomed to her new surroundings. With Antonin's help Robert managed to wrangle two tickets to the premiere of a play the following month. More than a premiere, the opening would surely prove to be an Event. In addition to the usual festivities associated with the premiere of any major play in Paris, this particular occasion was of special interest to Robert because of its subject. *Just Published (Vient de paraître)*, a four-act comedy by Edouard Bourdet, was a parody of the Parisian publishing world and, in particular, of the two most important publishers of the time, Bernard Grasset and Gaston Gallimard. It was even rumored that these two famous men might attend the opening. Since Robert had never seen either publisher before, except in the newspapers, he was determined to be there, too.

On the night of 25 November 1928 Robert and Cécile joined the elegant audience at the Théâtre de la Michodière for a show they would not soon forget. After finding their seats, Robert pointed to a box on the second floor at the left of the stage. Seated there was a short middle-aged man with brown hair and a large mustache, fidgeting uncomfortably and nervously picking at his fingernails. "See that man?" Robert whispered to his wife. "He's the one who discovered Marcel Proust. Bernard Grasset," Robert spoke almost reverently.

Just then another middle-aged man approached the loge on the other side of the stage, directly opposite Grasset. This man was slightly taller, more handsome, and clearly more gregarious. Several beautiful ladies surrounded him as he shook hands with one gentleman, then greeted and laughed with another. "And that's Gaston Gallimard, the man who stole Proust from Grasset." He grinned. "Do you know what they say about Gallimard?"

"What?"

"They say that Gaston is the first man to discover authors for the second time."

"You mean he just goes around to other publishers stealing their authors?" she asked.

"Whenever he can," he responded. "Whenever he possibly can. It's much easier than going out and actually finding them." He laughed.

"You can't be serious."

"Gallimard does whatever it takes to stay on top. He's the foremost publisher in France, maybe Europe, and he intends to stay that way."

"He doesn't know about you, then."

"Not yet, my dear, not yet. You know, there's a story about him. Gallimard was present at Proust's death a few years ago. Apparently it was quite a scene, a sort of literary death salon, with lots of people around the bedside of the dying Proust, and even an artist busy painting the entire scene. And just as Proust dies, Gallimard realizes he is standing next to none other than Jean Cocteau, you know, the playwright and novelist. So Gallimard just ignores the situation and asks Cocteau for permission to publish his new novel, *Thomas the Impostor (Thomas, l'imposteur)*. And Cocteau, seeing who has just made him the offer, says yes. They actually make the deal beside the still-warm corpse of Marcel Proust. Hard to believe. I think if Gallimard had had a contract then he might have whipped it out and placed it on Proust's forehead for Cocteau's signature."

"The publisher's benediction," Cécile responded, giggling.

"The writer is dead; long live the writer," said Robert in mock solemnity. "But you have to admit, Gaston Gallimard is one tough publisher, going after his next author even when the most famous writer in France is dying. He has no time for sentiment." Of course, Robert had no idea that in slightly less than one year Gallimard would attempt to steal one of Robert's own writers.

Cécile eyed Gallimard. A beautiful woman was bending over, earnestly talking to him as he sat in his loge, her arm on his shoulder. "Looks like he has time for women, though," she whispered.

"Gaston Gallimard always has time for beautiful women," her

husband responded. "And very fast cars, good theater, the best French restaurants. He's rich, you know, independently wealthy. Doesn't even need his publishing empire to make his living. They say he loves great literature. I think he loves only the literature he has published himself."

She laughed. "And Bernard Grasset?"

"I understand there is only one rule regarding Grasset: Don't mess with him! He can destroy an author with a few quick words. And temper, look out! But in spite of his tantrums, he makes remarkably good decisions. There's no doubt that he's a great publisher, probably as good as old Gaston—maybe better."

The play began, and the world of French publishing appeared on stage, with Grasset's name changed to Moscat, and Gallimard thinly disguised as Chamillard. At first the air seemed tense. Everyone knew that the playwright, Edouard Bourdet, had gotten the inspiration for his play while sitting in Grasset's waiting room. Intrigued by the comings and goings of writers, staff, and publisher, he began to take notes. Throughout the plot there are blatant manipulations by both publishers, shady money deals, attempted thefts of authors, literary prizes that the publishers manage to fix, literary judges who don't read the works they judge, and even the publishers themselves who haven't read their own publications.

But Bourdet was careful. He took potshots at the other French publishers as well. His humor was clever rather than harsh, gentle instead of fierce. And most important, Bourdet demonstrated that these two publishers, however keen their competition might be, clearly respected—even liked—each other. And that was true. In spite of certain tricks, there were rules to this publishing game, and both men followed them. At first members of the audience glanced up at Gallimard and Grasset before they dared to laugh. But when they saw both publishers chuckling, the audience relaxed and began to enjoy a great comedy.

Bourdet also parodied a publisher's tendency to inflate his sales figures. For example, Moscat tries to lure a writer to his publishing house by saying that he will publish twenty thousand copies of his novel. Then he adds, "And you realize that here, they are truly thousands . . . thousands of five hundred!" When the author expresses confusion at this number, Moscat continues: "Yes, because at Chamillard, for example, a thousand really means only 250." Here the two publishers began to join into the spirit of the evening and laughed and pointed at each other. The audience was delighted, and Bourdet, who had been pacing back and forth backstage, nervously wringing his hands and peeking from the wings at the two distinguished publishers, stopped worrying about a slander suit and began to enjoy the evening. The play was a hit!

As the newlyweds exited the theater, arm in arm, they passed a woman dressed in a long pleated blue silky gown with an equally long matching brocaded coat. I recognized her at once. Occupied in an animated conversation with two other people, she did not even notice the young couple. It was Jeanne Loviton. I looked for Pierre Frondaie, but he was nowhere in sight.

Although I was reluctant to leave the happy newlyweds, I was curious to see how the Frondaies were doing. And since Jeanne Loviton sometimes proved so difficult to trace, I decided to follow her right from the theater. She did not go directly home, but instead attended two glittering after-theater parties. She was mentioned in several society columns. She seemed to know everyone, was received with great respect—sometimes even awe. Jeanne Loviton, or Madame Frondaie, was clearly moving in much higher social circles than Robert Denoël. It was after 3:00 A.M. when she returned to the Frondaie mansion. A light was still shining in the library.

The stately white Frondaie mansion was located in an elegant Paris neighborhood with shady old trees lining the streets and here and there precise, well-tended gardens. It was the grandest mansion on that street, with beautiful gardens, a wide sweeping staircase, and a huge balcony across the back, providing views of the Seine. It was elegant, romantic. I tried to peek inside, but history afforded me only a good look at their library—where Pierre spent most of his time. It was an exquisite room of paintings and countless books with leather bindings neatly arranged in deep floor-to-ceiling shelves.

Near the center of the room stood a huge, deeply polished antique mahogany desk with two secret compartments. Pierre loved that desk and had written most of his plays and novels right there, seated in his comfortable leather chair with a high back. From there he could view his large fireplace whose mantel held ancient Chinese vases and figurines, or look out on the gardens through the tall, narrow windows with golden velvet drapes. The library's lustrous parquet floor was partially covered by a thick blue-and-gold Oriental rug. Against the darkly paneled wall were two large overstuffed chairs separated by a rich cherry library table with a heavy brass reading lamp. "My favorite room," murmured Pierre. I could see why.

I could imagine that Jeanne and Pierre must have been deeply happy together in such surroundings. Everything seemed perfect. I wondered if Pierre had been annoyed because his wife was often out so late without him. A small item in a gossip column of *The Literary News (Les Nouvelles littéraires)*, seemed to cast a shadow upon their bliss. Although her name was not mentioned, the article dealt with the beautiful wife of a "famous writer and playwright, known for his penchant for capes." Apparently this wife had, unbeknownst to her husband, taken his fabulous Hispano-Suiza out for a spin. And she was not alone at the time. She was driving with none other than Paul Valéry, Monsieur Teste himself, when she was involved in a minor traffic accident, denting a fender of the Hispano-Suiza. Monocle askew, but body intact, the shaken and embarrassed Valéry had an uncharacteristic "No comment," when a reporter happened on the scene and asked him what he thought about women drivers.

Sometimes angry voices could be heard coming from the Frondaie mansion. "You may not see him again! I forbid you to see him—or that insolent, egotistic Maurice Garçon!" Softer protestations of a female voice were also audible, but were overpowered by a deep male voice shouting "outrageous," "intolerable," "insufferable," and several "forbids."

So the man reputed to have a weakness for actresses was apparently having fidelity problems of his own. Then Jeanne abruptly quit her position as lawyer in the Garçon law office. Apparently there had been an either/or ultimatum from her husband. Was she having an affair with Garçon? I searched through piles of books and articles written by Garçon. As far as I could determine, Garçon willingly discussed every topic imaginable—except, of course, his own love life. That subject, the wily lawyer wisely avoided. Nor did I find any useful information in the writings of his friends and associates. Smart man, I thought. All that I had to link him romantically with Jeanne were the rages of her jealous husband. But clearly I already knew that Pierre Frondaie had, even aside from Maurice Garçon, several good reasons to be jealous.

In fact, he was not the only suspicious lover then. I soon discovered in a biography of Valéry's mistress, Catherine Pozzi, that she also sniffed betrayal at about the same time. "He has another woman," she stormed. "I can endure his wife, but not another. Not three, some Unseemly Trinity. Only God can be compatible with the number three!" And so, in 1928 Catherine Pozzi ended her long relationship with France's Official Poet. She burned everything that Paul Valéry had ever given her—all his letters, love poems, mementos.

Upon learning of Pozzi's bonfire, Paul Valéry sighed with relief. "Not everything should be saved for posterity," he once told an interviewer. "A man, even a famous man, has the intrinsic right to a personal life, to private letters and thoughts forever beyond the realm of public scrutiny." He had, in fact, made the concept of a famous man's right to privacy his own personal crusade. For Valéry, even death should not end that right. Pozzi and her poet had previously agreed that they would destroy all of their personal exchanges at the end of their relationship. And so it happened, to the great dismay and sorrow of many scholars and historians.

But Pozzi did keep one brief and vivid description of her poet at the time. And surely Valéry would have wished this entry in her diary also destroyed. First, she methodically listed his physical characteristics. And Valéry did not fare well in this description. According to his mistress he was a "small nervous shriveled man with bad teeth, sparse hair, and ugly misshapen hands." But it was in her description of his mental faculties that Pozzi became even more critical. She noted his intelligence, but combined it with a "fearful heart, and a protective sophism capable of biting criticism and hammering decrees given to anyone humble enough to accept his verbal blows." I knew already that some of the most famous literary men of France had quietly endured Valéry's scathing critiques. In fact, some men had never fully recovered from this poet's harsh, often relentless, criticism. Pozzi concluded that Valéry is "a strange friend of precise things, who doesn't like the truth." She decided that she couldn't love him anymore. There were simply too many faults of character, which she could no longer overlook. And although she did not yet know her rival's name, Jeanne Loviton was clearly one of Valéry's "flaws."

I returned to the elegant Frondaie library to look for Jeanne and arrived just in time to overhear a bitter argument. "Bills," Pierre snorted, pointing to a neat stack of papers sitting on his desk. "In the past month you have purchased enough jewelry, dresses, and shoes to outfit an entire theater production!"

"Darling, you do want me to look my best," she responded.

"Now this," he continued. "Decorators' expenses, wallpaper, new drapes, one outrageously expensive Oriental rug, Ming vases. Did they have to be Ming? And can this be right?" he said, pounding his fist on the next item, his dark eyes snapping. "Can you possibly have found a desk even larger and more costly than the one in this library? Apparently so," he sniffed. "Apparently the wife of a writer needs a bigger, better, more expensive desk than the writer himself!"

"I, too, am a writer," she responded.

"Since when?" he shouted.

"Since NOW!" She walked briskly out of the library, slamming the door behind her. I quietly retreated from her livid husband. Now I confirmed why it was so difficult to locate this woman, who had accompanied Denoël to the place of his murder the night of 2 December 1945, by searching for the name Jean Voilier. As of 1925, she hadn't even chosen that pseudonym yet.

She did not decide to become a writer, a novelist, until after she left her job with Garçon. And she launched her own writing career by turning the largest spare bedroom of the Frondaie mansion into her own sumptuous office. It was, if not more beautiful, certainly more costly than her husband's library. But she did not devote all of her time to writing. She had other matters to attend to: dress fittings, hair appointments, lavish parties, lunch with friends, and the theater. From the moment she married Pierre Frondaie, she expected and got the best theater seats in the house at no charge. It was considered an honor for her to be present. In the 1920s high-ranking French government officials often made the theater and its accompanying gatherings and fêtes a routine part of their social life. Many such officials selected leading ladies as their mistresses. As Madame Frondaie, Jeanne met the upper crust of Parisian society. She soon knew them all—artists, politicians, lawyers, the rich and powerful. For even before she married Pierre Frondaie, Jeanne knew the importance of money, power, and influence, and she was determined to make the most of her connections.

As for her husband's admonition to stop seeing Maurice Garçon and Paul Valéry, Jeanne was not very good with admonitions. She turned his decree into her discretion, remaining in close contact with both men—but quietly, carefully. She no longer took her famous poet out for a spin in her husband's Hispano-Suiza. And yes, she wrote. She wrote when she had nothing better to do. In her writing she began to castigate, berate, and disparage her husband. Pierre Frondaie, the writer out of step with the times, the critic of that new trend, surrealism, the man who still loved romantic writing in the twentieth century, became in his wife's writings Pierre Frondaie, the fool.

By now I had located several photographs of Jeanne Loviton. I took them out and carefully examined them, hoping they would bring her to life for me as she was in those glorious Parisian days. She was not beautiful, but aristocratic, patrician. Like her husband's previous wife, she often wore her brown hair back in a chignon. Many of her photos were taken in profile, revealing a regal elegance, fairly long nose, regular features, rich sumptuous blouses, and every hair carefully in place. I would later learn that Jeanne preferred pictures taken at least from the waist up. She had a flaw: large legs, which she took pains to minimize or camouflage. Nothing in her photos revealed her great attraction or physical charm. She had no Marilyn Monroe animal sexuality, and no Clara Bow cuteness. Instead, she seemed almost cold. I knew that she was intelligent, that she liked conversation and was good at it. But I couldn't yet determine what was so attractive about her. Was she witty, empathetic, loving? She certainly was an enigma to me. I left her writing a broad and hostile caricature of her husband's many foibles. She planned to use it later in her novel. I returned quietly to the less wealthy but far more colorful side of Paris, home of Les Trois Magots.

At his tiny publishing house/shop, Robert was everywhere. Day and night he worked on major projects, talking with authors, printing their works, looking for money, and reading new manuscripts. Only the figurines and lampshades, now shoved forlornly into a corner, escaped his attention. He continued to publish small editions, mostly at the authors' expense. Interestingly, even these very limited editions would one day become famous, a tribute to Robert's knack for literary discovery. But it would take decades for these works to gain recognition, and in the meantime, they did not make much money. Then Robert read a manuscript entitled *Hotel of the North (L'Hôtel du Nord)*, written by one of Irène Champigny's friends, Eugène Dabit, who was better known in the field of art than in literature.

"It's a wonderful book," Robert told Dabit. "I like the way you take the residents of the hotel and bring their lives together into a novel. I think we could make money with this book."

Dabit, however, was not so sure. He was four years older than Denoël and was not convinced that this young upstart was the right publisher for his manuscript. But he had already tried Grasset, Gallimard, and other major publishers, and they had all politely but firmly rejected him. He had even considered publishing the book himself. Then he had reluctantly shown it to Robert, whose great enthusiasm for the work was hard to resist.

Robert then suggested that they also publish a limited luxury edition containing some of Dabit's watercolors. "You are enormously talented in both fields," Robert told the hesitant author. "You could combine your watercolor gouaches with your novel. Imagine what a beautiful book you would have. And I know how to do it. I have already done it with Jean de Bosschère's book." He took out the exquisite book that Jean and he had so lovingly made and handed it to Dabit, who carefully examined each page, noting the care that had gone into its publication.

"Do you really think my work would sell?" he quietly asked, looking up at Robert.

"I know it would."

And so the deal was made. There was, of course, the matter of getting the money for publication. Both men borrowed from everyone they knew. In the end, Dabit's relatives put up most of the financing. Robert put everything he had into this publication, his first big printing. On 10 December 1929 the printer sent him three thousand copies of the book, along with a much more limited luxury edition. Cécile walked into Les Trois Magots the following day. She looked at the huge piles of books and boxes, scattered everywhere. There wasn't any room for customers, and barely room for Robert. He was alone, madly stacking, counting, and packing the boxes.

"I thought you might like to take me out to lunch," she suggested brightly.

"Can't today. Got to get these things to the bookstores right away. Antonin was just here. I think he is over at Champigny's gallery. Why don't you eat with him?" he suggested without even looking up. "You two can talk theater."

"I think I will," she said and left the shop.

Robert, who had served as the initial reader, then editor and publisher of *Hotel of the North* personally packed the books into boxes, carefully counting the contents and designating the future location of each container. Then he called a cab.

"This is gonna cost you extra," the cabby said, slowly scratching his head as Robert jammed as many boxes as he could into the cab, then squeezed himself inside. "I ain't no truck, ya know."

By the time the taxi had reached its first bookstore, Robert had charmed the driver into a lower price, hiring him by the day. The two of them drove all over Paris, stopping at bookstores where Robert delivered the books. He had already served as an advance man, talking the dealers into taking the book. Now he used his persuasive powers to get them displayed in the window, or in some other prominent place in each shop. And then they started to sell. In fact, they sold well.

As is customary, Robert sent free copies to important people, hoping they might favorably review the book and recommend it. And Dabit sent one copy to the man who had first rejected his manuscript: Gaston Gallimard. To his surprise, he received a prompt thank-you from this famous publisher, along with praise for the book. After all, the novel was no longer a forlorn manuscript that no one had read; it was becoming a hot commodity. To Eugène Dabit's astonishment and great pleasure, Gallimard also asked if he could meet with him. One of the biggest publishers in France wanted to meet personally with Eugène Dabit. Of course he would go. It was at that meeting that Gallimard stole him.

It was child's play, really. Gaston Gallimard simply praised Dabit's work, then offered him a generous contract along with a monthly stipend. Dabit leaped at the offer. As he later told Antonin over drinks at a sidewalk café, "I know that Robert did everything right. And he has gone to great lengths to make my book a success. But to be published by Gallimard—that's always been my dream. And now it's real. After all, it's my career, isn't it? In this world I have to look out for myself."

Until *Hotel of the North*, major publishers had simply ignored Robert's tiny publishing business. Why bother? Nearly every writer in Paris could find his own printing press if he really wanted to. Even Ernest Hemingway had access to a hand-run printing press in Paris, which dated from the seventeenth century. It was housed in a wine cellar on the quai d'Anjou and was still in active use. Hemingway sometimes set his latest manuscript in type, using the printing press to view his work in print. Sometimes a small publishing house in the late 1920s would publish only one author. Alice B. Toklas, for example, decided to establish a small press dedicated entirely to Gertrude Stein's works. Plain Editions was the result.

But this Dabit and his *Hotel of the North* were different; they were making money. Gaston Gallimard then got greedy. He not only wanted the author of this book, he decided he needed all future rights to *Hotel of the North* as well. To obtain those rights, he had to see this novice, Robert Denoël, himself. Gallimard did not call or write Robert to forewarn him of his intent. Instead, he used the element of surprise, ambush, making an unannounced personal visit to Les Trois Magots.

Robert was just getting ready to leave the shop and meet his wife for lunch when he brushed against a display shelf, which wobbled ominously, threatening to drop its contents of rare books onto the floor. Locating a screwdriver and lying on his back under the shelf, he had just started to tighten the screws when the great publisher entered Les Trois Magots. The publisher lying under the display cabinet jumped when he realized who was staring down at him, causing a clatter of glass—not exactly the impression he wished to make. While Robert slowly, carefully extricated himself from beneath the display and brushed off his clothes, Gallimard looked around—at the antiques, the books for sale, the gallery, and even at that tiny spot reserved for Denoël's publications. He smiled to himself. This was going to be easy.

After the introductions, the shaking of hands, and brief small talk, Gallimard got down to business. "Monsieur Denoël, my lawyers have informed me that your contract for all future rights to the *Hotel of the North* is simply not valid. If this case went to court, you would lose. Now I am a reasonable man. I am willing to make you some very generous concessions . . ."

"Monsieur Gallimard, let's be clear from the start. Not only do I not intend to give you any rights to Dabit's book, now or in the future, I don't intend to give you Eugène Dabit, either."

"Now let's be reasonable," said Gallimard. But Denoël was in no mood to be "reasonable." All of the older publisher's offers—free publicity, translation rights, other attractive concessions, and even significant money—were met with a resounding no.

Gallimard threw up his hands and abruptly left Les Trois Magots, promising that the battle had just begun. Forgetting about his lunch date with Cécile (he was already an hour late), Robert immediately stormed over to Dabit's studio. "I took your manuscript when everyone else rejected it. I did everything you asked of me and more. I worked twenty hours a day to make your novel a success. And now that it is a success, you leave me for Gaston Gallimard. Why?"

Dabit, who had been working on a watercolor, put down his brush and looked down. "You're right, Robert," Dabit admitted. "I could not have asked or expected more of you. And you have done a wonderful job. The problem is that I don't want to link my future to yours. Your future in publishing is just too uncertain."

"Stay with me," countered Robert, "and I will make you everything in my publishing house. You are and will always be first here."

"Robert," said the dejected Dabit. "I know. I know that you would make me first within your publishing house. It's just that . . . well . . . I'm afraid that I will be first because I am the only one."

In the end Denoël kept all future rights to *Hotel of the North*. But he lost his author. Gallimard's power, prestige, and generous contract to Dabit overcame the author's feelings of loyalty to his first publisher. By 20 January 1930, Denoël had sold fifteen hundred copies of Dabit's novel, plus twenty-five luxury books, with a new edition scheduled. Yet in spite of this success, Dabit signed with Gaston Gallimard on 3 February 1930, less than two months after his first novel's publication. Gallimard had acted quickly.

I came across the following sentences while researching French publishing houses:

Doesn't it seem legitimate to you that a publisher who gives an author his start, not being assured of recouping his investment, should at least have the future before him, and that he benefit to a certain degree from the launching he had some part in? Otherwise all the burden would be on the publisher, who might see the author, once successful, leave him for some bigger company.

Not Robert Denoël, but Gaston Gallimard himself wrote those words when one of his own authors, Roger Martin du Gard, was threatening to leave him. It was a tough business, publishing.

Although Gallimard stole Denoël's author, he did not win the battle. While there are some writers whose first book is merely a beginning to a whole career of writing, there are others who can write only one excellent book. At the time neither publisher could have foreseen that Dabit had already written his only great book. And Denoël had all the rights to it.

After the Gallimard and Dabit meetings, Robert returned home. His wife, dressed elegantly, was sitting in the living room, a romance novel in her hand. She looked up at him slowly. "Did you forget something, Robert? Something important?"

He touched his hand to his forehead and shut his eyes. "Oh God, I'm sorry. I stood you up, didn't I? It's just that . . ."

"Not the first time," she muttered. "I sat at Le Petit Gigot for more than an hour today waiting for you!"

"What can I do to make it up?" he asked.

She rose from her seat and slowly walked toward him. "You can remember me," she said softly. "You don't seem to remember me anymore. You remember your business appointments, your work engagements, everything but me. I want to be remembered, Robert."

"Of course, you're right," he said. "It's just that . . ."

"Our dates, our parties, our friends. We have no life together anymore, Robert. Is there someone else? Someone to help you take your mind off me?"

"No, my darling, there is no one else. It's just that . . . publishing . . . well, publishing—doing it right, I mean. It takes so much time to do it right."

"I've seen you and some of your women writers together. They practically fawn over you," she continued. "That little mademoiselle in your office yesterday, the one in the very tight pink outfit and her boudoir eyes, what do you suppose she wanted you to buy?"

"There is no one else but you," he repeated.

"There's more to life than books, Robert" she said. "Sometimes I think you deliberately foist me off onto others, just to get me out of your hair."

He pulled her close to him and held her quietly. "I'm sorry," he said.

The following day, while Robert was at work, there was a knock at the door. Cécile opened it to find a deliveryman holding a huge bouquet of pink roses. "For Madame Denoël," he stated. She smiled, took the flowers, then shut the door. Nestled inside the two dozen roses was a small card. It read, "I shall remember. All my love, Robert."

4

When Losing Is Winning

You will never be a publisher as long as you talk about sure
things.

Gaston Gallimard

Starting in the spring of 1929, a young man, aged twenty-seven,
often frequented Les Trois Magots. Although he spoke Parisian
French even better than Robert, he was not French. He was an American,
a connoisseur of books and music and fine wine. His name was
Bernard Steele. He watched Robert's comings and goings closely,
noting with particular interest that fourth section of the small establishment—Robert's
publishing house. Like nearly everyone else in
Paris, Steele was looking for a good investment. What distinguished
him from most others was that Steele was wealthy.

Soon the two men became acquainted. They liked each other.
Bernard admired Robert's dedication and nerve, especially in the face
of Gaston Gallimard. Even before he realized that Bernard had
money to invest, Robert appreciated Steele's knowledge of books, his
intelligence and savoir faire.

"If only I had the money to advertise," Robert told Bernard, "what
a difference that would make. Then I could really make a go of this
place."

"How much would it take?" asked Bernard.

They discussed various figures for some time, considering advertising, publishing costs, and the need for more space. For several days they sat in the back of Les Trois Magots, each with a notebook, busily writing. Finally, Robert put down his pen and concluded, "I would need at least 300,000 francs [more than $76,000] to really get started."

Bernard thought for a few moments. Then he smiled. "This could work," he said.

They officially formed their partnership in the spring of 1930, naming their business Les Editions Denoël et Steele. Bernard put up the capital, and Denoël ran the business as principal manager. Legally, however, both men headed the company and were equally responsible for it. Although neither man knew much about the day-to-day running of a business, what they lacked in business acumen, they made up for in their appreciation of literature.

Their first step was obvious. "If we are going to establish a great publishing house," said Bernard, "we need to find an adequate space for it without running into those damn lampshades and knick-knacks."

They scoured nearly all of Paris, looking for the perfect place to house their new business. That wasn't easy since they needed more room than most buildings afforded. Then one day Bernard rushed into Les Trois Magots. "I think I have found it," he said. "Well, not really it—more like them."

"What?" said Robert.

"Them. Not one building, but two—side-by-side. Both for sale now."

Bernard took Robert to rue Amélie to the site of an abandoned hosiery factory adjacent to a deconsecrated Protestant chapel. "We can pray in one side and make socks in the other," joked Bernard. They bought both buildings, officially turning them into Les Editions Denoël et Steele, located at 19, rue Amélie. Then they hired some help. By 1930 Robert Denoël had his publishing house. He remained the company's only reader. Although he retained Les Trois Magots, he readily gave up his duties as general secretary, salesman for Paris, salesman for the provinces, packer, designer, bookkeeper, distributor, production head, and production secretary. He hired others for those jobs. Still no one then ever expected him to succeed.

Steele's investment brought 19, rue Amélie to life. With the United States' stock market crash of 1929 and an ever more ominous global economic crisis, 1931 proved to be a difficult year for most French publishers. Because of Steele's investment, Robert Denoël was the exception. Finally, he could even advertise.

One of the new artistic fads at that time was called populism, which lauded works written by and about the common man. In 1931 Madame Antonin Coullet-Tessier established the Prize for the Populist Novel, to be awarded to the writer and work best representing the common man. During a discussion in Denoël's office, Robert, leaning back in his chair, his feet on his desk, asked Bernard, "Why couldn't we make Dabit fit the image of the common man? After all, *Hotel of the North* is about common people living together in a hotel."

Bernard put down his pen and grinned. "Dabit representing the common man? That's just about like making a duke a garbage collector." They both chuckled. "Dabit, the artist, the intellectual, the writer, with a shovel and hoe. Just think of it," Bernard continued. Both men could not stop laughing.

"Has he told you how much he hates any form of manual labor? He wouldn't know what to do with a hoe, except possibly paint a picture of it," Denoël continued, putting his feet down and holding his hands over his mouth in a vain effort stifle his mirth. Then he continued, "Do you know, Bernard, who actually *owns* The Hotel of the North?" Denoël paused for dramatic effect, "His parents!" They both shook with laughter.

"Oh, we have to do this, my friend," Steele continued. "Turning Dabit into an example of the common man will be a challenge, a true tribute to the power of advertising."

"The power of advertising," echoed his partner. "Let's turn Duke Dabit into a commoner."

And they did. They cleverly marketed both the book and its author as a pure example of populism. Their advertising paid off. In May 1931 the first winner of the Prize for the Populist Novel was announced: Eugène Dabit for *Hotel of the North*. As soon as Dabit won, the young publishers heavily advertised his book in journals and newspapers. The result was sales. Everyone wanted to read this new populist prizewinner. Gaston Gallimard was very annoyed.

In 1929, while Denoël was still occupied at Les Trois Magots, a man he had not yet met began writing in secret, feverishly, obsessively. And he continued to write, oblivious to anything else, as Denoël and Steele established their partnership and their publishing house. He wrote of death, of dreams, of haunting degradation, futile war, describing with heretofore unknown brutal eloquence and slang his fruitless search for the end of darkness. He was a medical doctor. His name was Dr. Louis-Ferdinand Destouches. His style was new, brilliant, shocking—his passion untethered. Although it is not clear exactly when Destouches finished his novel, he had begun to think about marketing it by the end of 1931.

Robert Denoël was not his first choice . . . or even his second or third. No, Dr. Louis-Ferdinand Destouches did not want to entrust his enormous manuscript to some young, inexperienced Belgian publisher. After all, who was this Robert Denoël anyway? And what did he know about literature . . . or publishing for that matter? Everyone knew that no banker in his right mind would ever have loaned Denoël any money. Dr. Destouches had no intention of submitting the manuscript he had worked on for so long to a publisher who might go bankrupt at any time.

But then Dr. Destouches didn't know much about publishing, either. In fact, the only publications this doctor had to his credit were a publicity brochure for Sanogyl Toothpaste and a few medical articles in various journals. Sanogyl Toothpaste, "Puerperal Infection and Antiviruses," and "Public Health in France" hardly made an impressive résumé for a novelist. Now Destouches believed he had written a masterpiece—and in fact, he had. But he had no idea how to market it. He did not realize that his *Journey to the End of the Night* (*Voyage au bout de la nuit*) would soon become an endless, mindless journey into the realm of publishing, editors, and readers—a nightmare of letters, rejections, suggestions, and delay.

He made several false starts. He thought of publishing his novel in the leftist journal *Monde* and gave it to one of its editors, Georges Altman. This bimonthly had already published one of Dr. Destouches' articles "Public Health in France" ("La Santé publique en France"), but that work hardly prepared Altman for the doctor's new, lengthy manuscript. The novel never appeared in *Monde*. Then Dr. Destouches sent his manuscript to a small publishing house, Les Editions Bossard. They rejected it. The work did not suit their formula; it was not right for their list. Then he submitted his *Journey* to the publishing house of Eugène Figuière. This establishment offered him a vanity publication. If Destouches would pay twelve thousand francs up front, Figuière would publish his work. Needless to say, Dr. Destouches refused their offer.

Dr. Destouches decided he would try Gaston Gallimard and wrote his first letter regarding his novel to Gallimard's literary journal *N.R.F.* (*La Nouvelle Revue française/New French Review*) on 9 December 1931. The Gallimard firm knew his name. It had already rejected two of his works: a play, *The Church* (*L'Eglise*) in 1927, and his doctoral dissertation, *"Sommelweis,"* in 1928. But the Gallimard rejection letters were not entirely negative, praising parts of his works and suggesting Detouches submit something else. And so even before his manuscript was fully typed, he wrote again to Gaston Gallimard describing his novel. Gallimard's literary secretary, Louis Chevasson, responded promptly enough, requesting a copy of the manuscript along with a brief summary of its contents.

Destouches did not immediately respond to Chevasson's request. He was irked—unsure how to provide a brief synopsis of a manuscript of more than eight hundred pages, and uncertain why this summary was needed. Finally he wrote Chevasson on 14 April 1932, sending him a copy of the manuscript along with the briefest sketch of its contents. He concluded his letter by saying, "It's the Goncourt Prize of 1932 given in an armchair to the happy publisher who decides to put this unparalleled work under contract." The author's confident prediction failed to impress anyone at the NRF. More letters ensued. An NRF reader, Benjamin Crémieux, was assigned to judge the manuscript and present a report to a literary committee that included Gaston Gallimard himself. But Crémieux was busy with other projects. By the time his report was due, he hadn't finished reading the manuscript. He simply gave the committee a brief summary of what he had read and suggested that the final decision on publication be delayed until others could read and critique it.

And so the manuscript was passed around. André Malraux read it. Emmanuel Berl read it. Others read it. Each reader had a different reaction to the work, along with various often-contradictory suggestions for cuts, corrections, and improvements. *Journey* was dying in committee. Destouches and Crémieux exchanged more letters. On 13 June 1932 Destouches wrote the NRF, complaining that it had held his manuscript for two months, "and I wonder if I can get it back or if you have still not found the time to read it?" Again the response from the NRF was vague, saying that the reader for the manuscript had not yet given his opinion. Finally, on 29 June 1932, Destouches wrote the NRF requesting the return of his manuscript. "Not having received your response, I have accepted the proposal of another publisher." Although he had not actually accepted another publisher's offer at the time he wrote that letter, he would do so on the following day. Even then the letters between the doctor and the NRF did not stop. But no offer by Gaston Gallimard and the NRF was forthcoming. And so Dr. Louis-Ferdinand Destouches slipped through the hands of Gaston Gallimard, ending up in the former hosiery factory and chapel that was now Denoël's new publishing house.

Destouches had read Dabit's *Hotel of the North.* He was impressed by Dabit's work, his style. Denoël's publication of Dabit influenced Destouches to submit his own novel to this new publisher. What happened next is still the subject of scholarly dispute. Robert Denoël himself recounted the story of his discovery of *Journey to the End of the*

Night. Whether this account is entirely true or hyped by Denoël is still unknown.

According to Denoël, he walked into his office early one evening intending to finish up a few odds and ends before going home. Sitting on his desk was an enormous package, wrapped in newspapers. While the package did have the correct address of Les Editions Denoël et Steele on it, Robert soon discovered that it also bore another tag: the address of Gaston Gallimard's publishing house. "One of Gallimard's rejects?" the young publisher asked himself. Curious, he opened the package and examined its contents. There, he found a huge manuscript of more than eight hundred carefully typed pages. Robert looked at the cover, examined briefly the inside page, then looked again at the newspaper wrapping. "Who sent this?" he said aloud.

Robert sat down at his desk, took the manuscript, and began to read. He had intended only to glance at it. But the work was extraordinary. "Seized from the first lines by the innovation of the author's tone, by his entire freedom, by this extraordinarily rich language, crammed with slang and images of an unparalleled rawness, I read *Journey* in one sitting. I spent the entire night reading it. And the following morning I started my search for the author of the book that I considered an unparalleled masterpiece."

Denoël then searched every inch of the newspaper wrapping. This time he found on one of the pieces of wrapping paper an address label bearing the name of a woman. Impossible, he thought. No woman could have written about war and battle in this way, using such crude language. But at least it was a start. He quickly sent a message to the woman asking her to visit him immediately. While he waited for her to respond, Robert sat down again at his desk and glanced briefly at some of the other manuscripts recently sent to him. "To my astonishment, there I discovered a novel that bore the name and address of the woman to whom I had just sent my message. The manuscript—with only a brief glance at it, I realized—the manuscript was insipid. What should I do? I did not want to hurt the only person who could inform me. She came to see me that afternoon, persuaded (alas!) that I had sent for her because I was going to publish her novel." When the woman knocked at his office door, Robert immediately ushered her in.

I tried to follow her into his office, but Robert quickly shut the door, preventing my entrance. I could only look through the glass in the door. I watched Denoël at work—smiling broadly, charming this woman. I remembered that Denoël had sometimes been called a chameleon, changing his attitude, his philosophy, even his appearance as the situation demanded. I had seen this publisher rumpled, slouched, hair askew, unhandsome, deeply engrossed in his work. But I had also seen him dazzling, impeccable, charming, debonair. Now he assumed his most engaging posture. Even standing outside the door, I was entranced.

I looked briefly at the author. She didn't have a chance against this skillful manipulator. Already her body language revealed her pleasure at his attentions. She crossed her legs, moving her skirt slightly above her knees, and smiled as she leaned toward the man who was now showering her with attention. I remembered the young man in the movie theater in one of Robert's early stories, turning his eyelid to produce tears in the hope of seduction. Clearly, this publisher had moved far beyond those early clumsy manipulation attempts. Now he was a master.

I had already seen some of the comments of other authors who had been ushered into Denoël's office. Writer Robert Poulet, for example, noted that Denoël had a habit of welcoming any author with a contract or money complaint into his office. There, Denoël would praise his disgruntled writer, laud his works, treat him as a cherished family member, and then take him into his confidence. In the face of all those compliments and confidences, the writer "no longer dared afterward to invoke the terms of the contract, which now suddenly seemed only an empty formality."

Now here was an unsuspecting author happily seated before a publisher who wanted something from her. It was all so simple. According to Denoël's own account of the incident, he quickly asked her if she knew the name of the author of that huge manuscript. At first she had said that she had no idea who the author could be. It took him an hour to pry the information out of her. Apparently after an hour of charm and compliments, poor Robert Denoël had looked so puzzled that when he again mentioned the unknown author of that manuscript, she simply had to help him. And he was so interested in what she had to say, hanging on her every word.

While Denoël lit her cigarette from a beautiful gold lighter he took from his pocket, then sat on the edge of his desk quite close to her, his blue eyes intense, his smile gentle, she confided to him, "I'm pretty sure that manuscript belongs to a neighbor of mine—a strange fellow, really—a doctor. You see, we both share the same maid. She must have used my paper to wrap up her slippers. She's always doing things like that. I imagine she left the paper at his place after she finished cleaning mine. It would be just like her . . . and he must have used that same paper to wrap his manuscript."

"You are a genius, Madame—a master detective!" Denoël told her, delighted. He leaned forward, moving even closer to her, and said softly, "You don't happen to know the name of this fellow, do you?"

She thought a moment. He held his breath. Then she said, "Destouches. Yes, Dr. Destouches. That's his name." Denoël was amazed by her memory, delighted by her every word—inwardly jubilant. They continued their conversation for about five more minutes. Then, beaming, Robert Denoël gently ushered the lady out of his office, with promises that she would be hearing from him soon. I watched her as she left Denoël's office. Clearly it had not been a difficult hour for her. Her face seemed slightly flushed as she shook hands with Denoël. She had a soft smile; her eyes sparkled. I looked at her again, walking nearly one block away from Denoël's publishing house. She was still smiling—perhaps even more broadly.

Right after her departure, Bernard Steele sauntered casually into Robert's office. "Bernard, Bernard, I have found it!" Robert shouted to his partner. He was pacing around his office, smiling, arms waving.

"Found what?" the somewhat startled Steele replied.

"You have to read it, Bernard." He reached over his desk and shoved the manuscript in Bernard's direction. "You can't understand until you read it. I have just discovered a masterpiece, gold, Bernard. It's wonderful! I've never read anything like it."

Bernard grinned and took the manuscript. "I've never seen you like this, Robert."

"That's because I have never been like this before. Read it! Read it! You will see."

As soon as Bernard and the manuscript had left the room, Robert quickly wrote to Dr. Destouches, asking for an appointment with him the following day. It was not until the message had been sent that he realized just how tired he was. He had not slept for more than thirty-six hours. A bed, sleep, and quiet, that's what he wanted now.

"Who is she?" was the greeting shouted at him as soon as he entered the door of their apartment. "This time I want the truth, Robert!"

"I was at the office," he responded slowly.

"All night? Publishing all night? Surely you can come up with something better than that."

"Please, Cécile, not now. I was at the office. I have just discovered a new, amazing writer. His name is—"

"I don't care what his name is. Was he with you all night? Who else was with you? Once again you didn't even bother to notify me that you wouldn't be home. I can't stand this, Robert. What about me?"

"I don't want to . . . I can't talk about it now."

"And just when will we talk about it, Robert? Next year?"

"Oh, what's the use." He left her standing there, went into the bedroom, slammed the door, and fell onto the bed without undressing. I could hear the sounds of glass breaking in the living room.

Dr. Destouches came to Denoël's office the next morning. His entrance made an indelible impression upon the young publisher. Denoël would later describe him in some detail. Destouches was tall, square-shouldered, with piercing gray-blue eyes, brownish blond hair, and severe features. According to Denoël, their first conversation was astonishing, lasting nearly two hours. Denoël would later say:

I can see him still, nervous, excited, his blue eyes hard, a penetrating stare, a little ragged, physically run-down. He had an especially striking gesture. His hand went back and forth as if he were wiping the slate clean, and at the same time, his index finger was pointing things out. He talked about the war, death, his book; one minute he would be carried away, the next he seemed blasé, like someone who has seen everything, with no illusions. He expressed himself always in a powerful, imagistic, sometimes hallucinatory way. The concept of death, his own and the world's, kept coming up in his conversation like a leitmotiv. He described humanity as starving for disaster, in love with slaughter. Sweat poured down his face, his gaze seemed burning.

At some point during that long first meeting, Robert Denoël offered Dr. Destouches a contract. Unlike the bumbling Gallimard bureaucracy, Denoël did not require time or committees to realize the merits of *Journey*. He did in one day what the NRF had not been able to accomplish in many months. On 30 June 1932 Dr. Destouches signed a standard contract with this new publisher. Wishing to keep his medical practice entirely separate from his literary career, Dr. Destouches selected a nom de plume. He decided upon the name of his mother and grandmother, Céline. It was Céline, then, who entered the writing stable of Robert Denoël in 1932. His presence there would be one of the best and one of the worst events in the history of Denoël's career.

By the terms of his contract, Céline would get a percentage of the sale of his novel. That percentage would rise according to the number of copies sold. At the maximum, Céline would receive 18 percent of the sale of the book after fifty thousand copies were sold. Although this figure was often used in standard contracts, so large a sale was generally considered to be unattainable, even for bestselling authors.

Now that he had signed Céline, Denoël was ecstatic. There was only one problem. Money. There wasn't enough of it to publish a large edition of this lengthy novel. And Denoël needed a large edition, not to mention significant advertising. "With the right timing, advertising, and publication," he told his partner, "we could win the Goncourt Prize with this one." The Goncourt Prize was the most important and most famous prize in all of French literature. It was hard to believe that this tiny enterprise, Les Editions Denoël et Steele, which had only been in existence for two years, was aiming for the biggest literary prize in France. Even more amazing, if they could find enough money for this project, their chances were excellent.

Although Bernard agreed that Céline's manuscript was remarkable and worth the investment, he confirmed that he didn't have enough money to finance the project. And neither of them knew of a wealthy patron who might be induced to grant them a loan. Then Bernard said, "I could call Mother." Bernard's mother had remarried, was wealthy, lived in the United States—and loved her son. Her name was Béatrice Hirshon.

Robert tapped his pen several times on his desk, thought a moment, then said, "It's worth a try."

After a very long and animated phone call, Béatrice Hirshon found herself in the publishing business. She became a legal shareholder on 1 October 1932, with a capital expansion of slightly over ninety-three thousand dollars. Since the Goncourt Prize was usually decided in late November, with the formal announcement of the prize in the first week of December, these new publishers had a mammoth task before them.

In addition to the overwhelming difficulties of producing a book that might win the Goncourt in such a short time, Denoël soon learned that he also had to contend with a very picky, difficult, and demanding writer. Céline was not about to just turn over his precious manuscript to a publisher, particularly when he believed that publishers were generally tasteless literary pimps to begin with. His biographer, Frédéric Vitoux, provides us with a few samples of Céline's apparently never-ending instructions to his new publisher: "Old man, I beg you, don't add one syllable to the text without telling me! You'd completely screw up the rhythm—I'm the only one who can

relocate it—I may seem like a gasbag but I know exactly what I want—
Not one syllable. Be careful with the cover too—No music-hallism—
No typographical sentimentalism, no classicism . . . a fairly somber,
discreet cover. That's my advice—Dark brown on black or maybe gray
on gray and uniform letters—somewhat thick. That's all—That's
enough impressionism." And on and on. Facing his author's bitter
opposition, outbursts, and anger, the beleaguered publisher managed
to cut Céline's manuscript from nearly 900 pages to 625. But just
as Céline had promised, there was a battle over the deletion of every
single paragraph, phrase, word.

Robert began advertising the novel even before it was published.
He put enticing little notices in various journals:

> JOURNEY TO THE END OF THE NIGHT
> **Keep this title in mind.**

That was all it said, but such an unusual ad for the times certainly
did capture the attention and curiosity of many readers. Denoël had
carefully studied the strategy and methods of that great publisher,
Bernard Grasset, to learn how to promote a novel. Unlike Céline,
he realized that without the proper advertising and promotion even
a masterpiece could remain undiscovered. He developed his plan for
touting this work with the same precision, thought, and skill as a
general plans a battle.

"What have we got to work with here?" Robert asked his partner
one day as they strolled to Bernard's office. "We've got controversy,
originality, innovation. We need to stress them all," he said. "And
we need to show the author as mature and experienced." Bernard
agreed. Robert developed a series of blurbs to put in every advertisement, such as moviegoers might see at a preview. "Vibrant, sensational, new, tailored to life, enormous, delirious, colorful, cruel,
exquisite, controversial," such were the words this publisher used to
entice readers. And the book could be had for only twenty-four

francs (about $6.11). Stretching his advertising budget to its maximum, he sprinkled large advertisements in newspapers and magazines to coincide with the novel's appearance in the third week of October 1932. He had only a little more than a month until the Goncourt committee met.

Robert Denoël realized the importance of word-of-mouth, the need to attract the interest of critics, journalists, and other people who might be able to give this work a boost. He wrote countless letters to journalists, describing his new masterpiece. He visited the important, the not-so-important, anyone who might promote his book. As his cynical new author summed up, "One can never grovel enough."

And when Céline's novel was actually nominated for the Goncourt, the two publishers increased their campaign.

"What can we do to soften up that jury?" asked Steele.

Robert thought for a moment, then said, "Why not publish a special numbered private edition, just for them?"

"And we could have Céline personally autograph each one, and write a special personal tribute to each member of the Goncourt jury." And so they did, specially publishing numbered editions for the jury, with a few extra copies for others who might aid their cause. And Céline, somewhat dazed and bewildered by all of these activities on behalf of his book, momentarily forgot his cynicism and wrote the tributes. He even agreed to some interviews. In short, Robert became one of those publishers caricatured in the play *Just Published*. He exaggerated his publication and sales figures, curried favor, got his author to do interviews and personally write to and meet some of the Goncourt jury members, and did whatever else he could think of to plug his book and win a prize.

In the far larger and plusher office of Gaston Gallimard, all was not well. To Gallimard's great displeasure, he heard rumors that Céline's novel was selling briskly. In fact, it was beginning to appear that this new publisher and his relatively unknown doctor might just win that prize—unless, of course, Gaston intervened. It wouldn't be the first time that a major publisher had fixed a literary prize. The play had joked about that, too. And taking the Goncourt Prize right out from under Denoël's nose would be fun. "It would give me a certain satisfaction," mused Gallimard, seated before his huge desk. The savvy older publisher moved quietly, behind the scenes.

At their preparatory luncheon on 30 November, the Goncourt jury (The Ten, as they were called) met to discuss their decision. And fairly quickly it was decided that Céline would have the prize for that year. In fact, it was even suggested that the official announcement be made at that time. However, the need for fanfare and the press overruled this proposal. No, the announcement of this important prize would have to wait another week. But everyone knew who the winner would be—or at least thought they knew. Even some members of the Goncourt jury warmly congratulated both Céline and Denoël.

Hurriedly, Denoël ordered special ribbons designed to go around Céline's novel, announcing it as the winner of the Goncourt. By 6 December nearly all of Paris knew the winner of the Goncourt. Critics wrote confident predictions in nearly all the journals and newspapers of the time. Some journalists even prematurely prepared articles about this new Goncourt winner.

On 7 December the Goncourt jury met at Drouant's restaurant, at the place Gaillon, where by tradition they would have a "luncheon" (an elaborate feast) and then vote for the 1932 winner of the Goncourt Prize. A crowd of onlookers, journalists, and photographers surrounded the restaurant. And within that anonymous crowd was one very nervous and excited writer, Céline himself, who at first stood beside his daughter and mother, then paced back and forth alone. He carried in his pocket a small spherical silver bell, which he had kept all his life. He always carried it with him as a talisman. Now he put his hand into that pocket and turned the bell over and over with his fingers, walking from one journalist to another, anxiously listening for news.

Above the main floor where the Goncourt jury, composed mostly of writers, would dine were members of another jury, composed of critics and journalists. They met at that place and time to decide and award the Théophraste Renaudot Prize for literature, given to a writer of great merit who had not received significant recognition for his work. Both the restaurant and its surroundings were packed.

Someone within the Goncourt jury suggested that instead of eating lunch first, it might be more enjoyable for all to take the vote first and then have their elegant meal. That way the press would not be kept waiting while they enjoyed their repast. So before they partook of their "Belon and Marennes oysters, broiled lobster, roast goose with chestnut stuffing, their Bordelaise mushrooms (cèpes), their Loïe Fuller ice cream and Succès cake, all washed down with blanc de blanc and Grands-Echézeaux 1915" they voted. And on the first ballot there was a clear winner: Guy Mazeline for his novel, *The Wolves (Les Loups)*, published, of course, by Gaston Gallimard. One of the members of the jury threw his napkin down onto the table and stormed out of the room. Others stared in disbelief.

As the winner was announced to the hushed crowd outside the restaurant, Céline took his little silver bell out of his pocket, threw it on the ground, and crushed it with his foot. His daughter, seeing his act, ran toward the bell, picked it up, and kept it. Oblivious to his mother and daughter, Céline disappeared into the crowd, alone and furious. He would be furious for much of the rest of his life.

No one on that Goncourt jury ever explained exactly what had happened to make Gallimard the winning publisher that day. There were many theories. Perhaps Hachette, which distributed Gallimard's books, had had a hand in the outcome. Gaston Gallimard sat at his huge oak desk in his elegant office and chuckled. He had many secrets, and he took great care that no one learn of them. He had not yet realized that this particular secret might blow up in his face.

Almost immediately that other jury upstairs selected Céline as the winner of the Renaudot Prize for his novel. But awarding the second prize to Céline satisfied no one, except, of course, for Gallimard. Everyone was astonished, outraged:

"How can such a thing happen?"

"That Goncourt jury was rigged."

"The Goncourt jury is no better than a marketplace where everything is for sale. And the biggest bidder gets the prize."

"It's a disgrace!" There were nods of agreement.

Although Gaston Gallimard foresaw that there might be some commotion over the outcome of the Goncourt, he seriously misjudged its size and intensity. A veritable scandal erupted almost overnight. And with that scandal came publicity—lots and lots of publicity—more, in fact, than Denoël's slim budget could ever have purchased. This obvious tampering with the Goncourt jury resulted in newspaper articles, critical essays, arguments, name-calling. Then came lawsuits for slander. For example, certain members of the Goncourt jury were called dangerous thieves, sellouts, and idiots. At one point there was even talk of a duel. The entire affair became a publicity bonanza. And people rushed out to see what all the fuss was about. They weren't as interested in *The Wolves*. They bought *Journey to the End of the Night*, the topic of the scandal.

In spite of Robert Denoël's inflated statements of the size and sales of his first edition, he had published only three thousand copies of Céline's novel. After all, he didn't really know if it would sell. Certainly its topic was dreary, and it was filled with slang, something new to the French reading public. Denoël had not been wrong to be cautious. Just ten days before the announcement of the Goncourt Prize, he had not even sold all of those three thousand copies.

He could not have possibly dreamed that just two months after the Goncourt Prize he would have sold more than fifty thousand copies of Céline's novel, with translation rights obtained by fourteen countries. In just one year Les Editions Denoël et Steele sold more than their wildest dreams—over 100,000 copies, with more sales promised. Denoël would later write, "From that very evening it was a great scandal in the press. For fifteen days only this event was discussed. We received more than 5000 newspaper articles about it." Sympathetic critics, outraged by the Goncourt decision, lauded the book everywhere in the press. As a result, just about everyone knew about the novel, its author, who had been unjustly denied the most important prize in French literature, and, of course, the publisher.

"We certainly did win when we lost that one," Robert told his partner. He was right. He had won. Thanks to Gaston Gallimard and that scandal, the resulting sales of Céline's novel established Les Editions Denoël et Steele as a truly significant Parisian publishing house. They were on their way.

Difficulties

The plain truth, I may as well admit it, is that I have never
been really right in the head.
Céline

*H*aving just read another article on Céline, Jeanne Loviton closed
the paper. "You know, Pierre," she said to her husband, "if you
would stop writing in such an old-fashioned way, if you would use a
little innovation in your novels, you could probably win the Goncourt."

He turned to her. "My novels keep you in jewels, my dear."

"Or perhaps I could win that prize," she mused. "Why not?"

"Your parties, your high-society duties, your shopping. That's
why not," he sniffed.

But still she wrote. She wrote when she had time. And she took special note of the circumstances surrounding that Goncourt. "It's not the
merits of the work that win the prize," she said to herself. "It's the skill
with which the book is marketed and the clout of those who tout it."

"And what do you think of this *Journey to the End of the Night*, Monsieur
Valéry?"

Valéry carefully adjusted his monocle, then smiled patronizingly. "I must confess I haven't read it. Too busy with mathematical calibrations and scientific interests, I suppose." Then he added in a low voice, "I doubt that I shall ever read it. His vulgar use of language, you understand." And he dismissed his interlocutor with a wave of his hand, turning to another admirer within the salon.

If Robert was ecstatic about the outcome of the Goncourt, Céline certainly was not. He was unwilling to admit, even to himself, just how much he had wanted that prize. He wanted praise for his years of work. He needed that praise. Missing that prize was, in Céline's eyes, a major betrayal, not just by the Goncourt jury or Gaston Gallimard, but by his own publisher as well. While Céline had lost the prize through no fault of his own, his own publisher was getting rich off him. And there was money connected with this prize. In losing the Goncourt, Céline had lost 500,000 francs. And now Robert Denoël was actually benefiting from Céline's loss. It was too much. Céline wrote a friend, "The Goncourt Prize is a flop. It is simply an affair between publishers." In the already dark mind of Céline, his thoughts grew ominously blacker.

Following his loss of the Goncourt, Céline's attitude and manner toward his publisher abruptly changed. Before that time, he had viewed Denoël as his friend. Although always difficult, he had tried to cooperate, had often been polite, and had shown his obvious pleasure in Denoël's appraisal of his book. Like Robert's other writers, Céline often visited his publisher's home, where, according to Cécile, "His place at the table was always set."

But now somehow things were different. In the winter of 1933 he sent his publisher a strange letter. In it he told Robert that he loathed intimacy and friendship. "It is one of the sides of life which disgusts me." He admitted that he had gotten swept up by the excitement of the Goncourt and had briefly lost his reserve. But now he had that reserve back. He rejected Robert's amity, adding, "We will never recover our friendship." Céline advised Robert to consider him from now on as "an excellent investment, nothing more, nothing less."

"I don't know what to make of this letter," Robert told his wife. But Cécile was not interested in the behavior of Céline. She offered no advice.

If Robert was concerned about Céline, his partner, Bernard, had another concern: Gaston Gallimard. Bernard told Robert, "In this city Gaston Gallimard is a force to be reckoned with. Be careful, Robert, he is like a giant squid. His tentacles reach everywhere."

Bernard Steele was right. Gaston Gallimard seemed to have influence everywhere. He had invested in the literary journal, *The Literary News* (*Les Nouvelles littéraires*), which was quite popular with a large readership. It would have taken a daring critic to disparage a Gallimard publication in this journal—and in fact, very few did. Gallimard controlled other journals as well. His impressive publishing house was an outgrowth of another literary journal, the *N.R.F.*, and had intimate ties to it. In addition to great wealth, Gallimard had important connections. His brother and later his son also worked in his publishing house, providing Gaston with the type of aid, loyalty, and support Denoël could never have imagined. Furthermore, he knew the power of influence and how to get and use it. He understood politics, bureaucrats, favors. Gaston Gallimard was privileged in every sense of the word: wealthy, attractive, elegant, shrewd—a knowledgeable businessman and a powerful enemy. He was an insider. He knew the rules. And now Gaston was Robert's keen enemy, first amazed, then annoyed, and then enraged by the outcome of the Goncourt fiasco.

He realized that he was largely responsible for the financial well-being that Robert now enjoyed. He hated the fact that Denoël had taken Céline during Gallimard's long indecision about *Journey*. "It's a theft," stormed Gaston. "Denoël took what should have been mine in the first place." But Gaston Gallimard was too smart to move quickly against his new competitor. He simply stretched out all of his tentacles and waited. He could afford to bide his time.

With the money from *Journey to the End of the Night* continuing to pour into its coffers, Les Editions Denoël et Steele now had the funds needed to expand and improve. Because of the publicity that Céline's novel and the Goncourt scandal had engendered, many talented writers began to send their manuscripts to this publishing house, and not just as a last resort. Denoël's reputation for quick and decisive action helped increase the number of excellent manuscripts sent his way. Wisely, Robert remained his company's only reader. His great talent continued to be his ability to recognize good literature when he saw it. With the money that he now had, he also increased his advertising.

I went to his office at 19, rue Amélie. Located in the deconsecrated chapel part of the building, it was very simple, sparsely furnished without decoration, like a reading or study room in a monastery—a place for quiet meditation. Robert was there, seated at a large table, head down, engrossed in a manuscript. As I quietly watched him, there was a knock at the door. *"Entrez,"* he said without looking up.

A middle-aged man carrying a large notebook entered. "Oh, I'm sorry," he said. I was looking for Robert Denoël."

Robert looked up from his reading, "I am Robert Denoël."

"Well then I must be looking for Monsieur Denoël, Sr. You know, the publisher."

"Mr. Denoël, Sr., is a professor in Liège, Monsieur. I am the publisher you are looking for," he said. He smiled broadly as he politely ushered his confused and embarrassed visitor into his office. It was not the first time that someone had assumed he was much too young to be such an important Parisian publisher. Robert still had a boyish elegance and charm about him. He was only thirty-two. Almost his entire staff, in fact, was young. In some of his advertisements, Robert described his firm as publishing "the best works by young writers." That goal remained constant throughout his career and proved to be hugely successful.

In addition to his expanding business, his family was also expanding. Cécile was pregnant. On 14 March 1933 she gave birth to their son. "We shall name him Robert," she said. He would be their only child.

"I hope that the baby will make her happier," Robert later told Bernard at the office. "I probably should have spent more time with her, but I have been so busy. Maybe the baby will make things better."

"I'm sure he will," said Bernard. In fact, he wasn't sure at all. He knew that although Cécile aspired to be a great actress, she had never auditioned, not even for a small part. He liked her. She was interesting, fun to be around, a good hostess, intelligent and friendly. But he knew she was unhappy, jealous of other women who found her husband so attractive, and jealous even of Robert's success. Bernard had witnessed some of her tantrums. It seemed to Bernard that her baby might not provide Cécile with the fulfillment she was seeking. But he said nothing to Robert.

"By the way," said Bernard. "I have been getting some really strange letters from our principal author lately. It's pretty clear that our friend, Céline, doesn't think much of me. As a matter of fact, he called me a thief."

"He called me a gluttonous parasite," said Robert.

"And he delights in misspelling my name, writing letters to Monsieur Steel." Bernard spelled the letters of his name to Robert, omitting the last *e*. "He can really be a nuisance. You know he is threatening us with court if we don't pay him more."

"You had better let Picq handle it. He seems to be the only member of our staff who doesn't enrage him," said Robert. He was referring to Auguste Picq, the only member of this small publishing house who had any experience in the day-to-day running of a business. Among other things, Picq kept the books for the company. He also excelled in unruffling the feathers of disgruntled authors, bookbinders, printers, or anyone else who had unpaid bills or monetary questions regarding this company. Although Picq was scrupulously honest, his job was made more difficult because Denoël did occasionally resort to sleights of hand in some of his fiscal dealings. After all, he was in a tough business. He always operated near the edge and did not hesitate to make an author or a supplier wait for his money in order to make his deals. The prompt, courteous letters of Monsieur Picq, along with his meticulous records, often served to reassure those owed money by Les Editions Denoël et Steele. Payment would be forthcoming; they simply needed a little patience. Picq, the bookkeeper, the honest businessman, the master letter writer, was a great asset to Denoël.

But sometimes even Picq could not salve the rages of their chief writer. Céline became increasingly convinced that his publishers knew nothing about literature. They were entirely incompetent and were taking advantage of him. In short, they were crooks. In fact, all publishers were pimps, thieves, stinking robbers. He wrote, "All in all, if you look around, you'll see any number of writers end their days as ragpickers, but it's a rare publisher who takes to sleeping under the bridges . . . a riot, isn't it?"

The anger went deeper than the simple loss of a literary prize. Reading biographies of him, along with his *Journey to the End of the Night,* I realized that this man had once been idealistic. Like many other young Frenchmen, he had once viewed World War I as something noble, virtuous, with a clear right and wrong—a war that could somehow improve man's condition. He felt that it was his duty to be a part of all that. And so he joined the cavalry, the Twelfth Cuirassiers. He volunteered before the war, then went to war and wrote about it. Aside from the fact that he had a horse, his descriptions of the horrors of war more closely resemble reports about the war in Vietnam than romanticized accounts of World War I.

He described himself as "an extra in this incredible international extravaganza, into which, I have to admit, I had leapt with enthusiasm." Then upon entering battle, he described his fear. "Could I, I thought, be the last coward on earth? How terrifying! . . . All alone with two million stark raving heroic madmen, armed to the eyeballs?" Then the gunfire: "Over our heads, two millimeters, maybe one millimeter from our temples, those long tempting lines of steel, that bullets make when they're out to kill you, were whistling through the hot summer air."

Céline, then, in his inimitable and innovative style, the style that had so impressed Denoël, wrote of battle:

With and without helmets, without horses, on motorcycles, bellowing, in cars, screeching, shooting, plotting, flying, kneeling,
digging, taking cover, bounding over trails, root-toot-tooting,
shut up on earth as if it were a loony bin, ready to demolish
everything on it, Germany, France, whole continents, everything
that breathes, destroy destroy, madder than mad dogs, worship-
ping their madness (which dogs don't), a hundred, a thousand
times madder than a thousand dogs, and a lot more vicious! A
pretty mess we were in! No doubt about it, this crusade I'd let
myself in for was the apocalypse!

And the result of the battle? A better place to live, a new order?
The only results for Céline were death and destruction. He described
death everywhere. The death of one man, a captain leaning against
a tree: "He was holding his pants in both hands and vomiting. . . .
Bleeding all over and rolling his eyes . . . There was nobody with
him. He was through. . . . 'Mama! Mama!' he was sniveling, all the
while dying and pissing blood." In a letter to his parents he described
the deaths of many: "Nothing new on the battlefield almost in the
same line of fire for 3 days the dead are continually replaced by the
living to the point where they form little hillocks that are burned
and at a certain point you can cross the Meuse without getting your
feet wet over the bodies of Germans who tried to get through and
whom our artillery swallowed up tirelessly."

He wondered just exactly what this war was all about. "Maybe our
colonel knew why they were shooting, maybe the Germans knew, but
I, so help me, hadn't the vaguest idea. As far back as I could search
my memory, I hadn't done a thing to the Germans, I'd always treated
them friendly and polite."

And finally, the result of war. "You come out of jail alive, out of
a war you don't! The rest is blarney." For Céline no one comes out
of a war the same as he was when he entered. If he isn't killed, he is
wounded. And if he is not physically wounded, he is certainly mentally damaged. Insanity. There was a great deal of it in *Journey to the
End of the Night*. As Céline said, "At a time when the world is upside

down and it's thought insane to ask why you're being murdered, it obviously requires no great effort to pass for a lunatic." Then he continued, "Dazed by the war, we had developed a different kind of madness: fear. The heads and tails of the war."

I reminded myself that Céline's *Journey to the End of the Night* was fiction, that its central character was a man named Bardamu. But the story very closely paralleled Céline's own life. Bardamu even became a medical doctor. I was inclined to agree with one of Robert's friends, Carlos Rim, who met Céline shortly after reading his novel. When he saw the author, Rim concluded he was actually seeing Bardamu in the flesh: "furious, cynical, ingenuous, and gullible."

Many scholars, psychiatrists, and psychologists have attempted to put a name to Céline's mental state following the publication of his novel and to trace its delirious descent in his future works. Céline would have laughed and cursed them all. I put away my own suspicions of post-traumatic stress disorder and read many of their works, looking carefully at their diagnoses, all rich in scientific jargon—yet all somehow inconclusive. Perhaps Céline said it best in his novel, "The plain truth, I may as well admit it, is that I have never been really right in the head."

In the war he suffered a head wound, although it was the injury to his arm that most concerned his doctors. There was even serious talk of amputation. But the wound to his head would bother him for the rest of his life. As Bardamu, he alludes to that injury, saying, "I preferred my own kind of death, the kind that comes late . . . in twenty years . . . thirty . . . maybe more . . . to this death they were trying to deal me right away . . . eating Flanders mud, my whole mouth full of it, fuller than full, split to the ears by a shell fragment." His ears, a shell exploding directly beside his ears, a shell fragment. The explosion had blown him off his horse. A bit of blood flowing out of his left ear was all that remained of this horror. At first the doctors didn't even notice it.

Then the headaches started, horrible, profound, resulting in insomnia, dizziness. They would continue and worsen throughout his life. But it was those ear noises that bothered him the most. "You have tinnitus," the doctors told him. Céline described it better: "I can say that I have slept only in fits since November 14 . . . I've learned to get along with my ear noises . . . I listen to them become trombones, full orchestras, marshaling yards . . . it's a game! . . . if you move your mattress . . . show some little sign of impatience, you're lost, you go crazy. . . ." He sometimes described it as a train in his ear, then "whistles . . . drums . . . blasts of steam," and always, always the echo of that exploding shell right next to him. No, not next to him anymore—inside his head.

Because of his arm, he was honorably discharged from the military. He had escaped the war. As Céline, or rather Bardamu, put it, "The army finally dropped me. I'd saved my guts, but my brains were scrambled for good."

I ran across another description of Céline in his early days with Robert Denoël. Writer Robert Poulet described him as he appeared in Denoël's office. He called him a *"grand diable,"* then described his closed expression, his sneering bottom lip. The term *grand diable* has two possible meanings in French. Literally, it means "great devil," but it can also mean "a tall, lanky fellow." While Céline was tall and lanky, I thought the literal meaning also fit him. And if Céline were that great devil, Robert would soon be unwittingly cast in the role of Faust.

I knew that Céline went to jail shortly after Robert Denoël's death—but not for shooting his publisher. Céline was in Denmark at the time of Denoël's murder. He was not one of my suspects, and never had been . . . except, of course, for the setting of the stage. When it comes to laying the groundwork for the murder of Robert Denoël, Céline has no equal. In fact, had it not been for Céline, there probably would have been no murder at all.

The hatred, the ear noises, the headaches, his vivid descriptions of the horrors of war were nothing compared to what Céline planned to do next. Yes, Poulet was right on both counts. Céline was a *grand diable*. But it was not just Céline's madness and the instability of Cécile that Robert had to contend with in the early 1930s. There was yet another man who contributed to the setting of the stage for the murder of Robert Denoël. And this gifted genius was certifiable.

6

Affairs, Psychology, Games, and Madness

> In your fear of what my piercing mind might detect, you
> have done your best to have me locked up as a madman.
> *Antonin Artaud*, The Cenci

Constantly occupied with his business, Robert encouraged his wife almost from her arrival in Paris to become acquainted with the poet, artist, writer, and actor Antonin. This handsome, passionate man was one of Robert's first Paris acquaintances. Like Cécile, Antonin loved the theater. He had written plays and philosophical treatises on theater, and had acted on stage and in silent film with some success. His striking, almost plastic face was perfect for silent film, revealing all sorts of emotions, without the need for words. No one imagined then (except for Robert Denoël) the tremendous impact this man would have upon the philosophy of contemporary theater. For this actor/author was the now-celebrated Antonin Artaud.

While Céline often used a psychotic, sometimes delirious writing style and showed paranoid symptoms himself, he was never officially pronounced insane. Antonin, on the other hand, had been mad since childhood, certifiably insane. However, Antonin's madness was not directed against others—at least not at that time. There was no malice in his mental imbalance then. In fact, many have stated that it was Artaud's insanity that made him interesting. His very genius may have lurked somewhere within his mental instability—a brilliance that was profoundly artistic and creative.

Antonin Artaud knew sanitariums. He spent long periods of his youth within their walls, for "rests," as they were called. Some of his "rests" lasted many months. And during that time Antonin passed the hours quietly—reading, painting, writing, dreaming. Then while he was "resting" in a sanitarium in Neuchâtel, Switzerland, he met Dr. Daudel. This doctor was determined to cure Antonin Artaud of his mental difficulties. And he knew exactly how he would accomplish this feat. In May 1919, when Antonin was twenty-two, Dr. Daudel introduced his patient to opium.

The muse controlling the mad genius within Antonin was delighted, entranced, charmed by the drug, and hungry for it. And thanks to opium, Antonin and his muse knew ecstasy—his creative impulses flew into rapture. Because of Dr. Daudel's magic medicine, Antonin, already insane, became addicted to drugs. The anguish and despair of addiction would come later. No matter—by then Artaud sought any drug he could find. He was a gentle man, a poet, a philosopher, a dreamer—a junkie.

If anything came close to his passion for drugs, it was theater. Antonin Artaud loved acting, reading plays, writing and thinking about them. Even the smell of a theater entranced him. And the stage, that miraculous space, what wonders it held! He acted on it, wrote about it, and decorated it, his magic altar, with amazing, innovative set designs. There was nothing Antonin Artaud did not like about the theater, except for closing night. It was only natural that Cécile and Antonin would become friends. And certainly at first Robert encouraged their relationship, thinking that Antonin might help her get started in the theater, or at least encourage her to audition.

Cécile's first meeting with Antonin had been awkward. At Robert's suggestion, they met for lunch at a small nearby café. Robert introduced them outside the restaurant, then unexpectedly excused himself and hurried off on publishing business. They sat down at a small table on the sidewalk. The street was pleasant, colorful, not too crowded, and the day was glorious, warm, cloudless. They ordered some red wine, and began to talk. Antonin was shy. Cécile felt nervous. "So you have worked in the Paris theater," she said.

"I have worked in lots of places," he responded. "Now mostly I write."

"About the theater?" she asked.

"Sometimes. I used to be a poet, you know. I gave that up when the surrealists threw me out. Did you know I was once a surrealist? Then it all got political. I don't much care for the political," he admitted, shifting uncomfortably in his chair and playing with an ashtray.

"I'm not very political myself," she responded. "I hope you go back to poetry. I like poetry."

Artaud was silent, then changed the subject. "I'm really interested in the occult, you know—the supernatural." He paused a moment. "Do you believe in spells?"

"Well, I never really thought much about them one way or the other."

"I do," he said. "Sometimes I can see them at night, sailing across the sky, leaving gray mists behind them. But I don't know yet who casts them or how to cast one myself."

Uncertain just how to respond, Cécile smiled briefly and tried to think of something to say. "Do you write a lot?" she finally asked.

"Oh yes," he said. "An awfully lot. If I don't, my head will burst. The ideas will come out of my ears if I don't write them down." He smiled sheepishly. "Dr. Allendy, my analyst, says that sometimes I get so engrossed by an idea, I think I *am* the idea. He says I should be careful about that. But it's so perfectly clear when I actually am the idea, and not me. My best works seem to come out of me that way." And then the waiter came with their wine. At first Cécile did not know what to make of Antonin. She found him endearing, fragile in a charming sort of way, and very handsome. She hoped they would meet again.

In 1929 Robert published (at the author's expense) one of Artaud's most significant treatises, *Art and Death* (*l'Art et la mort*). Robert even convinced his friend Jean de Bosschère to create the frontispiece for Artaud's work. It was reviewed that summer in *The Literary News*, but not favorably. The only positive remarks that critic Jean Cassou made about this book concerned the frontispiece. Cassou decided that Jean de Bosschère was "one of the most curious and keenly original men of our times." As for Artaud's work, Cassou concluded, "The entire piece, right up to the effort of expression, is utterly hopeless." It would be decades before the true value of Artaud's *Art and Death* was recognized. In the meantime, Artaud was spending his money on drugs, was often without funds, and was emotionally and physically needy.

Artaud soon moved into Robert's circle of friends. He loved Irène Champigny. They often discussed the occult. "You are truly clairvoyant," he told her. "Your power, your perceptions are phenomenal!" Artaud was welcomed within Irène's literary and artistic circle; he had a sense of belonging. Then he went further. One day when he had no more money at all, he showed up at Robert's door. Of course, the Denoëls invited him in. But he stayed . . . and stayed until finally Cécile, sensing that he had nowhere else to go, invited him to spend the night. And that was it. He moved in with them. While Cécile may have enjoyed his attentions and company, Robert clearly did not, especially when he saw the way Antonin looked at his wife. He had not expected that. And Robert noticed that Cécile, who had been cold and accusing toward him lately, smiled at Antonin in such a charming manner.

Robert walked quickly and quietly past Artaud, once again sleeping on the couch, and into the kitchen where Cécile was fixing breakfast. "How could this happen?" he whispered, pointing to Artaud. She shrugged. "And how will we get rid of our parasite now that he has claimed our couch?"

"Can't you find work for him?"

"I want that man out of here," he said in a stage whisper.

Robert did find work for Artaud. He decided to commission Antonin to write a French adaptation of *The Monk*, a novel written by Matthew Gregory Lewis in 1794. Robert knew that Antonin would

like the work because it was very dramatic, frightening, and sometimes bizarre and sadistic. Antonin always enjoyed such novels. After
giving him an advance and pointing to a very affordable apartment
nearby, Robert eased his "parasite" off his couch—but not out of his
life.

One day Antonin entered Denoël's office on the rue Amélie with
another idea. He smiled brightly at his publisher. "I noticed that
there is a large back room that you are not presently using," Antonin
began.

Robert, engrossed in a manuscript, hardly looked up. "Oh that.
At present it's our conference room," he said.

"But there are times when it is empty, especially at night. Right?"

"That's correct. Why?"

"I was wondering if I might be able to use it twice a week, but
only in the evenings."

"Why?" his publisher asked, now looking squarely at Artaud.

"For acting lessons and classes in film and drama," Antonin replied. He paused a moment, then, not looking at his publisher, he
softly admitted, "I could really use the money."

"On Tuesday and Thursday evenings you can have it rent-free,"
Robert said, thinking of his couch.

And so for a brief period Les Editions Denoël et Steele also
became the location for Antonin's lessons on theater. The project
failed for lack of students, due to the extreme eccentricity of the
teacher.

There were other projects, too, mostly adaptations and transla-
tions, which the beleaguered publisher sent Antonin's way in an effort to help him get on his feet. Then Robert had a brilliant idea.
Ever since he came to Paris and met Irène Champigny, he had wanted
to establish a series of publications dedicated to psychology and certain areas of the occult. At that time there was no clear delineation
between the occult and psychology, since the latter had not yet clearly
defined itself as a serious scientific study or established rules of
ethics. In fact, at that time one could hang out a shingle as a psy-
chologist with no training in the field at all. What better way to find

out about psychologists and psychiatrists in Paris than from a man who regularly used them?

Robert consulted Antonin about publishing a psychological series. Antonin encouraged him to do so. He perched on the side of Robert's desk and discussed the project. "You know, Robert, psychology is a popular topic these days. And everyone wants to know about psychoanalysis. And now there is more interest in the occult than ever. You could attract a huge readership with this project."

"Can you introduce me to some people who might be willing to contribute articles to this series?"

Antonin certainly could and did. He introduced both Robert and Bernard Steele to the unusual world of psychology in France in the 1930s. Antonin's first introduction may have been to the strangest psychiatrist of the day, his psychoanalyst, the intelligent and eccentric Dr. René Allendy.

Dr. Allendy was a man of many interests: alchemy and the occult, modern art, allopathy, flagellation, theater, surrealism, Freud's psychoanalysis, numerology, and mysticism. The celebrated diarist Anaïs Nin was also one of his patients—and one of his lovers. Several of Nin's other lovers, as well as her husband, the wealthy banker Hugh Guiler, were also Allendy's patients. Dr. René Allendy analyzed them all, not together, but singly. I wondered who analyzed Allendy.

Looking through Anaïs Nin's voluminous diaries, I noticed that she liked to refer to games, role playing, what seemed for her to be acting in real life. Petite, elegant, and beautiful, she thrived on the attentions of men (and sometimes women) . . . and on these often sexually charged games.

I learned from her diary and the reports of some of the other "players" that the major game, the main tournament, was held at dinner at the Allendy house every Sunday. Antonin was always there. Anxious to meet Artaud, Nin had begged her psychoanalyst to introduce them. But Allendy was worried. He knew that Nin loved to play, to flirt, to change herself like a chameleon. She once wrote in her diary that she had given her soul "for taking fantasies seriously, for living life as a theatre, for loving costumes and changes of selves, for wearing masks and disguises."

Dr. Allendy warned Nin, "Do not play with Artaud. He is too miserable, too poor."

"I am only interested in his genius," she responded.

"But then be a friend, not a coquette," he pleaded.

"In literary relationships I am very masculine."

"But your silhouette is decidedly not masculine," Allendy responded.

In the end René Allendy gave in and, against his better judgment, invited her to meet Artaud. And then, like Artaud, Nin became one of the regulars at the Allendy Sunday dinners. Wanting to observe one of Allendy's elaborate and game-filled feasts, I decided to attend, too.

I was surprised to discover that Dr. Allendy and his wife lived on the same street where Jeanne Loviton would one day reside. The Allendy mansion was located just down the street from her future home, at 67, rue de l'Assomption. I rang the bell. A maid appeared and escorted me into a dark paneled hallway, then into a sumptuous drawing room where I sat in a heavily cushioned dark brown velvet armchair. On the wall opposite my chair was an exquisite gold curtain. I knew from my reading that the curtain was a Chinese brocade, and that behind it was Allendy's office. Nothing hidden or dramatic about Dr. René Allendy, I thought. He and his wife were already in the drawing room, as was Artaud, engaged in animated conversation with both of them. Artaud's arms waved wildly. I watched their discussion while the other players arrived, smiling and greeting each other as if they were old friends.

Anaïs Nin arrived last, impeccably dressed in a black silk suit with white blouse, high black heels, sheer black silk stockings, short white gloves, a small black silk purse, and a tiny matching chou hat tipped to one side of her head, with a veil draped just over her eyes, accentuating her bright red lips. She looked smashing, right out of a bandbox, I thought—or ready to step center stage. But more than her dress, her lipstick, and her diva entrance, it was her eyes that most intrigued me. They were green and, according to Artaud, "sometimes violet." But their color was not what most interested me. She had sharp black-penciled eyebrows, thick eyeliner, heavy dark eye shadow, and long black false eyelashes. Her eyes were so dramatic behind her veil that she seemed to be wearing a mask. Her entrance was met with approving stares from everyone. Even René Allendy's wife, Yvonne, seemed impressed. Nin's husband, the ever patient and indulgent Hugh Guiler, had arrived before her and strode quickly over to greet his wife.

There would be only six for dinner that afternoon: Artaud, Nin and her husband, the elegant Bernard Steele, and the Allendys. Then a butler arrived and invited us to the dining room. I quietly followed the others and watched them as they sat down to what would be a long, lavish dinner. In her diary, Nin described them all. Yvonne, "heavy, earth-formed, active, intelligent, martial, dominant," sat at one end of the table. Her husband, René, "with a secret, pearly laughter . . . head in his shoulders like a bull," sat at the other. On René's left were Anaïs and Bernard, "young, handsome, full, heavy featured." On René's right sat Artaud "with hallucinated eyes. The sharpness, the pain-carved features. The man-dreamer, diabolical and innocent, frail, nervous, potent." And next to Artaud sat Nin's husband, Hugh. Nin did not waste too many words describing her Hugo that day. "Inert" and "crushed" sufficed. Transfixed, I stared at them all as they began their complex, hurtful game. I wondered why Hugh Guiler attended, sitting there, sad, shaken, quietly watching his wife's lovers pretend.

Each man at the table that day was either in love with or deeply attracted to Anaïs Nin, and all were probably sleeping with her at that time, with the possible exception of Artaud, who certainly wanted to. Anaïs Nin, of course, knew this—and so did her profoundly jealous psychiatrist. Did the others know? Did Yvonne? They were all acting so civilized. To make this game even more interesting, Anaïs began discussing Henry Miller. "Poor Henry," she said. "He has been working so hard and so long on his *Tropic of Cancer*. He needs a well-deserved rest." What Nin and her psychiatrist knew, of course, was that Henry Miller was also one of Nin's lovers—and so was, for that matter, Miller's wife, June. Nin would later immortalize their tangled loves and lives in her work, *Henry and June.*

Over the second course, fresh salmon steaks baked with butter and shallots, then steeped in heavy cream, Bernard Steele asked René Allendy if he would consider contributing to the psychology series at Les Editions Denoël et Steele. "I would be delighted to," René replied. "I have several important and timely topics which I think might interest you." Nin's mind wandered as Bernard and René talked about the series. She stared at her lover/psychiatrist.

"I am dazzled," she later wrote in her diary. "I am afraid everybody will see how much I love him. He has remembered that I smoke Sultane cigarettes. He has the eyes of a child who is being told fairy tales."

Over the roast partridge with truffles Steele managed to get Dr. René Allendy to suggest other contributors to the series: Dr. René Laforgue, Dr. Otto Rank (with whom Nin would later have a passionate and multi-continent affair), and others. Yes, such a series could be done and done well. The psychiatrist was sure of that.

Then came a crisp green salad and more games. Allendy knew the private secrets and sufferings of all of his guests, with the exception of Steele. Yet before the alluring Nin, this doctor seemed powerless. "To my surprise, I am witty, malicious, piquant," wrote Nin. "But I cannot talk to Allendy because I have such a mad impulse to kiss his long-lashed eyes and his woman's mouth."

The white-gloved butler brought in a huge tray of cheese: Brie, Saint-Marcellin, Boursin, Roquefort, chèvre, and Beaufort. Nin took a Sultane from the little silver tray near her. Her doctor rose to light it. "His hand trembles when he lights my cigarette, and he gives me an ashtray as if I were an imperious and impatient queen. I am so afraid of my love for him that I turn toward Mrs. Allendy and charm her by understanding her great contribution to the ascension of Allendy. Her secret contribution without glow or form or beauty (the tyranny of a household mechanism!)."

I wondered how they would finish this meal, and what magnificent dessert the butler would bring. Then I looked at Artaud. He was smitten. He had not taken his eyes off the alluring Nin the entire evening. He wanted her. His doctor knew it. Nin knew it. Four men—all politely eating together, all wanting the same woman who was coyly seated before them, along with Yvonne, the "household mechanism." I left before the end of their meal. I was tired of their game and sad for Artaud.

Antonin Artaud had had miserable luck in love. In fact, some of his previous romances could have gone down in the annals of love's worst disasters. And here was another calamity in the making. The mad Antonin Artaud in love with the deeply neurotic, very unfaithful, and narcissistic Anaïs Nin. A match made in hell, I muttered to myself.

Bernard Steele and Robert Denoël did get the people they needed for their psychological series, and it became enormously popular and successful. Dr. Allendy provided unusual and interesting works, and so did Otto Rank, René Laforgue, and others whom these doctors had recommended. Denoël even published works by Freud. And Bernard Steele got a brief affair with Anaïs Nin in the bargain. As for Antonin, he fell more deeply for the bewitching Nin. Dr. Allendy's warning to Nin not to play games with Artaud went unheeded. Games could be such fun. A painter once said of Artaud, "His own suffering did exist, but he enjoyed it. . . . Artaud had told himself: 'It is I who will play Artaud.' " It was the role of a lifetime.

And so Artaud and Nin began a mad role-playing whirl together. He played the madman, the gentle poet, the philosopher, the wit, the jealous lover, the actor, the rebel. And she played her roles as well—love goddess, panther, woman warrior, writer, the all-knowing beauty—at once compassionate and treacherous. Soon, they started to miss cues, to misinterpret the other's motivation. Artaud once told Nin, "The difference between you and other women [is that] you breathe in carbon dioxide and exhale oxygen." He was playing the wit. She mistook him for lover. Their play together failed in part because both hogged center stage. Each wanted the soliloquy.

Much of what happened between Anaïs Nin and Antonin Artaud occurred in 1933, the same year that Cécile Denoël had her baby. After Nin and Artaud had finished their exciting, tragic drama together, Artaud frequently visited the Denoël household, seeking solace and company. Excited about the success of his psychological series, Robert Denoël decided to create a theatrical series to showcase new works by young playwrights. He discussed his project with Artaud and sought his advice. Bleary-eyed, smiling, vacuous, Artaud slumped in a chair in Robert's office. Slurring his words, he tried to answer his publisher's questions, but he was incoherent.

Worried, Robert gave Artaud money in return for his promise to rid himself once and for all of his drug habit. Artaud promised—a junkie's oath. In fact, he spent Denoël's money on a nice hotel in the south of France—and, of course, on drugs. Les Editions Denoël et Steele published Artaud's *Second Manifesto of the Theater of Cruelty* (*Le Second Manifeste du théâtre de la cruauté*), without much success. Bernard Steele even backed him in a theatrical enterprise, called the Anonymous Society of the Theater of Cruelty, which would provide money for a theatrical company dedicated to Artaud's ideas. Steele felt sure that he could raise the 650,000 francs needed for this project, but he couldn't.

Robert didn't have much time to watch over the floundering Artaud. He was more concerned with Céline. After all that publicity over the Goncourt scandal, Robert hoped to bring out a new Céline book as quickly as possible. He encouraged Céline to write, maybe a short book this time. The petulant principal author did not respond to his publisher's urgings. Well then, perhaps Céline could give his publisher some sort of plot outline for his next book—a schedule perhaps? Céline remained silent, producing no schedule at all, not even a possible topic. Would Céline consent to give some interviews, to keep his name in print? This time Céline spoke: "Never!" He would do nothing to help his "pimp," except perhaps sue the bastard for more money. That he would, and did, do. Robert was frantic. He had under contract a literary genius who wouldn't write.

If Céline viewed his publisher as a literary know-nothing and refused to cooperate, there were other able writers within the Denoël stable eager to sell their manuscripts. From its inception, Les Editions Denoël et Steele began taking literary prizes away from the Gallimard firm. In addition to Dabit's Prize for the Populist Novel of 1931, Denoël won the Renaudot Prize for 1931 and 1932 with novels by Philippe Hériat (*L'Innocent*) and, of course, Céline's *Journey to the End of the Night*. Again in 1932 Denoël snatched the Courteline Prize (for a comic novel or novel of manners) away from Gallimard with Marcel Sauvage's *The End of Paris* (*La Fin de Paris*). He captured the Renaudot Prize again in 1933 with Charles Braibant's novel, *The King Is Sleeping* (*Le Roi dort*). Seeing the prizes his publisher was winning, Céline narrowed his eyes and sniffed, drawing down his lower lip in derision. He had had quite enough of literary prizes.

While his wife tended the baby and consoled Artaud, Robert turned his thoughts to expansion. He began to make plans to turn his antique shop/bookstore, Les Trois Magots, into a real publishing house specializing in popular novels and light reading. By 1934 his shop officially became Les Editions de la Bourdonnais. As new authors, projects, and ideas poured into his publishing house, Robert quietly acquired other publishing firms that faced severe financial problems or bankruptcy due to the weakened economy. He purchased Les Editions des Cahiers libres and Les Editions de la Connaissance de René-Louis Doyon at bargain prices.

While Cécile Denoël still made no serious attempts to become an actress, Antonin Artaud, freshly back from his "cure" in the south of France, had regained his theatrical passion. He returned with a plan. To illustrate his theories, Artaud decided to write a play, or rather to adapt one. And he would stage it, perform in it, and direct it. In fact, he would be in complete control over the entire project at all times. And in that play he would demonstrate his innovative creative ideas about contemporary theater. He would show all of Paris exactly what he meant by the Theater of Cruelty. Artaud wanted this play to be his masterpiece, the centerpiece for his original thought. Excited, he began to write.

He decided to adapt a tragedy by Shelley, *The Cenci*, and to incorporate some of Stendhal's *Italian Chronicles* (*Chroniques italiennes*) into his play. He entitled it *Les Cenci*. He reserved the role of the cruel, murderous, incestuous Count Cenci for himself. The story is simple and gruesome. An Italian nobleman, Count Cenci, becomes obsessed by his daughter; he lusts after her and violates her. In revenge his daughter, with some help from her family, assassinates her father and is ultimately executed for her act. In this play Artaud was not interested in personal character development or psychology, preferring to show instead the forces of destiny, what he called a "cosmic cruelty," within the plot. He had a grand idea. All he needed to pull it off was money . . . along with the mental strength, courage, and determination to control the entire huge production while acting in the starring role.

Artaud finished writing his play in February 1935. Now he needed to find serious backing for his production. As was often done in Paris at the time, Antonin decided to give a reading of his play before a group of wealthy potential contributors. He invited Bernard Steele; Robert and Cécile Denoël; celebrated writer André Gide; a wealthy Russian woman, Iya Abdy; René and Yvonne Allendy; and other impressive notables.

As she was getting ready for Artaud's reading, Cécile spoke to her husband. "This could be my chance, Robert. This could really be my chance! You know how I have longed to act. And here is my good friend, Antonin, casting for his play. He knows I could play the part of the wife . . . or even the daughter. I would be perfect for either part, Robert. Really I would," she said as she applied her makeup and combed her hair.

Robert sighed. "Perhaps you are right," he said. He smiled at her, his theatrical wife who aspired to be an actress without ever going to auditions. Waiting for her, he sat on the bed and smoked a cigarette, then asked, "Is that what you really want? To be in Artaud's play?"

"More than anything else in the world, Robert."

"Then perhaps I could help you," he said.

Artaud's reading took place in February 1935 in the beautiful home of Jean-Marie Conty. After carefully explaining the purpose of his play, Artaud read it aloud, acting each part. There would be refreshments and discussions afterward. Following the performance, two very important backers offered their support: Iya Abdy and Robert Denoël. But there were strings attached to each offer—acting parts in return for money. Robert Denoël purchased the role of Cenci's wife, Lucrétia, for his own wife. And Iya Abdy purchased the role of Cenci's daughter for herself. Both women were thrilled.

Although Artaud would have liked a more experienced actress than Cécile to play Cenci's wife, it was Iya Abdy in the part of the Cenci's daughter that really troubled him. For one thing, Abdy was middle-aged—and looked it—making her far too old for the part. And then there was the problem of her Russian accent. So the lead female role in Artaud's drama, Cenci's beautiful young daughter, would be played by a middle-aged woman with a strong Russian accent. Artaud's control had already slipped considerably. Yet he couldn't refuse Abdy . . . and her money.

Another difficulty concerned the theater itself. Although there were several theaters in Paris that suited his concepts of scene design, all were reserved at the time when he wished to schedule his production. The only available theater was the Folies-Wagram, constructed for light operettas and ill suited to his impressive scenic plans. More compromise. Reluctantly, Artaud reserved the Folies-Wagram for his production in May. He would need to change some of his designs.

In some of the court records concerning the murder of Robert Denoël, I discovered a letter revealing information about Artaud's personal life at the time he was working on *Les Cenci*. It was written by Robert Denoël to his wife. In that letter, I learned to my astonishment that while Artaud was directing his play, he had another romance, again with a married woman, one who, like Nin, loved games, role playing, the theatrical. This time the object of his love was the wife of his publisher, Cécile Denoël. It soon became apparent to the entire cast of *Les Cenci* that their director and star was carrying on with one of his actresses. One day Robert Denoël slipped into

the back of the theater where they were rehearsing. And, unbeknownst to Antonin and Cécile, he watched them.

They flirted openly, rested backstage together, exchanged tender
looks and secrets, behaved like lovers in front of the cast. Then
Robert went backstage. Standing quietly by the curtain, he watched
Artaud, who normally withdrew from personal human contact, kiss
his wife. At home that evening Robert was strangely tense, silent.
Cécile, who had not seen him at the theater that day, pretended not
to notice. Or perhaps she really didn't notice at all. She was excited:
Her life was now important, new, and then there was Antonin. He
was different, charismatic, even magnetic. Cécile Denoël was ro-
mancing this handsome, fascinating, and talented author, director,
and star of *Les Cenci*. And everyone knew. She didn't yet realize that
her husband knew, too.

And he knew so much more. In that letter, written many years
later, he told Cécile that he had loved and been faithful to her for
many years. But she had, in his eyes, inexcusably betrayed him. What
bothered him most was not that she had had discreet affairs, but
rather her choice of lovers. Invariably, she became romantically involved with someone who was in her husband's employ. Robert believed that there had been several such affairs. She had repeatedly
made her husband a cuckold within his own business establishment.
How many within Les Editions Denoël et Steele knew of her indis-
cretions, Denoël could not guess. He felt belittled, humiliated within
his own company. And now there was this thing, this romance or
possible affair with Artaud (whom he had repeatedly helped) right
under his nose—and in front of the cast that Robert had helped to
finance. He said nothing at the time. But he was enraged. And
each time he watched Cécile and Antonin together, his resentment
deepened.

In the spring of 1935 Antonin and Cécile became more passionate
toward each other, while Robert observed them. Robert wrote, "You
loved him. He loved you. Were you his mistress? Perhaps yes, without
doubt yes, perhaps no. I witnessed your extravagant loves, your quar-

rels, your reconciliations, your mutual tenderness. . . . You seem able to love only those who take something from me. That is very curious. Your loves attained their paroxysm, with dramatic scenes, yelling etc. . . . at the time of *Les Cenci* when they cost me the most."

I attended one of the rehearsals for Artaud's play. Artaud was everywhere, giving directions to stagehands and actors at the same time. Stopping, pacing, starting to explain his theories to his cast, and being interrupted by a publicity problem, Artaud was frantic. He stormed, yelled, shrieked at his actors, then softened and started all over again. "Every movement must be choreographed. You must work as a whole, a team, like a dance," he told them. "The gestures and movements are just as important as the text." But they weren't working together. They were arguing. Often they didn't even listen to Artaud.

While Artaud was explaining his theories, Iya Abdy and the not-yet-famous Jean-Louis Barrault were arguing—no, fighting, yelling at each other. In sheer disgust Barrault told her, "You will never be right for this part, Iya. You're too damned old!" Then he stormed off the stage.

Artaud was beside himself. "Iya, you are garbling your lines. You are sounding like a Russian countess. Watch your accent!" Already annoyed, she shouted back at her director. Artaud retreated. He couldn't get the troupe to gel, to listen to him, to come together. In fact, he couldn't even get them to understand his concepts. And if they didn't understand, how could they communicate his ideas to the audience? There was not much time left until the premiere, on 6 May. He needed to do so much before then: programs, advertising, advance notices, tickets, ushers, scenery, rehearsals, sound, lighting, acting, interviews, and, of course, raising more money. He had already gone over budget. Then a peaceful thought entered his mind, overtaking it, throwing out all of his other worries: opium. He just needed some opium and everything would be all right. Opium was what he needed now—or better yet, heroin.

Dr. Allendy was growing more and more concerned about Artaud. He knew something that most of the actors didn't: as part of his insanity, when Artaud became truly focused and intense about an idea or a character, he actually became that idea or character in his mind. Allendy had treated Artaud when he believed that he actually *was* surrealism, that somehow he embodied it entirely. And Allendy vividly remembered what happened in 1933 when Robert Denoël, in another effort to help Artaud financially, commissioned Artaud to write a biography of the Roman emperor Heliogabalus. Artaud became so engrossed by the story of this mad young emperor who ruled Rome through debauchery and cruelty that for a while Artaud actually became Heliogabalus—at least in his mind. Dr. Allendy and Robert Denoël both had quite a time with him then.

And now Artaud was playing Count Cenci, not a nice fellow at all—an incestuous rapist and murderer, in fact. Allendy was right to be worried. I remembered that Artaud had alluded to his identification problem in his first meeting with Cécile. I wondered if she remembered that conversation, too. I had already read his play. I knew that two women (Iya and Cécile) could possibly be hurt (or worse) if Artaud actually became Count Cenci. But certainly he wouldn't, he couldn't. . . .

Of course I attended the premiere of *Les Cenci*. I wanted to see what happened. The evening of 6 May 1935, I entered the main portals of the theater, Les Folies-Wagram. Wanting to see all of the dignitaries arrive, I arrived early and stood for a long time by the door, watching. Robert Denoël, too, was early. He seemed serious, preoccupied, as he entered. I also recognized the Allendys, Bernard Steele, and a few other notables. Consulting my files, I managed to locate Princess Georges of Greece, Count Etienne de Beaumont, Dr. Thuyer-Landry, and the Princesses of Polignac. I did not see Anaïs Nin, although as the crowds became denser, I could have missed her. The attire was very formal. The women wore beautiful long gowns, punctuated with jewelry, which looked to be mostly pearls and diamonds.

I took a program and realized only then how large that cast really was. No wonder Artaud had had such difficulty keeping so many people in line. There were twenty-five actors playing thirty-one parts.

And there were so many scene changes. It was a four-act play with ten *tableaux*—ten scenes. And sound—it was the French theater's first attempt at stereophonic sound. The costumes, the scenery, the lighting, all were innovative and (I soon learned as the play began) spectacular. I looked for Cécile's name in the program for the part of Lucrétia. I saw that she was using a stage name: Cécile Bressant, very close to her maiden name, Brusson.

I became nervous as soon as the play began. Artaud was so agitated. His acting seemed somehow bigger even than the awful Count Cenci. I took a closer look at him. In spite of heavy makeup, he looked exhausted. Then he appeared to get a second wind, he fell more into his role, his features became more exaggerated, his voice grew louder, and his eyes seemed too big for their sockets. I wasn't sure. Was he still an actor, or had he turned into Count Cenci? I would soon find out.

Artaud, the actor, was supposed to lunge at Cécile, the actress. He was supposed to put his hands around her throat and say, "Not content with murder, you make use of criminal slander. In your fear of what my piercing mind might detect, you have done your best to have me locked up as a madman." Then he was supposed to pretend to strangle her.

And she was supposed to struggle with him and say, "I am suffocating."

Only this time Artaud wasn't Artaud anymore. He wasn't an actor, either. And he certainly wasn't pretending. He became for that moment the awful Count Cenci. He rushed at Cécile and seized her by the throat. Transfixed, I watched the scene unfold. Cécile wasn't acting anymore, either. Terrified, she was fighting for her life. She managed to get out a hoarse, rasping "I am suffocating," before she dropped to the floor. I watched the scene again, this time looking at the audience. Both Robert Denoël and René Allendy rose from their seats during this scene and started for the stage. Then Artaud caught himself and became the actor playing the role again.

Cécile's neck bore the imprint of Antonin's hands. Backstage, several people tended her. She was crying quietly, trembling. Later the red reminder of that incident turned blue. At each of the re-maining performances, a stagehand carefully applied a thick layer of makeup to Cécile's neck, to cover the bruises. But there was no permanent damage. She was all right. And most of the audience did not know what had happened. Critics later claimed that scene was overacted. They did not realize the scene had not been acted at all.

The first performance seemed to be a success. Artaud was ecstatic. After the play he and several others went to Montparnasse to celebrate at La Coupole. An acquaintance saw him arrive. "He was walking very quickly, at the head of several of his friends who were out of breath just following him. I heard happy voices, laughter. The entire com-pany seemed triumphant as they rushed into the establishment." Their triumph lasted only until they read the reviews.

Most of the critics hated the play. "I do not believe that one could play the part of Cenci (the incestuous father) more badly."

"He [Artaud] is a horrible actor."

"Artaud mocks us with this play."

The play closed after only seventeen performances. Right up to closing night, Artaud frantically sought more money to keep it open. But such harsh reviews served to keep audiences and future possible investors away.

Robert Denoël lost a small fortune with the closing of Artaud's play. He also effectively lost his wife. He didn't leave her at the time. And for a while she went on as if nothing had happened. But Robert's attitude toward his wife changed. Following *Les Cenci,* Robert wrote in that private letter to his wife, "Little by little this dramatic atmosphere in which you made me live, those constant dramatic scenes caused me to lose interest in you. I did not even perceive it myself. . . . I began to look at the women who surrounded you. And I had several brief affairs with them. These adventures permitted me to more easily support our common life together, which was becoming more and more sterile with each passing day." His business and his son remained profoundly important to Robert. But as for his wife, he really didn't care anymore. While he had affairs with his wife's friends, Cécile continued to have affairs with the men (mostly authors) who worked for her husband. Each seemed out to spite the other.

And Artaud? He felt an extreme need to go away, to be anywhere that was not France—not Paris—the farther away the better. And soon he did leave France. He went to Cuba, then Mexico, then back to Europe, to Brussels, then to Ireland. He was angry, furious with those who didn't understand him and who had panned his play. He cast spells on them. He made death threats. He decorated small pieces of paper with special symbols, colors, and curses, then attacked the papers, often destroying them and burning them with his cigarettes. He believed such actions would physically harm the object of his curse. He became more dangerous, more threatening to himself and to others. He was also hallucinating, often seeing dark, violent, horrible things. On 30 September 1937 he returned to France on the SS *Washington*—in a straitjacket. He would spend the next eight years and eight months incarcerated in various French insane asylums. He was in an asylum the night that Denoël was murdered.

During Artaud's harrowing period of travel and exile, he continued to work and in fact produced a masterpiece: *The Theater and Its Double* (*Le Théâtre et son double*). Robert Denoël had helped Artaud almost from their very first meeting in the 1920s. He had published his early works; commissioned him to write other works when Artaud needed money; allowed his publishing house to be used for Artaud's drama lessons; permitted Artaud to live with him; loaned him money; tried to get him off drugs; and invested in his theater productions. He had even looked the other way when Artaud romanced his wife. And now Artaud had a genuine masterpiece that needed a publisher. On 7 February 1938 *The Theater and Its Double* was published— by Gaston Gallimard.

7

Céline, France, and the Jews

Christ cannot possibly have been a Jew. I don't have to
prove that scientifically. It is a fact!

Paul Joseph Goebbels

*W*ishing to run away from anything connected to his failure of *Les
Cenci*, Artaud not only left France, he also left (at least for a while)
the friends who had supported him in this theatrical disaster. I could
find no evidence that he wrote to Robert or Cécile while he was
abroad. Instead, he wrote to his friend Jean Paulhan, keeping him
abreast of his writing. And Paulhan worked for Gaston Gallimard.
Probably because Gallimard had had nothing to do with *Les Cenci*, he
won the publishing rights to Artaud's masterpiece.

In spite of the loss of Artaud's *The Theater and Its Double* to Gaston
Gallimard, the progress of Les Editions Denoël et Steele during the
1930s was astonishing. Denoël's Psychological Library was a success,
as was his theater series, the Three Masks Collection. He continued
to produce exquisite books on art, and added books on history and
civilization, as well as many thoughtful essays. As for the novel, Denoël was now publishing some of the most distinguished French writers of the twentieth century. Most of his authors were discovered and
launched by Denoël himself.

Year after year he won just about every literary prize that was offered, with the exception of the one he most wanted, the Goncourt. After the Céline fiasco, that ultimate prize continued to elude him. But his reputation for decisiveness and innovation, along with the excellence of his publications, secured his fame. No longer did he have to wait until a manuscript was rejected by every other publishing house in Paris before he could see it. Now he was often the first choice for the submission of new manuscripts. Gaston Gallimard was beside himself.

In my research of the 1930s I discovered many descriptions of Robert Denoël. Almost invariably these accounts portray him as intelligent, energetic, persuasive, and distinguished. Many of his contemporaries noticed his eyes in particular, bright blue and sparkling with interest and enthusiasm behind his round glasses. He seemed to posses many of the same attractive traits as his enemy, Gallimard. Both men had a certain charisma, diplomacy, politeness. As he became established, he also demonstrated some of Gallimard's shrewdness—a touch of trickery or deceit perhaps. With Gallimard and Denoël, their cards were never entirely on the table, their next move never clear.

In sharp contrast to descriptions of Denoël's demeanor, I discovered that those who met Céline in the 1930s were taken by his dour expression. Hatred, cynicism, and anger were reflected on his face. His hands, his body, his stance all served to punctuate Céline's distain and scorn, particularly for his publishers. Some biographers of Céline have suggested that it was all a game, that Céline and Denoël were really friends then. Looking at their letters and the words others heard them say, I cannot agree. They were antagonists. Denoël even admitted to his friend Denis Saurot, "Céline has on several occasions written me letters the unbelievable violence of which seems to me to be entirely mad." Céline's relationship with Denoël was constantly antagonistic, sometimes outrageous, and often litigious. In fact, there is considerable evidence that they may have hated each other, each in a different way.

In addition to the constant battles over money, Céline despised

Robert's charisma, his diplomacy, his good looks, and the way he used them to get what he wanted. Céline was fond of mimicking his publisher in front of others. He was good at it, too. He used his hands just as his publisher did and imitated his expressions and gestures in blatantly derisive mockery. Then he would flounce around, wave his arms and say in an exaggerated sugary imitation of Denoël's voice and Belgian accent, "But yes, of course, certainly, my good friend. You can always count on me." Then he would grovel, smile, bow very low, and sneer as only Céline, returning to himself, could sneer. Céline continually attacked his publisher's honesty, his intentions, his intelligence, and his integrity.

For Robert Denoël, one of Céline's most disturbing traits was that this author accused him publicly of not knowing anything about good writing, and worse, of not even valuing it. Céline let everyone know that he considered Denoël to be nothing more than an ignorant, money-grubbing, pimping crook. Denoël did not attempt to defend himself. He suffered his principal writer's epithets in silence.

Céline's accusations, contempt, and mockery hurt Denoël's reputation with his other writers. For example, Eugène Dabit, now with Gallimard, greatly admired Céline's first novel, particularly its fresh, crude style. He believed Céline to be a kindred spirit. Céline's charges against his publisher served to salve Dabit's conscience about leaving Denoël for the prestige and security of Gallimard. Dabit then concluded in his own mind that maybe he really did have good reasons to leave Denoël after all. He conveniently forgot all that Robert had done to get *Hotel of the North* published and promoted. He even forgot about his populist literary prize. Instead, Dabit followed Céline's lead and decided that Denoël was underhanded.

This situation came to a head after a Hungarian translator assured Dabit that he had sent Denoël the money for the translation rights to *Hotel of the North*. Dabit marched into Les Editions Denoël et Steele and quickly entered Denoël's office unannounced. Reading at his desk, Robert glanced up, then smiled.

"Where's my money?" Dabit asked.

"What money?"

"The money you got from that Hungarian translator. Where is it? I want it." Dabit stormed.

"Oh that," responded Denoël. "It hasn't come in yet."

"You're lying," Dabit shouted. "I know you're lying, you cheat. I want my money."

Denoël rose from his desk, walked quickly over to Dabit, grabbed his shirt, and punched him in the face. The startled Dabit pushed him off, but Denoël lunged again, hitting him several times. Too surprised to defend himself, Dabit swung wildly at Denoël while retreating toward the door. Enraged, Denoël just stood there watching his former author leave. This unfortunate incident was formally closed after an exchange of very tense, guarded letters between the two combatants and a check from Denoël. In reality the rift never closed.

Céline admitted in a letter written to his friend, Evelyne Pollet, that he was on "the worst possible terms" with his publisher. He was wrong. It got worse—much worse. The not certifiably mad, but ominously dangerous Céline provided new sources of difficulty for Denoël when, nearly four years after the publication of *Journey*, he submitted the manuscript for his second novel, *Death on the Installment Plan (Mort à crédit)*. If *Journey* contained coarse language and slang, this new manuscript far outdid it in sheer vulgarity. While the first novel recounted a fruitless search for life's meaning, the second became something of a journey to the most profound depths of the misery and humiliation of childhood—supposedly Céline's own childhood.

Without respite, Céline litters his pages with examples of extreme domestic violence, beatings, shouting and screaming, bigotry, brutality, belittlement, and excrement—plenty of excrement. Describing his parents, he says. "They huddled up in their misery, disintegrating, lacerating themselves with despair, shrinking so as to offer less surface." And they engaged in constant name-calling. For example, the father tells his son, "Suffering asshole Christ almighty! My poor dear, what did we do to produce such vermin? As corrupt as three dozen

jailbirds! . . . Profligate! Scoundrel! Idler! And then some! He's calamity personified!"

In addition to his obscenity, Céline's style journeyed into the
realm of the incomprehensible, with abrupt changes from past to
present tense, fragmented sentences, coarse slang throughout, and
strange ellipses. Robert grew pale upon reading it, turning each page
with a new sense of tension and worry. Céline basked in his publisher's discomfiture. He later described to Robert Poulet, with exaggerated gestures and mimicking tone, their first meeting to discuss
the manuscript. Mocking Denoël, he assumed an intensely worried
and severe look, then said in his best imitation of a Belgian accent,
"I believe you may have gone too far this time." Then Céline laughed
uproariously, a laugh that has been described as a "clownish and
paranoid cackle that seized him."

He wrongly assumed that it was the style that had most upset his
publisher. Although Denoël did want a clearer style in certain places,
he worried in particular that the work was pornographic, that they
would get in trouble with the law if they published it as is.

Denoël used all of his diplomacy.

Céline despised Denoël's use of diplomacy.

Denoël used all of his tact and careful reasoning.

Céline hated Denoël's use of tact and careful reasoning.

"We don't want to be charged with pornography," Denoël quietly
explained to his fuming author. "We have carefully acquired important sympathies. Let's not alienate them," he said. His explanations
had the effect of pouring gasoline onto an already roaring fire.

Perhaps the only good that came from their heated, protracted,
fierce, vitriolic disagreement is that there is no evidence that either
man punched the other in the face. Denoël desperately tried to temper some of the more virulent and obscene passages and tone down
the most violent scenes in the manuscript. Céline steadfastly refused
to alter one word. As if this weren't bad enough, the printer decided
to enter the fray by refusing to print three of the manuscript's most
obscene pages. Fights, name-calling, proposals, counterproposals,

threats, counterthreats—all ended in stalemate. Even the printer refused to budge. Denoël would not publish the work as it was; Céline would change absolutely nothing. And each man claimed the other had won.

In the end both men won—and lost. The book was published in the summer of 1936 with blank spaces representing what the author wanted to include and what Denoël and the printer had deleted. However, 117 copies were numbered and printed in the unexpurgated version to be sold to collectors of rare editions.

If there was no agreement among Céline, Denoël, and the printer, there was amazing consensus among the critics regarding the merits of this work. Although today it is considered something of a dark and innovative masterpiece, most of the critics of the time disparaged it, not only for its obscenity and difficult style, but also for its very premise. In this work Céline demonstrated his belief in the absolute baseness of humanity. For him, mankind had no intrinsic value, nothing to lift it beyond the rawest animal instincts. The book was relentlessly pessimistic. Some even claimed its unceasing horror and gloom became monotonous. "Abject," "sordid," "ignominious," "corruptive," "disgusting," "boring"—these were the adjectives the critics used to describe Céline's novel. For most of them, *Death on the Installment Plan* was "a product of sewers."

This time there was no scandal to pique the reader's interest. And the critics certainly weren't recommending it. Even the intellectuals of the time expressed either disgust or indifference to Céline's new novel. If Denoël didn't do something, he was going to have a total flop on his hands. What he did was unprecedented. He defended this man who was constantly attacking and belittling him. He wrote a thirty-two-page pamphlet entitled *Justification for "Death on the Installment Plan" (Apologie de "Mort à crédit")* in which he defended his author's style and his literary concepts. Not only that, he also defended Céline's refusal to do what was generally expected of any writer who had just published a book, i.e., give interviews, visit literary salons, write articles, or tout his book in any way in order to sell more copies. He compared the criticisms of Céline's novels to those of other innovative authors and musicians of the past: Beethoven, Flaubert, Balzac, and Zola, among others. Finally, he cited the individual charges of several important critics and responded to each in turn.

Denoël had just had a protracted, bitter battle with his author over the very things the critics were complaining about: his unremitting gloom, his obscenity, and his sometimes incomprehensible style. Then he turned around and published a work that eloquently defended Céline on all counts. Not only that, but he also defended Céline's right not to do anything to try to sell his book—when Denoël had tried valiantly to get him to help promote it. Of course, the readers of Denoël's ardent defense did not know the publisher's true feelings. They did not know that Denoël was simply doing his job as a publisher, playing the publishing game, trying desperately to sell a book. On the contrary, most believed that Robert Denoël was in true harmony and accord with his author—a belief that would not serve Robert well in the future. By defending Céline so strongly, he inadvertently joined his own views with those of Céline. Denoël and Céline in perfect agreement—that was the public perception.

Denoël published three thousand copies of his defense, hoping to stir up some controversy, spark some interest in the novel. He failed. Not even Céline himself was impressed by his publisher's unprecedented action. He simply added another name to his Denoël name-calling repertoire. To "crook," "lazybones," "pimp," "thief," "ignoramus," and "parasite," he added "zebra." His publisher was a zebra, a man who stressed the white when it served his needs, or emphasized the black when it suited him to do so. Denoël, the zebra, played the double game. "Zebra" was Céline's first epithet that really suited his publisher. In fact, the zebra characteristic of playing both sides, going either way on an issue while promoting a book, was Denoël's very definition of what a good publisher should be. And Gaston Gallimard agreed with this concept. He, too, was a zebra, a master of the double game.

It was clear to Bernard Steele and Robert Denoël that they had a principal writer who was out of control. Céline had insulted, threatened, abused, and, whenever possible, embarrassed both men on a fairly constant basis since the loss of the Goncourt Prize in 1932. But Céline's castigation and accusations against Bernard Steele were much more bitter and intense. Neither publisher could have guessed why simply by reading that first manuscript that he had submitted to them. There is really no evidence of it in *Journey to the End of the Night*. Nor is there much evidence of it in *Death on the Installment Plan*. What both men could not have known then was that Céline had created or invented a reason for his feelings of anger, a reason for everything that had ever gone wrong or was going to go wrong with him or with the entire world. That reason was the Jew. Although his major works had not yet clearly shown it, Céline was profoundly anti-Semitic. And Bernard Steele was a Jew. It is indeed ironic that Bernard Steele, along with his Jewish mother, Béatrice Hirshon, provided the financial backing to launch the literary career of Louis-Ferdinand Céline.

I wanted to believe that Céline was some half-baked fanatic on the fringe of society expressing views that no one else articulated or believed. But that wasn't true. Most French people shared some of Céline's anti-Semitic viewpoints at that time. He directed much of his anti-Semitism at his Jewish publisher, Bernard Steele. In fact, he despised him. He hated his youth, his good looks, his intelligence, his savoir faire. Most of all, Céline hated Steele's wealth and his aristocratic tendencies.

Then there was the problem of accents. Robert Denoël was never able to eradicate entirely his Belgian accent. But Céline also had an undesirable accent, and he was quite aware of it. He spoke a definite lower-class Parisian French, exacerbated by the slang he had picked up while treating his patients (often the destitute, alcoholics, and undesirables) in his Clichy clinic. Bernard Steele spoke flawless upper-class Parisian French with no trace of his American origins. Céline hated Steele's perfect French, and by this time he was none too fond of Americans, either. To Céline's great annoyance, Steele seemed to know about everything. He was not just a connoisseur of fine wine but was reputed to be able to recognize by taste not only the type of wine and its origin, but sometimes even the year it had been made. Steele represented just about everything that Céline absolutely loathed. And what's more, Steele, too, was making money from Céline's work.

Bernard Steele patiently endured Céline's sullen hatred, accusations, and denigration for four long years (1932–36). In the space of that time Céline's bigotry and intolerance of the Jews grew into a mad passion culminating in the belief that in order to save France itself, Jews must lose all power within the country. They must be expelled . . . or worse. And so, in a climate of growing anti-Semitism throughout France, a darkening political situation in Europe itself, and a vituperative anti-Semitic principal writer within his publishing house, Steele withdrew his financial support from Robert Denoël. Bernard and Robert talked for nearly two hours in Denoël's office at 19, rue Amélie on a cold December night in 1936—almost nine years to the day before Robert's murder.

"What can I do to induce you to stay?" asked Robert.

"I am not sure you can do anything, or that you should do anything," his partner responded. "I know how Céline is. You can't stop his attacks. And they're getting worse—for both of us, they're getting worse. Sometimes I think he's a roaring lunatic . . . gone mad, and the world with him. I can't stay here anymore. I'm not happy here." He took out a cigarette, lit it, and smoked, not saying anything.

Robert tried to find the right words. He needed his partner. They had worked well together; they had been a success. "I could threaten to drop Céline," he suggested.

"You can't threaten Céline. You need him too much. Besides, Céline loves threats, thrives on them. And if he left, he would go straight to Gaston Gallimard. And old Gaston would welcome him with open arms. Céline knows that. Then what would you do? He's still your biggest moneymaker."

"I don't want you to go," said Robert. "You have been invaluable. I need you."

"And part of me doesn't want to go either. Robert, you have been a great friend. But it's more than just Céline. It's France. France—my home. I've never seen this kind of hatred before. It's . . . I'm not comfortable here anymore. I need a change. Sometimes I don't even feel safe. And I believe the time will come when I really won't be safe here. I can feel it. France has changed, just like Germany."

"You're going to leave France?" asked Robert.

"I'm a Jew. An American Jew. It's time I went back to the States." They were both silent for some time. Then Robert sighed deeply and said, "I wish you the best. You do know that you will always be welcome to return as my partner—anytime you wish."

"Thank you," Bernard replied. "It's been quite a ride, hasn't it?" They shook hands and Bernard left the deconsecrated chapel for the last time.

Reluctantly, Denoël bought out the shares of Steele and his mother on 30 December 1936, leaving his firm flirting with bankruptcy. The official reason given for Steele's departure was that the two partners could no longer agree on the direction of the firm. I checked with two of Robert's employees at the time. They also knew and confirmed the real reason for Steele's departure. As one employee, Max Dorian, put it, "Céline mistreated the Jews, democratic ideals, . . . and his impressions of America were not exactly favorable. Now Bernard Steele, although he was liberal in his ideas, was just the same a good American, good democrat . . . and of Jewish origin!" Les Editions Denoël et Steele became simply Les Editions Denoël. Before he left for the United States, Bernard phoned Robert to say good-bye.

"Be careful, Robert," his ex-partner warned him. "I think Céline has some monstrous plans up his sleeve."

"I can take care of myself," responded Robert. "Bon voyage, my good friend, and good luck."

Bernard was right to leave—right on both counts. Céline did have a monstrous plan up his sleeve, and France had clearly changed. All over that country anti-Semitic organizations were springing up. The year 1936 saw the establishment of Jean Boissel's Universal Anti-Jewish League (Ligue anti-juive universelle), which many French leaders and intellectuals supported. Dozens of other organizations and so-called civic groups espousing anti-Semitism as part of their charters were also founded.

Even French laws began to reflect the country's growing anti-Semitism. In 1936 a law was passed requiring that "all immigrant refugees prove that they were victims of political persecution before being allowed even temporary residence in France." This law made it more difficult for German Jews and others to flee their country. Jews in Germany were already losing their human rights, their businesses, and their citizenship. In many places they were already denied access to stores, to food, to towns, to public schools. Proving political persecution should have been simple for a German Jew. But it wasn't. French bureaucrats saw to that.

While Bernard Steele was sailing for America, Céline sent his only publisher yet another letter threatening Denoël with another court battle over money. This time Robert himself responded: "You know, it might not be in your own self-interest to litigate Les Editions Denoël into bankruptcy." Céline, of course, was not impressed.

I found a description of Céline in 1936, written by Pierre de Boisdeffre. He said, "Céline was considered to be a popular novelist, gruff, but good-hearted, tender in spite of his hardheadedness. Wrong, he was a madman: no one had yet realized it." It was probably true; yet no one comprehended Céline's mental state, except, of course, for Bernard Steele, Robert Denoël, and a few employees within their publishing house. And now Bernard had dropped out of the game. But Robert, as determined as ever, refused to fold.

Often Céline wrote as an outlet for his physical pain and passions. When the buzzing in his ears got too great, when his dizzying headaches overwhelmed him, when his head throbbed and his insomnia became insufferable, he would shut himself away from people. Then he would sit alone at his desk, very still, almost motionless lest he jar his screaming head, and he would write. And the venom and hatred in his mind would spill forth from him onto the paper, and he would be comforted; his pain would lessen. Amid Hitler's rise, new global crises, the growing threat of another war, and his own increasing pain and hatred, Céline, that great devil, conceived a plan. Why not combine his hatred, his fear, his pain, and his writing skills into one long polemical diatribe to show the world its errors?

And so he began to write. To his amazement, the words, the sentences and paragraphs flowed easily from him, spurting like blood from a gaping wound. The other two novels had taken years to write; his words had come slowly, painfully. Now words dripped from his mind, then rushed freely, feverishly, and as he wrote he began to feel better. In only a few months he had completed his 384-page work, which he entitled *Trifles for a Massacre (Bagatelles pour un massacre)*. And just exactly what he had written was not clear to anyone.

Céline did not even try to invent a name for the book's hero. Céline's protagonist was Céline himself, as both unwitting recipient of evil and as the master of black and vituperative humor. He castigated nearly everything in this work, ridiculing the refined world of letters and literature, criticizing Communist Russia, and berating the English as snobs. His piercing, harsh eye took aim at the indifference and decadence of the French themselves. He ridiculed France's institutions, taking special jabs at what he called France's ridiculous and outmoded educational system. One device he repeatedly used was to start with himself as the poor, sometimes comical, innocent victim, and then expand this concept to include other victims, then all of France, and finally the entire world as victim. And victim of what? The Jew, of course.

What he said was an insane mixture of deadly serious anti-Semitic charges amply mixed with the clearly preposterous. On the one hand, he did claim that to tolerate the Jew was to submit to total Jewish domination, decadence, and even death. Often he echoed, sometimes even plagiarized, the words of earlier anti-Semites. But then, as only Céline could do, he seemed to make a wild detour, resulting in a confusing and sometimes darkly humorous journey into the land of nonsense. He claimed, for example, that the pope was Jewish. And so were, for that matter, the entire House of Lords in England and all of the Soviet leaders of Russia. According to Céline, Racine was Jewish, as was Virginia Woolf. All of the French Bourbon monarchs were Jewish. That virtually all of his readers would know that his claims were entirely false did not matter—or perhaps that was the very point. Much of his work was written as a dark, vile joke, with anyone that Céline particularly disliked being automatically defined as Jewish.

In particular, Céline hated literary critics. After all, they had turned their backs on him at the last minute and awarded the Goncourt Prize of 1932 to another. Then they had panned his second novel. "They are all stupid jerks! All of them bloody stupid jerks, Jews! All are failures, hicks, outrages!" His book was a catharsis of rage.

If Robert Denoël did not know what to make of this book, he was not alone. Neither did the critics. Reviews were lukewarm and mixed, with no significant differences among various political factions, primarily because no one was sure what Céline had really written. A vile and serious anti-Semitic attack? Or a clever, mean, ridiculous joke with Céline himself cast in the role of the dark bard of black humor? Whatever he meant, and in spite of the critics, the public loved it. The book was a hit. The twenty-thousand-copy first edition sold quickly. Within just a few years this book sold over seventy-five thousand copies, with each copy selling at about $6.67 or higher, a very good price for a book at that time. And once again, thanks to Céline, significant money began pouring into his publisher's coffers.

I wanted to find out what Denoël's reaction had been to this book, just as I had discovered his initial reactions to Céline's first two novels. I looked everywhere. Finally, I had to concede that sometimes, in spite of all the work that a researcher does, in spite of intense effort to find a definitive answer, it does not reveal itself. I had hoped to listen in on that conversation between author and publisher regarding *Trifles for a Massacre*. I believed that if I heard that discussion, I would know and understand Denoël so much better. In particular, I wanted to know Robert's reaction to Céline's anti-Semitism. Was this publisher, like so many of his friends, also deeply anti-Semitic? Instead of an answer to my questions, I found nothing. All that I managed to find was one simple clue, a poor bedraggled ribbon, one that had apparently gone around the first editions as they went to bookstores. On that ribbon was only this: "For a good laugh in the trenches." Ironically, the press release announcing this book came out on Christmas day, 1937, and it too carried that same statement.

Then I began to suspect that my failure to find even one clue, one hint of a meeting between publisher and author might have been an accurate reflection of what actually happened. Maybe there hadn't been a meeting. Perhaps Denoël, realizing that anything he said about the manuscript would cause a major uproar, said nothing. It made sense. Denoël avoided another huge and probably fruitless confrontation by keeping silent. Once I accepted the possibility of no discussion between author and publisher about the book, something that Céline said years later to the American scholar (also Jewish) Milton Hindus now made sense. "I used to go to poor Denoël—I would not even permit him to read my manuscripts—I used to tell him—one million cash! And we would make the exchange—I like to work that way—straightforward—it's for me to judge the quality of the work and not the job of a shitty publisher."

Céline lied. He lied to everyone on a regular basis. As Hindus put it, "Céline is as tightly packed with lies as a boil is with puss." And when he wasn't lying, he exaggerated. Many of his early biographers were taken in, to their later dismay, by his lies. And certainly part of what he had said to Hindus was a lie, for Robert Denoël had carefully, painstakingly gone over the manuscripts of his first two novels. But maybe there was a kernel of truth in Céline's remark. Perhaps his publisher no longer tried to edit Céline's manuscripts, knowing that such an attempt would only lead to chaos.

Carefully filing away my information on Denoël's tribulations, I decided to look again into the Frondaie/Loviton household. I soon learned that 1936, that awful year for Denoël in which Céline became totally uncontrollable and Bernard Steele left the partnership, was a year of change for Pierre Frondaie and his wife as well. As I visited them both in that year, I realized that, unlike his still beautiful and young wife, Frondaie looked older. He was wearing glasses now with huge black frames. But his voice and stance remained as young as ever. He was fifty-two. His plays and novels were still hugely successful. Now he was contemplating a monumental work, *A History of Love Through the Ages*, in which he would describe and examine some of the world's greatest loves and lovers, both real and fictional. As for love at home, there was very little of it. Pierre and Jeanne had traveled extensively together, and both had enjoyed that. They had both worked on novels in the same house, if not together. But more and more, there were quarrels, fights, and separations. Although they often argued over money, love and fidelity were becoming even more critical issues between them. Pierre was certain that Jeanne had lovers.

His wife confused him. She was so ambitious, so secretive. And she took such care to cultivate the friendships of influential people. "You never know when you will need the help of important friends," she told him.

Pierre Frondaie once told an interviewer, "I have never in my life known how to cultivate useful relationships; what's more, I often neglect my own interests in order to live as a poet. That's what explains why I don't have my own theater, like Bernstein, or that I am not yet in the Académie [française] like Pierre Benoit!" It was true. He would rather be alone or traveling than seeking to curry favor in order to increase his own fame or prestige. And with his passionate, outspoken temperament, he was better at making enemies than friends. He had in fact made a lot of enemies.

By 1935 Jeanne was more absent than present in the Frondaie household. Often Pierre didn't even know where she was. All that he received from his wife on a regular basis was a continual barrage of bills for ball gowns, Chanel suits, hats, shoes, furs, new coiffures, jewelry, perfume; the list was endless. "You do want me to look my best, darling" had become a tawdry phrase for him, grown old with use. The real problem was that he still loved her. But this couldn't go on. He would go bankrupt paying the bills for a wife who preferred the company of others (sometimes the beds of others) to his own. No. The marriage could not continue. They divorced on 11 February 1936. Paul Valéry was waiting.

On that very same day (11 February) Jeanne went to a party at the home of some friends. Her hostess, knowing of her divorce that day, seated her at dinner next to a small balding man with large round glasses. He was something of a lady's man, known for his brilliant conversation and wonderful sense of humor. This man was one of the most celebrated playwrights of France, Jean Giraudoux. Loviton's hostess also knew that Giraudoux had just ended an affair of his own— an eleven-year passionate affair with a woman named Anita (who was now in Argentina). Perhaps they might hit it off, their hostess thought. They liked each other right from the start. Their affair began that night. At about the same time, Jeanne had yet another affair with celebrated writer and poet Saint-John Perse. As for Valéry, he and Jeanne too were engaged in an affair. And although some scholars have tried to suggest that their affair was purely platonic, their words, their letters, and the observations of those who knew them suggest otherwise. Furthermore, the three affairs clearly overlapped. It is fair to say that Jeanne Loviton was not grieving very much over her failed marriage, or for the loss of Pierre Frondaie. She had emerged from that marriage with money, influence, contacts, savoir faire—and one completed novel.

Having read that first novel, I believe it is fair to say that if Jeanne Loviton had submitted it to Robert Denoël, he would have pronounced it "insipid." Even his Editions de la Bourdonnais, specializing in light and popular reading, would probably have politely but firmly rejected it. No, she could not rely upon merit to get her first book published. But contacts and influence—she had plenty of those.

Jeanne Loviton's first novel, *Beauty; the Major Reason (Beauté, raison majeur)*, was published in the spring of 1936 by Emile-Paul Frères, Pierre Frondaie's own publisher. And although Jeanne never admitted that her former husband used his influence to get her first book published, Pierre Frondaie himself certainly alluded to it in an interview some months later. "I greatly loved a woman who wrote a novel, a roman à clef, in which she disparaged me," he admitted. "Then she was rejected by two publishers. In spite of what she had said about me in her novel, I felt bad for her. So secretly I used my influence to get her novel published." Now Jeanne Loviton was a published novelist, the ex-wife of a famous and important writer who still cared for her, and the mistress of three scions of French literature. What more could she want?

A house. Jeanne Loviton wanted her own home. After carefully looking at nearly all the expensive residences in Paris, she selected a large, elegant home with a small carriage house and a beautiful private garden, located at 11, rue de l'Assomption. Then she hired a maid to cook and keep the house, and a combination chauffeur and gardener. Although her instructions to the maid/cook were quite detailed and specific, those of the chauffeur/gardener were even more demanding, particularly regarding the garden. "I want beautiful flowers blooming here from early spring until late fall," she ordered. "Your job is to keep this garden perfect and colorful always. Is that understood?"

"Oui, Madame." There was a specific reason for her interest in that garden, as I would soon discover.

After the furniture had been carefully positioned, all the paintings tastefully hung, and the china set in place—and after all the shrubs had been sculpted, the rosebushes (now in full bloom) pruned and fertilized, and other flowers tended—Jeanne invited her dear friend, the man who had stood on the sidelines, patiently waiting throughout her marriage—the Official Poet of France—to a little lunch, which her cook had spent days preparing. He was her first guest in her new home. After the maid answered the door and announced him, Jeanne came to receive him in her beautiful foyer, taking both of his outstretched hands into hers and kissing him gently on the lips. If it was an old man who had knocked at that door, that man now was growing younger, almost by the minute. His face broadened into a handsome smile, his shoulders straightened, his beautiful blue eyes sparkled. He pulled her close to him and held her silently against him for a few moments. The man of words could not describe his happiness then. He was like a child hugging a treasured teddy close to him . . . wanting to hold onto that moment forever. He loved her. He had loved her for so long.

"I have a surprise for you," she said.

"What?" he asked.

"But first you must look at my house." She took him by the hand and led him into every room, pointing here and there, asking if he liked this or that. The overwhelmed Valéry followed her, smiling, and exclaiming with satisfaction and pleasure at times.

"You have done wonders here," he said.

"Now for the surprise," she said. "Follow me." She led him down a narrow hallway, then out the back door. And there before him was the most wonderful, private, inviting garden that Paul Valéry had ever seen. Reds, pinks, greens, variegated leaves, yellows all showered his eyes with color. And at the center of that garden, lending a beautiful exotic touch to the entire area, stood a lovely stand of bamboo. But it was the quietness, the solitude, the privacy of it all that most enchanted him. The garden offered no view to outsiders from any direction. It would become Paul Valéry's favorite place, his secret place. He would think there, reflect there, write there. He would make love there, be in love there, and experience the most profound joy of his entire life right there in the hidden garden of 11, rue de l'Assomption. He loved her surprise. His joy renewed him.

The aging poet awoke from his reverie. The man who had written his best works so many years ago, who had shelved future projects, later to abandon them entirely, the poet without verse who contented himself with writing prefaces for others or giving a lecture now and then, revived. He was no longer an old man without ideas—one past his prime. He was richly mature and experienced, a man in his mid-sixties with the best yet to come. He was in love. The whole world stood before him. Suddenly he had so many projects ahead of him, so much to do. And there was his muse, his Jeanne, beside him.

In 1936 Paul Valéry really began writing and working again. First, of course, he wrote to his love, his Jeanne. He wrote her nearly every day, beautiful letters and notes and verses, which sang of his joy and devotion to her. He wrote Jeanne Loviton more than eleven hundred letters and more than 133 poems praising her and exulting in their love together. Then he began his projects.

He decided to write a play. He would entitle it *Mon Faust*. He would model the play's heroine, Lust (a name having a much less sexual connotation in French than in English), after Jeanne. He decided that part of his entire life's philosophy was incorrect. The love of a woman was no longer something to eschew, some horrible fate to face with submission. It was instead the most profound experience a man could have. More than that, a woman's love was divine, perhaps as close as man could get on earth to God. He said, "To be one in two persons, that is, in sum, to be something like God." He also decided to write an intimate book on love, which he would call the *Coronilla*. He could let Frondaie recount the history of love. Valéry intended in his work to show exactly what love is.

One beautiful summer day, Paul was writing in Jeanne's garden. She was reading nearby. Suddenly he looked up, then said, "Suppose we write a book together."

"What sort of book?" she asked.

He smiled at her. "A book on love, of course."

"But there are so many books on love already," she replied. "How would ours be different?"

"Are you implying that our love is ordinary?" he joked.

"Hardly ordinary, my dear, but if we wrote a book on love, I would want it to be unique, unusual." Valéry began to cough. "I know that Yvette has made some lemonade," she said. "I'll get some. Perhaps it will soothe your throat." She got up and went into the house.

While she was gone, Paul glanced at the garden, watched a little gray bird in one of the shrubs, then looked down again at his work. All at once he began to smile, then chuckled. "I've got it!" he said upon her return. "We shall write a book of love letters."

"But what would be so unusual about that?" she asked. "We are always writing love letters."

"But this would be different," he said, still smiling. "This time I would write the woman's letters and you would write from the man's point of view. It would be very amusing for us."

She laughed. "Do you think we could pull it off? Fool people?"

"Of course," he replied. Clearly, the idea appealed to them both. But it was simply one of so many of Valéry's ideas then. He was overwhelmed with new thoughts, insights, and feelings, and he still had lectures to give, appearances to make, and prefaces to write. Of course, his love for Jeanne took up so much of his time. When he wasn't with her, he was writing to her—or about her—and thinking of her always. And when she wasn't with him, she was with her many friends, including Giraudoux and Saint-John Perse.

I remembered how much Paul Valéry loved secrets. He was himself a kind of player, but not of the double game that Gallimard and Denoël engaged in. Valéry loved the game of words, the double entendre, the secret message and hidden meaning. He had always loved such secrets. In particular, he liked to use secret names and meanings for the women he admired. In 1925 he described the beauty and grace of prima ballerina Anna Pavlova, as she danced *Swan Lake*. He referred to her as Athikte. She would know and recognize that name. She had once been called that name, long ago and in another country. But others would not know. He liked that. Calling her Athikte was like sharing a secret with her, a private intimacy.

He expanded his use of secret names during his affair with Catherine Pozzi. He called her "Béatrice," "bice" "Bce," "B," "Laure" "C.K.," "Karin," and "Eurydiké." He used these names in his *Notebooks*. Sometimes he just referred to her as "the women (*les femmes*)."

With Jeanne Loviton he went even further. He called himself "the Assumptionist" (a religious and historical reference) because she lived on the rue de l'Assomption. Since her phone was on the Jasmine line, he called her "my Jasmine." He also named her "Rose," "Calypso," and "Polydore," each with its own secret meaning. I remembered that he even went beyond mere words, using complicated mathematical symbols and numbers to refer to her. After all, his love for her should also include mathematics, abstraction.

Then he decided mythology could best describe their love. He was writing again in that beautiful secret garden when Jeanne came out to see how he was progressing. He looked up from his work, then stood and embraced her tenderly in their garden. "You are my Héra," he whispered softly.

"And you are my Zeus," she responded quickly. She knew that the mythological Héra was the queen of the heavens and, interestingly, both wife and sister of Zeus, supreme god of the heavens. Her response greatly pleased the aging poet.

He kissed her. From then on he often called her Héra. Had he forgotten the double side of this goddess? Héra presided over birth. And certainly Valéry appeared reborn. His new projects, too, could symbolize births—the birth of creativity and new ideas. But there was a darker side to this goddess. She could be severe, vindictive. She had persecuted Zeus and had relentlessly pursued her enemies. She could be hateful, mean-spirited. Most of all, the goddess Héra was not to be trusted. She was a goddess of deception and duplicity. Had Valéry merely overlooked this side of Héra? Or did he have a premonition?

The two lovers did not cowrite the book of love letters that Paul had proposed. Instead, Jeanne had another project in mind. She decided to write her second novel. And this time at her side was Paul Valéry who willingly, joyfully corrected her drafts. With all of her influential friends, plus the help of one of the ablest writers in France, she intended to win the Goncourt, or at least some other significant literary prize. As she had in her first novel, she used the pseudonym Jean Voilier. Voilier in French means sailing ship, or sail-maker. Interesting, I thought, especially considering the fact that Denoël had used Marin (sailor) as his nom de plume. She would use her pseudonym quite often in her later life.

It was clear that by the late 1930s Paul Valéry was deeply, possibly foolishly, in love with Jeanne Loviton and that he would have done just about anything for her. He had decided that she was responsible for his renewed vigor and interest in writing. "I have found in you my source of energy. It's a fact," he wrote to her. They happily worked on her novel together; he asked her only for "an insignificant little kiss in recompense for my vigil and corrections." Her novel, entitled *Days of Light* (*Jours de lumière*), recounted her travels in Ireland and the United States. Emile-Paul Frères (Frondaie's publisher) published it in 1938.

Immediately after the novel's publication, Jeanne Loviton and Paul Valéry launched a serious, lengthy campaign to get the book nominated for a literary prize. Valéry's letters to her in 1938 are filled with campaign strategies and schemes. He told her the names of the people he had contacted regarding her book. And although I did not have her responses, it was clear from his letters that she was giving him the names of more possible contacts and other promotional suggestions. For Jeanne Loviton there were always more ways to use her lover's power and prestige—more people to phone or write to or even to see personally on behalf of her book. If she was using her aging poet, it was clear that he was perfectly willing to be used. He did everything he could to promote her book and to get it nominated for a literary prize—and that was quite a lot.

Although the University of Michigan has millions of books, it had not seen fit to order either one of Jeanne Loviton's novels. I laughed. I ordered *Days of Light* on interlibrary loan. After several weeks, it arrived from the New York Public Library. When I opened the book, I laughed again. Apparently the amazing and huge New York Public Library had not deliberately ordered it, either. For on the inside page was a dedication written by Jeanne Loviton (Jean Voilier) herself. It was dedicated to a publisher, a Mr. Shuster. I could not help but wonder: Was it really a Mr. Schuster she was writing to? Surely she had not misspelled his name. And the dedication clearly indicated she hoped he would publish a translation of the novel in the United States. Apparently Mr. Shuster had been unimpressed with the book and had turned it over to the New York Public Library, which in turn had sent it to me. I suspected I might be the only person to have actually read it in the last thirty years. And once again, Robert Denoël would have pronounced it "insipid," which is what made her campaign to win a literary prize so remarkable.

The Valéry/Loviton literary campaign was actually working. Thanks to their tireless energy and use of influence, the book was nominated for the prestigious Fémina Prize. Jeanne's picture appeared in newspapers, along with such other notables as Jean-Paul Sartre and Pierre-Jean Launay (published by Denoël), also nominated for various literary prizes at that time. One newspaper article also claimed that she was once a very famous lawyer. That statement certainly stretched the truth. But the real exaggeration was that her work was in the same league with the other nominees. In reality such statements were a tribute primarily to Paul Valéry's connections. She didn't win. Valéry took special care to comfort his Héra. "There will be other times," he said, gently stroking her cheek. "Someday everyone will recognize your talent as I do. Just wait and see." I left Paul Valéry in 1938, seated with Jeanne on a red velvet love seat in the living room of 11, rue de l'Assomption, softly consoling her.

War and Occupation

> Everyone, when there's a war in the air, learns to live with
> a new element: falsehood.
>
> *Jean Giraudoux*

I entered the data I had on Robert Denoël in the mid-1930s into
my computer. As he always did when I was in my office, my enormous
black cat, Rupert, sat on my desk, watching me, his big green eyes
slowly blinking, then shutting entirely. As he dozed, he stretched full
length over a pile of my research. I ignored the cat, even after he
awoke and methodically began to scoot all of my pens and paper clips
onto the floor. I refused to play his game. I let them fall. Annoyed,
he stood directly in front of the computer screen. That always got
my attention. I stroked the cat, listening to the rumble of his purr,
but still my mind was elsewhere. Can one list World War II as a
contributing factor in a murder? That's pretty absurd, I mused.
World War II directly contributed to millions of deaths. Even sitting
safely in a nice peaceful office, petting a placid cat, I could not escape
the feeling of ominous and frightening horror that was inexorably
drifting toward France in the late 1930s. I wanted to shout warnings
to the French, particularly French leaders, who still steadfastly refused to see and recognize what was coming. As for anti-Semitism in

France, it was generally accepted, growing stronger and more virulent. Yet few people protested against it.

From June 1936 to June 1937 a Jew, Léon Blum, of the Popular Front, headed the French government. His brief rise to power served to intensify anti-Semitic feelings in France and seemed to lend credence to those who charged that all of France was controlled by a small Jewish coterie. In 1936 Blum was attacked by a group of anti-Semitic royalist thugs and nearly beaten to death. Céline's anti-Semitic *Trifles for a Massacre* (*Bagatelles pour un massacre*) came out at the end of 1937. Three months after its publication France passed a law saying that aliens, including eighteen thousand Jews, could either leave France or do only farm work. Two months later a new law specified that all immigrants be refused entrance into France unless they had enough funds to emigrate again overseas. Since nearly all the assets of German Jewish refugees had already been confiscated by the Nazis, Jewish escape from Germany into France became nearly impossible.

Every level of French society became infected with a deeply anti-Semitic bias: the workers, the bourgeoisie, royalists, Communists, rich and poor, intellectuals, members of the extreme Right and Left— all castigated the Jew. On that issue, most factions united. The Jew was generally considered to be the source of France's economic, political, and moral problems. Worse, most believed that the Jew was leading France into yet another hideous war. Even the Catholic Church in the late 1930s was largely anti-Semitic, supporting the anti-Jewish right-wing Action française and continuing to teach Jewish deicide in its catechisms until 1942.

And in Germany it was worse. By the end of 1937 most German Jews had lost their human rights, their businesses, and their citizenship. They were denied access to stores, to food, to towns, to public schools, parks, museums, and libraries. They could not own land. They could not associate with non-Jews. Dachau, Buchenwald, and other concentration camps were already built and operating. Auschwitz, Belsec, and Treblinka would soon follow. Book burnings of

Jewish authors and those perceived to be Jewish sympathizers began
in Germany as early as 1933. Books by Thomas Mann, Albert Ein-
stein, Jack London, Helen Keller, André Gide, Upton Sinclair,
H. G. Wells, Sigmund Freud, Emile Zola, and Marcel Proust, among
others, were enthusiastically burned and banned for being either Jewish or somehow subversive of German ideals. Jews were denied access
to the arts or to professions. By 1937 countless Jews were fleeing
Germany, seeking refuge, and France was not helping them.

On 12 March 1938 Hitler occupied Austria. France made no attempt to stop him. On 12 September Hitler claimed the Sudeten-
land. France's head of state, Daladier, urged the Czechs to yield to
Hitler. About two weeks later England's Neville Chamberlain gave in
to Hitler's wishes at the Munich Conference. Then came 7 November
1938. On that date in Paris a German Jewish refugee (aged seventeen)
shot and killed the third secretary of the German embassy. His intention had been to kill the German ambassador as a protest against
the German treatment of Jews, and in particular, their treatment of
his father, whom the Germans had deported to Poland in a boxcar.
In Germany the result of this act was the Week of the Broken Glass.
It began on 9 November. Although the Nazis claimed it was a "spontaneous demonstration," Hitler's henchman, Paul Joseph Goebbels,
ordered it. He called for the burning of all Jewish synagogues provided that the fires would not endanger German property; the destruction of Jewish businesses and private dwellings without any
interference by the police; the arrest of "as many Jews, especially rich
ones, . . . as can be accommodated in the existing prisons," followed
by their deportation to concentration camps. As famed historian of
this period William L. Shirer reports, "It was a night of horror
throughout Germany. Synagogues, Jewish homes and shops went up
in flames and several Jews, men, women and children, were shot or
otherwise slain while trying to escape burning to death." The horror
continued throughout the week with murders, rapes, and destruction.
Although exact figures of the carnage are still not clear, it is estimated
that about 7,500 Jewish businesses were entirely destroyed. It was
also asserted in a report sent to Göring on 11 November that "119

synagogues were set on fire, and another 76 completely destroyed . . . 20,000 Jews were arrested." Then Jews were forced to clean up and pay (whenever possible) for the mess.

Only a few days later (24 November 1938), also in Paris, Robert Denoël published Céline's second anti-Semitic book, *The School of Cadavers (l'Ecole des cadavres)*. This work was an even more frenzied attack on France's degeneration and on its chief cause, the Jew. According to Céline's biographer, Frédéric Vitoux, Céline's book "descends into a vortex of madness. Words pile upon words, sucked into a revelry, an alliterative delirium, an abusive music, shimmering insults, a euphonic ebb and flow of his fears." Vitoux continues by saying that Céline's book was a descent into "hatred or unequivocal dementia." Once again there were no attempts at logic and no actual facts to support his claims. Céline in this work called for the total extermination of Jews ("stock pens for Jewish killings") and the creation of an Aryan state with a Franco-German army. And he decried those journalists who claimed that another war would not come as "Pencil-necked shitslingers!"

At the same time that Hitler was invading Prague, Céline was advocating the creation of a Franco-German Union that would ultimately lead to a Confederation of Aryan States of Europe. Because of his desire to unify France with Hitler's Germany, the work was not as successful as his *Trifles for a Massacre*. But it made money. And there is no doubt that Robert Denoël badly needed that money to keep his publishing house in business.

It would be easy to condemn Robert Denoël as the worst of anti-Semites. But to do so would be to overlook a major tenet of French publishing at that time. Robert Denoël, Gaston Gallimard, and other French publishers believed that it was not their job to judge the moral probity of their publications. The very same publishers often published works of disparate political views. It was not uncommon for a Jew and an anti-Semite or a Communist and Fascist to use the same publisher.

In fact, publishing writers with varied and conflicting views was considered to be the hallmark of good publishing. Gaston Gallimard had long subscribed to this tenet. He often stated, "I am a publisher. I publish everything: Léon Blum [left-wing Jewish leader of France] as well as Léon Daudet [right-wing anti-Semite], Léon Daudet as well as Léon Blum." And in fact, he did. By the early 1930s he was publishing Fascist and anti-Fascist literature, pro-Jewish and anti-Semitic literature, works by Communists and anti-Communists. Always an excellent player of the double game, Gaston Gallimard was proud of the diversity of his publications.

Robert Denoël, too, enjoyed the double game. Along with Céline's anti-Semitic works, he published several prominent Jewish writers. Steele and Artaud had translated *The Case of Mr. Crump (Crime passionnel)*, by Ludwig Lewisohn, which contained several pro-Jewish themes. Denoël published Freud and other distinguished Jews in his Psychological Library series. In 1936 he published Pierre Goemare's *When Israel Returns to Its Homeland (Quand Israël rentre chez soi)*, which correctly predicted the future creation of a Jewish state. Ironically, the Russian Jew Elsa Triolet translated Céline's *Journey to the End of the Night* into Russian for Robert Denoël. And in 1936, when Céline denounced all things Russian and Communist in his work *Mea Culpa*, the Communist Louis Aragon won the prestigious Renaudot Prize for his novel *The Fashionable District (Les Beaux quartiers)*, also published by Denoël and Steele.

But just how far can this double game go? Should a publisher's freedom extend to publishing books promoting murder? No matter how much humor existed within the pages of *Trifles for a Massacre*, no matter how many utterly ludicrous statements it contained, Céline in this book also advocated the mass murder of Jews. "Then you want to kill all the Jews?" Céline not only answers yes to that question in this book, he adds, "If you want some veal in the adventure, let's bleed the Jews." And in *The School of Cadavers* he reaffirms his belief in the necessity of Jewish extermination. Was there nothing a publisher should censor?

It was generally assumed that there was no difference between the philosophy of Céline and that of his publisher; Denoël's *Justification for "Death on the Installment Plan"* had seen to that. Céline's writings then served to ostracize his publisher from certain more moderate circles. Even some of Robert's friends were aghast. Following the publication of *The School of Cadavers*, Irène Champigny, largely responsible for helping Robert to get established when he first came to Paris, announced that she had had quite enough of Robert Denoël and "his German Céline."

Robert never succeeded in becoming truly Parisian. He never managed to lose his Belgian ways, still speaking in a heavy Belgian French. He often preferred the company of other Belgians like himself. No matter how well his publishing house did, Robert Denoël himself remained an outsider. He rarely socialized with other French publishers. The one publisher he did befriend was an outsider like himself, Sven Nielson. Parisians tended to look down upon foreigners and provincials. They were somehow just not up to snuff. Robert feared that no matter what his accomplishments might be, he would always remain somehow not quite good enough for Paris, in spite of his phenomenal success.

Then came 1939. Had not the wily Gaston Gallimard used all of his powers of persuasion and a very attractive contract to lure another principal writer, Philippe Hériat, away from the Denoël stable, Robert would have won all of the most significant literary prizes for that year. Although Hériat had already published four books with Denoël, he could not resist Gallimard's generous offer. And so in 1939 he published *Spoiled Children (Les Enfants gâtés)* with the older publisher. To Gallimard's great pleasure, Hériat won the Goncourt for that year— the one prize that continued to elude Denoël.

In spite of all signs to the contrary, France still refused to prepare for what was to come. By 1939 there could be little doubt of the expansionist intentions of the Rome-Berlin-Tokyo Axis. Hitler and Mussolini backed the Spanish nationalists, causing the fall of Madrid and ultimately leading to the replacement of the Spanish Republic by the Fascist Franco. Now Spain, Italy, and Germany, all bordering France, were Fascist. Yet France, that most reluctant of warriors, still refused to become overly alarmed or to prepare adequately to defend itself.

In fact, it wasn't even clear exactly which side France wanted to take. Hoping to end France's "degenerate ways" and return to simpler times, many French people found Fascism attractive. They believed that Fascism would "purify the nation" and restore French morality and prosperity. Besides, France had no great love for Great Britain. In the 1930s the English often resorted to diplomatic jousting between Germany and France, playing one off against the other. The idea of becoming Great Britain's ally was almost as distasteful to the French as the notion of going to war in the first place. There was simply no consensus in France, a nation divided on every point except one: almost no one wanted to go to war. "Peace at any price" was not just a British slogan.

Amid British and French hesitation and concessions, the balance of power shifted to the Fascists. In 1939 the combined forces of France and Great Britain did not come close to the enormous might of the Luftwaffe, the German air force. Hitler and Mussolini recognized the weakness and reluctance of both nations, and very soon they once again took advantage. By March 1939 Hitler had occupied all of Czechoslovakia, and Mussolini seized Albania the following month. Then on 22 May of that same year Hitler and Mussolini signed their mutual assistance treaty, the Pact of Steel.

Yet France persisted in ignoring the situation and hoping for peace. The scene became almost surreal. While all around them soldiers invaded, killed, and seized, the French concentrated on the triumph of one of Jeanne Loviton's lovers, Jean Giraudoux, with his new play, *Ondine*. Theater attendance in general was quite high. The French sought entertainment, went to museums, bought books and works of art. They abstractly discussed Marcel Déat's new article "Must We Die for Danzig?" Déat's answer, of course, was "No!" France was determined not to engage in yet another war. Like a half-blind horse with heavy blinkers, France refused to look.

Always chiefly concerned with his business, Robert Denoël was not looking too closely at the political scene, either. He did take one wise step. He withdrew both of Céline's anti-Semitic, often pro-German, and blatantly pacifist books from distribution. They were too inflammatory for the times. What Céline had written as part of his delirium was coming true. Then Robert made a risky choice. He decided to establish a deeply patriotic series entitled *Our Combat (Notre Combat)*. He founded this series in 1939, using able writers to serve as contributors. It quickly became popular. Denoël did not foresee what might happen to a publisher of such a patriotic work if the country should fall to the Nazis. As for Céline, he had begun in 1938 to deposit his gold into foreign banks—his hedge against the future. Although he claimed his one wish was not to flee France, he began to prepare for such a possibility. Robert Denoël took no such precautions.

That philosophy about a publisher's right to publish anything without censorship returned to trouble this publisher. In *The School of Cadavers* Céline had called a certain Dr. Roquès a Jew. But then Céline had a habit of calling everyone he disliked a Jew, including many dead writers and monarchs. However, Dr. Roquès was very much alive. And he wasn't a Jew, and he took offense. One day while sitting in his monastic office reading yet another manuscript, Denoël received a legal document stating that he and his author, Céline, were being sued.

"This can't be right," Denoël told his lawyer. "I can't be held accountable for every crackpot thing that Céline says." His lawyer agreed.

Unfortunately, the courts did not. Dr. Roquès won his case. On 21 June both author and publisher were convicted of "defamation, public injury, and complicity" by the Twelfth Chamber of the Court of Summary Jurisdiction. Dr. Roquès was awarded two thousand francs in damages with each man paying an additional two-hundred-franc fine. Worse for Denoël, he had to remove Céline's false charge from the book and pay two hundred francs per day for any delay of the suppression of the remark. With this ruling, the courts clearly ignored former publishing philosophies, now making publishers accountable for the statements of their authors. This court decision carried ominous warnings to all French publishers.

On 23 August 1939 Hitler signed a nonaggression pact with

Stalin. In effect, this agreement permitted Hitler to invade Poland without fear of reprisal from Russia. On 1 September Hitler's armies marched into Poland, its Luftwaffe bombing Polish cities. Desperate, Chamberlain issued Hitler an ultimatum. But Hitler was in no mood for ultimatums. Finally, faced with no alternative, Great Britain and France, along with Australia and New Zealand, declared war two days later.

Then came a period of lull. There were skirmishes, battles, but nothing spectacular. Hitler was preparing. And even after France's declaration of war, there was no coming together of its people, and no commanding French leader to urge the nation to unite. De Gaulle was not the inspiration then that he later became for France. As Céline remarked, no one ever saw "Charlot [Céline's nickname for De Gaulle] in the trenches with a bazooka, fighting off the Kraut tanks!" The Communists in France did not want to fight, and neither did the members of the extreme Right. In fact, being generally pro-Fascist, the extreme Right often cheered France's losses. Even in war France remained a nation divided. Only about two decades earlier the French had gone to war united in courage and determination. And they had won that war, that so-called Great War, at the price of being slaughtered, their industries left in shambles. They had no desire to repeat the past. Robert Denoël, still a Belgian citizen, remained at the helm of his business during this time, nervously watching as events beyond his control unfolded. His own country had not yet mobilized.

Everything changed on 10 May 1940. Hitler had wisely bided his time. During that period of lull he recalled his armored tank units (German panzers) from Poland and regrouped them. Then he gathered his troops—105 divisions in all. After everything was ready, Hitler launched one of the most impressive German offensives ever known. Belgium was only one of Hitler's targets. On 11 May, as Hitler invaded Belgium, Denoël turned his business over to the faithful and competent Auguste Picq, his head accountant, who had been with him almost from the beginning. I remembered that it was Picq who had diplomatically answered so many of Céline's nasty letters over monetary disputes. Denoël returned immediately to Belgium to serve in its armed forces. Apparently because of his brief experience as a medical student, he was assigned to the Second Medical Corps in Gand, Belgium. But the German forces were just too powerful. Almost immediately, his unit was forced to retreat, apparently spending some time in Narbonne.

The German advances came from France's north and east, with German panzers leading the way and the Luftwaffe strafing and bombing from above. France's air force was no match for them. The enormous German infantry followed the panzers. France's defense soon proved to be in as much disarray as its resolve. By 8 June the Germans reached the Seine. A rout ensued. Céline was part of that retreat, along with his future wife, two orphaned infants (one of whom Céline found on the side of the road), and an old woman who clung throughout everything to her bottles of wine. Céline later stated, "I did the retreat myself, like many another, I chased the French army all the way from Bezons to La Rochelle, but I could never catch up."

With the French army in the lead, with soldiers throwing their weapons away and running or riding, with no one in command, with civilians on bicycles, motorbikes, in cars, trucks, walking, running, with carts, carrying children, clutching valuables, everyone madly headed in one direction—south—urged on by repeated strafing from German aircraft. Many vehicles were stranded on the roads, out of gas. Gas, there was no gas. The black market controlled the gas. People drove until they ran out of gas, then abandoned their vehicles, got out and ran. They slept in barns, in ditches, in fields, and then they got up and ran again. Céline stated, "I saw forty-ton tanks shove our orphans aside, force us into the beanfields in their dash for cover, a juggernaut free-for-all, a thundering panic of scrap iron. Charge of the lightweight brigade!" He concluded, "You can't make this sort of thing up. This is no ugly treachery. There were 15 million of us who saw it."

Officially, Paris fell on 14 June 1940. The City of Light was dark, and for the most part deserted. Would Hitler destroy that beautiful gem? Would he set it all on fire as he had so recently done to the property of his own Jewish population? Hitler understood the divisions and ambivalence existing among the French people. He knew that to set their famous city ablaze might serve to unify the French against him. He had a better plan. A docile and cooperative French populace would best suit his interests. They would be much easier to control while he attended to other matters—other campaigns, other nations. No, Hitler would control France rather than destroy it. First, he divided France into two parts. German troops occupied Paris and the northern two-thirds of France. A puppet French government located in Vichy, a sleepy little town more famous then for its spas and mineral waters than for its politics, was established and legitimized in the south. Now Hitler needed a prominent, distinguished French leader to serve as his puppet. Who better than a decorated World War I hero?

The Germans found their man in the person of Marshal Philippe Pétain, a brilliant and able retired French general of the Great War. Pétain was eighty-four years old when he assumed the office of chief of state at Vichy in 1940. Nearly all of the people of France loved and revered him. Apparently, he sincerely believed that by collaborating with the Germans he could actually help the French, restore order, repair the damage done by the invasion, facilitate the release of French prisoners of war, and temper German harshness. He believed, as did many others, that he could play the double game, i.e., pleasing the Germans while at the same time really serving the interests of France. Although he may have begun his job as leader of France under the Occupation with the best of intentions, he became a German pawn in this national drama. Some, in fact, noticed that the aged Pétain sometimes fell asleep at inappropriate moments. Others saw him stare with a blank face at his papers, apparently paralyzed by them. These actions on the part of Pétain led some to whisper that his mind was "senile," or at the very least, "closed due to old age."

Robert Denoël's native land, Belgium, sued for armistice on 24

May 1940, even before the fall of France, and would remain under German occupation until the end of the war. It took some time for Robert to be discharged and to return to Paris. Although exact dates of his return vary, he was clearly in Paris by August. His wife and Picq had already informed him that the Germans had shut down his business. There was a huge padlock on the door, along with a sign forbidding entrance. Robert also knew before his return that the Germans were looking for him, a fact that may have helped to cloud his exact date of return. It seems that there were some questions the Germans wanted answered—questions about some of his publications, particularly about that new patriotic series, *Our Combat*. So one of the foremost publishers in Paris returned secretly to his place of business, quickly walking down the rue Amélie and glancing only briefly at his publishing house as he passed by. He didn't return to his home. He was wanted. He stayed with friends, changing his residence often.

First, through his friends, he managed to arrange a secret meeting with Auguste Picq. Picq appeared one day at the back door of the house where Robert was staying. After greeting each other as old friends, they sat at the kitchen table while Picq set about the difficult task of bringing Robert up to date. "Robert, they took some stock," he said.

"They took our stock? Why? How much?"

"Quite a lot, I'm afraid. And they want to arrest you, you know."

"Why?"

"Well, as they put it, for the publication of *Our Combat* and certain other works they have deemed unsuitable to the German cause."

"What other books?" Robert asked.

"I believe the number of what they call anti-German books that you have published totals forty-one."

Stunned, Robert shook his head, sat silent for a moment, then asked, "Just how much stock did they take?"

Picq took out his notes, glanced at them, then silently handed them to Robert. After studying them a moment, he looked at Picq. "They took one-third of my company!" he said. "Just like that, they have stolen about one-third of my business—more than 1,700,000 francs!" He put the papers down, incredulous. "And now they want to arrest me. Have they arrested other publishers?"

"The publishing house Sorlot is shut down, I'm not sure why. Grasset is still open. But then I understand that Bernard Grasset has some pro-German sentiment. Gaston Gallimard left Paris as soon as the war started. I heard he and his entourage went to Normandy, then Carcassonne. There are rumors that he's back now. I'm not sure exactly what's going on with Gallimard's publishing business right now. I also understand that that small Jewish-owned publishing company, Ferenczi, has been totally taken over. I'm not sure about the others."

"So what do I do now?" Robert asked his accountant. "And how do I get my money back? Right now I can't even see my wife and son or show my face on a Paris street. And how do I keep the rest of my company safe from these thieves?"

Picq thought a moment, then said, "You won't ever get the money back, Robert. The Germans told me they took the money as punishment—fines for your anti-German books. But as for the rest of the assets, what they don't find they can't take. Also, there is a man, a German, who might be able to help you get back into publishing legally. I have already made a few inquiries. In the meantime, you need to find a safe place for your remaining assets."

"I'll do that," said Robert. The two men shook hands, and Picq quietly left his employer.

Robert then decided to break into his own publishing house on the rue Amélie. And he knew exactly how he would gain entrance— the secret passageway. There really was a secret passageway, not used for over twenty years. Part of the hosiery shop that existed before Robert and Bernard Steele transformed it into their publishing house had extended into another building, which was now a telephone apparatus business. The passageway was still there, now boarded up and used mostly for storage. Robert was a friend of the owner, Robert Beauzemont. And one fine late August morning in 1940 Robert Denoël slipped unnoticed into Beauzemont's store.

Beauzemont stared in surprise at the publisher. "You haven't seen me," Denoël told him.

"I haven't seen you." Beauzemont smiled.

"Mind if I reopen that passageway?"

"I haven't seen you," continued Beauzemont, "and I know nothing about a passageway."

"I will keep everything in place; I'll just loosen the nails on the door. No one will notice."

"Notice what?" Beauzemont said. "I see nothing, I hear nothing, I know nothing. It's the only way to run a business these days. I'm glad you're okay and that you're back."

"I'm not back, you haven't seen me, remember?" Denoël winked. The two old friends said no more. Robert entered his publishing house, making sure the secret passageway looked the same as before. He took his accounts, retrieved the rest of his assets, which he had carefully hidden before his departure to Belgium, and, after waiting until a customer left, returned to the telephone store. Then, lowering his hat, he exited without a word, just another businessman looking for a new phone.

Although the Germans knew about Les Editions Denoël, they didn't realize that Robert also owned that smaller publishing company devoted to the publication of light reading, Les Editions de la Bourdonnais. Having no interest in romance and popular novels, since they posed no threat to German goals, the Nazis left that publishing house alone. After carefully hiding the rest of his assets, Robert returned to his smaller publishing house. He carefully set up a secret office, with curtains over the windows, and another door allowing a quick exit if needed. There he ran his entire business, maintaining contact with his regular authors, planning new strategies, and attempting to extricate himself from his difficulties with the Germans.

As for Robert Beauzemont, he had a new customer, one who frequently entered his telephone apparatus store when no one else was there, who sometimes carefully examined Beauzemont's merchandise, then vanished. During these visits neither man spoke to the other as a friend. Robert Denoël became a shadow. His residence, his whereabouts, his business activities, his wealth—all were unknown. He was wanted by the Nazis, a hunted man. His crime? Publishing Jewish authors and patriotic French books.

Meanwhile Auguste Picq, a middle-aged businessman, an accountant, also entered the world of secret dealings himself. He had to. He wanted to help his boss solve his problems with the Nazis so that both could get on with the business of publishing. He made very discreet inquiries of those he trusted. Again and again, one name, the name of a German who was supposedly sympathetic to France, surfaced as someone who might be able to help Denoël. That name was Otto Abetz. After several delicate discussions with Picq, Abetz agreed to meet with Denoël. He also promised not to arrest him—at least not at the meeting.

"So I now have the word of a Nazi that he won't arrest me, cart me off to prison or a concentration camp, or have me shot. Should I trust him, this Nazi?" Denoël asked Picq.

Picq shrugged. "I am told that he is very clever. I am told he has a French wife. I am told he admires books, French books. I know he is a connoisseur of art. As for trusting him, what other choice do you have?"

The meeting was arranged at a neutral place, in the back of a small café that Robert knew about. Abetz had promised to come alone. On the way to his meeting, Robert passed a large poster. He looked at it and frowned. It was a huge picture of a handsome German soldier, blond, kind, smiling. He was feeding three hungry French children. The caption read, "You who have been abandoned—have confidence in the German soldier!" For about half an hour Robert sat alone, nursing a glass of red wine, tense, nervous, waiting. Then Abetz appeared, alone as promised. Robert rose from the table, they shook hands, then sat down again. The waiter quickly appeared, and Abetz ordered wine. Denoël noticed that Abetz spoke impeccable French. In many ways he resembled that German on the poster, except that he was thinner, more angular, and somewhat older. In his speech and mannerisms he seemed almost more French

Publisher Robert Denoël in the early 1930s. © ROGER-VIOLLET

Sketch of Jeanne Loviton (Jean Voilier). All photos of this woman located by the author were ultimately owned by her estate and not permitted for use in this book. © 2001 SONYA DELANEY, MIDDLE GEORGIA ARTS ASSOCIATION

Louis-Ferdinand Céline in front of his home at Meudon, France, around 1955. © ROGER-VIOLLET

Publisher Gaston Gallimard. © ROGER-VIOLLET

Pierre Frondaie, standing with script and pointer in hand, at a rehearsal of his *Blanche Câline* at Théâtre Michel in 1913. © LA PETITE ILLUSTRATION

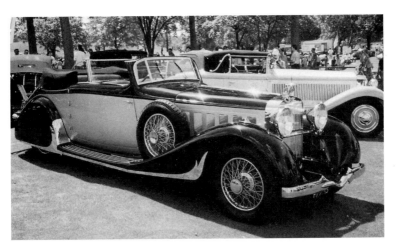

A slightly later model Hispano-Suiza (foreground), but looking almost exactly the same as the car Frondaie made famous in his 1925 novel, *L'Homme à l'Hispano*. Frondaie described this automobile as "a grand blue-blooded automobile, the beast of pure luxury, able to rip through the countryside." PHOTO BY BILL VANCE; USED WITH PERMISSION OF ERAMOSA VALLEY PUBLISHING

The first author
Robert Denoël pub‑
lished, artist and
writer Jean de
Bosschère. PHOTO
USED WITH PERMISSION
OF ALAIN BILOT

Sketch of Robert Denoël
by Jean de Bosschère, as
found in *Portraits d'Amis*.
The artist describes
Denoël as "one of the
rare publishers whose tal‑
ent equals that of the
authors that he accepts."
PHOTO USED WITH PER‑
MISSION OF ALAIN BILOT

Paul Valéry, Official Poet of France. © ROGER-VIOLLET

Antonin Artaud in
Les Cenci, 1935.
© ROGER-VIOLLET

Two of Denoël's important authors, Elsa Triolet and Louis Aragon (carrying topcoat). © ROGER-VIOLLET

Publisher Bernard Grasset, seated between his two lawyers. Tried and found guilty of collaboration, he awaits his sentence. © AFP PHOTO

than German. To Robert's surprise, he praised several books that Les Editions Denoël had published. After the waiter brought the wine, they ended their small talk, and Abetz began. He leaned forward across the table, smiled at Denoël, and quietly said, "I understand that you are in some difficulty now with certain German officials. You have published some books that are not in the German interest."

"I am prepared," said Robert, "to do whatever is necessary to cooperate with German interests in the future."

"Good, good," replied Abetz. "We, like you, are interested in the publication of good literature—great literature. It seems prudent to both French and German interests to publish great German works in French and great French works in German. That way we shall educate and enlighten both of our populaces." Denoël agreed. "We need publishers like you," Abetz continued, "as long as you will cooperate."

"You can count on me, Monsieur," Robert responded.

"Then in that case, I shall see what I can do for you," Abetz said. "You will soon learn that all French publishers are cooperating. It is in the best interest of everyone concerned, and especially in the interest of the great literature of both our countries that they do." Then Abetz rose and left.

Robert later told Picq, "I didn't even mention the 1,700,000 francs those robbers already stole from me. Maybe I should have."

"You should not have," Picq retorted. "You can't afford to offend the only man I could find who might be able to help you."

"They want my total cooperation."

"Have you listened to the radio lately, Robert? Cooperate is just a fancy word for obey. You have no other choice."

"The double game."

"What?" Picq asked.

"My other choice is the double game. In a way, we are all playing the double game. Oh, I will cooperate with them. And then again I won't. Just as they will rob me on the one hand and 'see what they can do' about my case on the other. It's all just a double game. I will tell them what they want to hear."

"Be careful, Robert," his employee told him.

"I intend to be very careful," Robert responded.

While Robert was still waiting for the Germans either to arrest him or allow him to return to his business, other French publishers learned what was in store for them. The Germans decided not to dictate their wishes, but rather to use a carrot-and-stick approach that would force French publishers to police themselves. In September 1940 these publishers learned that they would become their own censors. It would be up to French publishers themselves to decide what should and should not be published—according to German guidelines, of course. These publishers were to omit from publication anything that might show Germany in a bad light, any work or author already censored within Germany, any foreign author who might not be sympathetic to German interests, and all Jewish authors. If a publisher was undecided about a work, he could opt to have it read and judged by a German censor. And as a special incentive, those publishers who were the most cooperative would be rewarded. Their reward would be that increasingly hard-to-obtain commodity, paper. On the other hand, those who failed to comply completely with German expectations faced severe reprisals.

There was no meaningful protest against this censorship by any French publisher. Almost without exception or discussion, they readily agreed to the German proposal. The Association of French Publishers quickly signed the censorship agreement. By so doing, each publisher technically collaborated with the enemy. But in 1940 collaboration in France was considered by most to be good, necessary, positive. Pétain was telling his countrymen that to collaborate with the Germans would ensure a brighter future for all of France. As he said on the radio to the French people on 24 October 1940, "It is *in honor* and to maintain French unity—a unity of ten centuries—in the setting of a constructive activity for a new European order that I enter today upon the path of collaboration." These words, coming from one of the most respected men in France, were a stroke of Nazi genius. Most people agreed with the Catholic cardinal who exclaimed, "Pétain is France and France is Pétain."

Books that French publishers deemed unworthy of publication were placed on the Otto List, probably named for the German ambassador in Paris, the same man who had met privately with Robert Denoël, Otto Abetz. On 15 October 1940, on Abetz's recommendation, the Germans permitted Robert to reopen his business—in return for his cooperation. "And what happens if the Nazis lose the war?"

"What?" Picq said.

"The Nazis make me publish their works, then leave me with a bag of Fascist Nazi books in my catalogue. What then?"

Picq thought a moment. "Do they have to go into your catalogue?"

On 16 December 1939 Denoël had purchased the stock and assets of a small publishing company called Lively Publicity (La Publicité vivante). Although he had intended simply to absorb this company into Les Editions Denoël, historical events caused him to rethink his initial decision. No, he decided to keep that company separate. In November 1940 he changed the name of this company to New French Editions (Les Nouvelles Editions Françaises). The problem was he didn't really have a separate building for the company. He had simply bought out its stock. Robert solved that problem by listing this new company's address as 21, rue Amélie, the address of that same telephone apparatus store next door to his publishing house. He claimed the assets of this company to be twenty-five thousand francs. This publishing house, which even his friends described as "very theoretical," allowed him to create a separate catalogue for the pro-German works that the Nazis expected him to publish. He also placed Céline's anti-Semitic works in this catalogue. And for good measure, Denoël listed there some children's books he had published.

With the creation of this publishing house whose initials (NEF) are quite similar to Gaston Gallimard's NRF, one finds a strange mixture of Jeannot the rabbit and Martin the big bear (both creations of Thornton Burgess), interspersed with the ardently anti-Semitic literature of Céline and other pro-Nazi and anti-Semitic works. Denoël published *How to Recognize a Jew? (Comment reconnaître le Juif?)* by

Professor Montadon; *Medicine and the Jews (La Médecine et les Juifs)* by Dr. Querrioux; *The Press and the Jews (La Presse et les Juifs)* by L. Pemjean; and *The Tribes of the Cinema and the Theater (Les Tribus du cinéma et du théâtre)* by Lucien Rebatet. He also threw in Hitler's *Speeches (Discours)* and works by other Nazi writers.

By using this ploy, Denoël was able to keep his catalogue for Les Editions Denoël relatively free of anti-Semitic, Nazi, and other German-inspired works. He kept his very capable stable of writers intact. In fact, by December 1940 Denoël was complaining because there would be no Goncourt Prize for that year. He believed that he had a contender for this prize with Jean Rogissart's *The Iron and the Forest (Le Fer et la forêt)*.

By controlling the radio, the press, journals, and the books that the French read, and by using the French themselves in all of these communications, the Germans cleverly made it appear that France itself approved of German collaboration, that the right outcome had already happened to France, that Franco-German collaboration was a permanent solution, and that France would ultimately be better off as a result. Considering the ideological confusion and conflicting ideas in France before the war, it was a relief to many to have France, under the guidance of the Nazis, finally pointing in one direction. Everywhere, the Nazis told the French that this collaboration would result in a new, stronger, and better France, united with Germany and ready for a new order. Those Nazis were clever.

Although Gaston Gallimard fared much better than Robert Denoël in 1940, he was also facing some difficult problems. Upon his return to his publishing duties following the fall of Paris, Gallimard found that one of his authors, the charming, elegant, talented, Fascist anti-Semite Pierre Drieu La Rochelle had now taken on a new importance. Drieu La Rochelle had become great friends with none other than Otto Abetz. And for both men that wonderful word in 1940, collaboration, was beginning to find another avenue of expression.

Abetz was serious when he suggested to Robert Denoël that great works of literature by French and German authors should be readily available in both French and German for the consumption of both countries. Abetz admired both cultures.

Then Abetz decided that Drieu should head a literary journal dedicated to French and German artistic and intellectual collaboration. After some discussion, Abetz and Drieu decided that the easiest way to accomplish this goal was to use the already famous and long-running *New French Review (N.R.F.)* of Gaston Gallimard. All they had to do was to convince Gallimard of the necessity of such a publication and to replace the former editor of the *N.R.F.* (Artaud's friend, Jean Paulhan) with Drieu. As it turned out, Gallimard was not hard to convince. He realized that having German patronage for the *N.R.F.* could also greatly benefit and protect his publishing business. Paulhan pleaded with Gallimard to change the name of the distinguished *N.R.F.*, since it was now clearly under German control. But Gallimard refused to do so. With Drieu La Rochelle as editor of the *N.R.F.*, this journal, an important element of Gallimard's publishing empire, now had Fascist, pro-German, Nazi, and anti-Semitic goals.

It was not long before the influence and patronage that Drieu enjoyed not only with Abetz, but also with the equally cultured aide at the German Propaganda Department, Gerhard Heller, proved quite helpful to Gallimard. Even before the first edition of Drieu's *N.R.F.* came out in early December 1940, the Germans threatened to close Gallimard's publishing house unless he gave 51 percent of its control to a German publisher. But Gallimard was able to point out to the Nazis that he already had a pro-Fascist, pro-Nazi anti-Semite (Drieu La Rochelle) at the helm of his *N.R.F.*, as well as Otto Abetz's guidance. Apparently, Drieu and Abetz were enough; no shutdown or takeover of Les Editions Gallimard ever occurred.

Céline, too, returned to Paris in the fall of 1940 after some hair-raising experiences that were bizarre enough to have come out of his own more delirious writings. In 1939 he worked as a doctor aboard the *Chella,* a ship serving as a troop transport. One night this ship rammed a British torpedo gunboat, loaded with explosives, that was sailing without lights. The British gunboat exploded almost immediately, killing some twenty crew members. As Céline's biographer Frédéric Vitoux notes, "Picture a military ship sunk by a civilian ship, and the English going down just a few furlongs from Gibraltar, sunk by their allies the French."

After the ship disaster, Céline worked as a doctor in a refugee camp near La Rochelle. Then in October 1940 he came back to Paris, humiliated and shocked, in spite of his dire predictions, by what had happened to France. He viewed with some consternation the new "elite" of Paris, composed primarily of French collaborators and German officers. Yet to his surprise he was greeted as a wise prophet, one who had foreseen and predicted the war and its consequences. Drieu La Rochelle praised him, as did that other notable French Fascist writer, Lucien Rebatet. Even better for Céline, the now pro-German press sought to print his slightest comments, asked him to expound upon his positions, and provided him space to print whatever he wished. Céline, delighted, did not disappoint them.

And so by the late fall of 1940 Gallimard and Denoël were again in command of their publishing houses. Things were returning to some semblance of normal, except, of course, that a different nation was now in control. As Christmas approached, a new rhyme passed from mouth to mouth, whispered quietly on Paris streets:

> The Virgin Mary has been evacuated.
> Saint Joseph is in a concentration camp.
> The Three Kings are in London.
> The ox is in Berlin.
> The ass is in Rome.
> So there will be no Christmas this year.

But although Les Editions Denoël remained open, its publisher still faced serious problems.

"If you add up all of my debts right now, how much do I owe my creditors?" Robert asked Picq.

For two days Picq carefully examined all of Robert's financial records. Then sadly Picq told his boss, "Robert, you are presently 800,000 francs in debt." The sum was staggering. It was clear that if Robert did not find some money—and soon—he would lose his business.

9

Early Occupation Years

Collaboration is: You give me your watch, and I will tell
you what time it is.

Jean Galtier-Boissière

Winter in Paris in 1941. It's beautiful with snow slowly falling. So
much of Paris looks just the same as it did before the Occupation;
massive gray buildings, narrow winding streets, open shops. Let's take
a walk in this wonderland. Let's visit the lovely sixteenth district, and
stroll down the stately street called Villa Saïd. All of it seems just the
same—untouched. But don't look too closely. And whatever you do,
ignore those men. See them taking a smoke on the front steps of
that beautiful mansion over there? And don't listen too carefully.
Mostly the thick walls of that mansion stifle the sounds. But sometimes the neighbors awaken in the middle of the night to such hideous screams. Let's walk quickly by, I will tell you about it later. . . .

Those men at the mansion of Villa Saïd are members of the
Gestapo. They use that mansion to torture anyone suspected of re-
sisting. It's all perfectly legal, of course. I heard rumors that the
mansion once belonged to a delightful cultured Jewish family. No
one knows where they are now. Céline calls the mansion "the Dental
Institute," because . . . well, you know. Everyone knows. But isn't
Paris beautiful!

. . .

I tried to imagine what it must be like to attempt to run a business when all the rules had changed. I tried to imagine Robert Denoël being polite in his dealings with the very same people who had stolen 1,700,000 francs from him. Other streets, too, had houses or places that struck terror into the Frenchman's heart: rue Lauriston, place des Etats-Unis, avenue Foch, and rue des Saussaies. The only indication from the outside of the constant torture, extortion, and often murder that went on within these dwellings were the steel screens placed in front of each window. Then, of course, there was the rue Le Sueur, home of the famous Dr. Petiot's furnace. Dr. Petiot supposedly provided escape from occupied France for Jews and others sought by the Gestapo. For those able to pay his steep price, Dr. Petiot promised to provide them a safe way to get to South America. His rich clients came to his door with payment, as well as with suitcases filled with their valuables (gold, jewels, art). Once they crossed Dr. Petiot's threshold, they (and all of their luggage) were never seen again. Dr. Petiot invited them in, asphyxiated them, cut them up, and burned them in his furnace.

I remembered that unlike most other Parisians, Robert had grown up under German occupation . . . when the Germans seized Liège in World War I. He had witnessed the cruelty and watched his father's struggle to keep his enormous family together during those awful years. And now he had a wife and young son in the same predicament. As soon as the Germans no longer sought his arrest, Robert returned to his family. He would remain with his wife and son throughout the Occupation.

The French were cooperating with the Nazis at every turn in 1941. Sometimes they even outdid the Germans. For example, without any Nazi pressure, the new Vichy government passed a law excluding all Jews from any significant positions within the courts, the government, the army, public life, and the arts (primarily movies and theater). In addition, any Jewish immigrant could be incarcerated for the crime of being a Jewish immigrant. And why not put French government leaders who served before the fall of France on trial? Vichy France energetically set about this task, too, with the establishment of its Riom Court.

Now that Denoël had hidden the remainder of his stock, reopened his publishing house, and devised a way to separate the pro-German and anti-Semitic works the Nazis expected him to publish, by channeling them through a second phony publishing house, his central problem was money. Desperate to acquire operating capital, Robert sought funds everywhere, and from just about anyone, with the exception of other French publishers. He could not countenance the possibility of another French publisher gaining control over his establishment. He first applied for a loan of one million francs from the French Crédit National for the funding of four patriotic collections. This request became so steeped in bureaucracy that Denoël was already seeking other options before the loan was refused in August 1941.

He had more luck with a German publisher who was looking for a French contact for the publication of art books. On 22 July 1941 Denoël and the German publisher Wilhelm Andermann signed a contract. Denoël ceded to Andermann 360 shares of Les Editions Denoël (which was five shares less than his own stock) at 500 francs per share. In addition to the purchase of stock, Andermann also provided Denoël with a loan of two million francs. With that money Robert paid off his 800,000 francs in debts and used the rest to get his business running again.

Then Robert Denoël published. In the face of German victories and control, he reissued Céline's *Trifles for a Massacre* and *The School of Cadavers*. Hitler was winning the war, and Céline was popular, considered an insightful writer and an enlightened prophet. In February 1941 Céline contributed another depressing and critical work to Les Editions Denoël: *A Fine Mess (Les Beaux Draps)*. Although this work, too, was deeply anti-Semitic, its main focus was not the Jew. Instead, Céline took special aim at French institutions, especially education, and at the Catholic Church, all of which, according to Céline, were in a deplorable state. Robert also published significant literature in

1941, including Albert Paraz's *The Completely Naked King (Le Roi tout nu)* and Paul Vialar's *The House Under the Sea (La Maison sous la mer)*. Always expanding, always working near the edge, Robert envisioned the establishment of a musical library, sought to improve children's literature, and continued to make important contributions in the fields of psychology, theater, politics, and art. Like those who pretended not to hear the screams coming from the Villa Saïd mansion, he tried to ignore the war. He was, after all, a businessman, a publisher.

I decided to pay another visit to Jeanne Loviton's home, looking for Paul Valéry and for her. I found her in her library, seated at that beautiful desk she had purchased when she was the wife of Pierre Frondaie. She was writing. But Valéry was not with her. I checked several literary and artistic salons. He was not there, either. Looking at records of his itinerary, I saw that he was in Paris—somewhere. Checking his diaries, I looked for him at his own residence. No, he wasn't at home. Although his health was poor (he had a severe case of bronchitis), he wasn't in a hospital, either. Where was he? I sought out his friends. No one had seen him for weeks. I looked into the restaurants and cafés he frequented, the galleries, clubs, salons, shops, the florist where he often bought flowers for Jeanne. I searched for him in gossip columns in various newspapers. He wasn't there.

I backed up two months and looked for him then. I searched his appointment books, his diaries, and of course the poetry he had written to Jeanne. Finally, I located him via one of the notes he had written to Jeanne, thanking her for a wonderful evening at her home. I went to II, rue de l'Assomption that same evening. He was sitting with Jeanne on a wonderful plush couch before the fireplace. His arm was around her shoulder as both looked into the warm fire. "You are my Supreme Rose, pride of my winter," he told her. She smiled, leaning her head against his shoulder. I watched them as they sat quietly, peacefully together.

Then, still looking at the fire, she said, "Paul . . ."

"Yes, my darling?"

"Let's do something fun together. But something that would be meaningful, too."

"Certainly, of course," he replied. "What do you have in mind?"

"Well, I am thinking of writing a new book," she said.

"What sort of book, my dear?"

"A book about war—and peace."

"I believe Tolstoy has beaten you to that particular work." He chuckled.

"I'm serious," she said, laughing too.

"Well, we could certainly use some good advice about war and particularly about peace these days," he responded. "Do you want me to help you write it?"

"Not exactly," she said. "Oh, I need your advice, your counsel, as always, but this time I would like something else, too."

"What?" he said, straightening and turning to look directly at her.

"I am half afraid to ask you," she said, smiling coyly.

"You can ask anything of me. You know that. And if it is in my power, I shall give it to you. Now what do you want? Tell me."

"You are such a wonderful artist. If I wrote a simple book about how to find peace in this world, would you honor me by illustrating it for me?" She looked directly at him now, eyes bright with excitement.

He was taken aback. "Illustrate? You want me to illustrate your book?"

"It would be such fun. We would be working together on something important. It would be our own little masterpiece."

He thought a moment. "You know that I am not very good at drawing," he said finally.

"Nonsense," she replied. "You have drawn wonderful pictures for me. And I have seen some of your work on display. You touch people with your art. You touch me."

Clearly flattered by her remark, he was silent for a few moments. Then he said, "If my Héra desires my artwork, then she will have it."

Joyfully she embraced him.

With that information I was able to find him two months later. He was at a friend's studio in Montmartre—busily drawing. I watched him. He was muttering to himself, "Damn dogs," he said. "She knows I can't draw dogs." He was obviously tired and old. He coughed a lot; sometimes he had to stop his work and sit and hack. He held his ribs as if they hurt from all his coughing. His stomach almost always hurt. Then he would light another cigarette and start drawing again. He had told his Héra, "This work both attracts and terrifies me." He spent months trying to draw exactly what she wanted. She would praise him, and he would smile. And then she would make suggestions, something more here or there, perhaps. And he would work some more. The Official Poet of France, clearly near the end of his life, had become the Official Illustrator for his Mistress.

He could feel it sometimes, his own death creeping up on him, silently drifting around his body, sniffing him. He hated that feeling. If he thought of Héra, it went away. He thought of Héra often. And in his mind she came to represent for him his defense against death. In his poetry he wrote of her as his special protector against his own mortality. But part of him knew. In spite of all of his love for her, part of him realized that the mountain of love he gave her was not equally returned. She was still young. She was busy. She had other interests. As one of his friends remarked about Valéry, "Old age was coming. He who had conserved a youthful air and an adolescent vivacity for so long, his later photographs show that he had truly aged; he was worn out." In spite of her youth and health and the fact that it was she who first suggested this project, Jeanne Loviton did not spend nearly as much time on her text as her lover spent on his illustrations.

The result of their efforts was a slim tome called *The Open City* (*Ville ouverte*), published by Emile-Paul Frères in 1942. Once again I tried to obtain this work from the mammoth holdings in both art and literature at the University of Michigan. And once again this university had decided it didn't need this book. I obtained it from interlibrary loan. I opened the book and found that Jeanne Loviton had dedicated it to Paul Valéry. Then I read it. The very thin plot deals with a French soldier and a dog who meet a German soldier in an evacuated and otherwise totally empty French town. Ultimately, the French soldier, the German soldier, and even the dog (who often seems much smarter than the men) realize that there is no reason why they cannot all get along together. In fact, there is no reason why France and Germany cannot get along together, too. I could understand why the University of Michigan had passed on this book. It was blatantly collaborationist, badly written, simplistic, trite.

That Jeanne Loviton was careless in this work can be seen just by looking at the frontispiece. There she quotes the following: "A man never sees a man without pleasure." While at first glance this quote might seem quite apt, the author of that statement was Robespierre— that fanatic of the French Revolution who was personally responsible for countless hundreds of deaths. Apparently, Jeanne overlooked the irony, and Paul Valéry was either too in love or too old and sick to notice. During the course of my research on Valéry, I had seen many of his drawings. Most of them were interesting, some evocative and passionate. But his lithographs in *The Open City* seemed adolescent. I had to concede that Valéry was right. He couldn't draw dogs. His earlier sketches of castles, ships, and mermaids were much better.

I wondered if Valéry was senile. He was, after all, seventy-one and ill (his Héra was only thirty-nine). It was hard for me to reconcile the sarcastic and piercing Valéry of earlier years, who had deeply wounded André Breton and other able writers with his severe literary analyses, with the man who would lend his name to *The Open City*. Yet after checking several of the works he wrote around 1942, I saw that he was still quite sharp. Clearly his mental faculties had not significantly diminished. He still spent hours, days, sometimes longer, working on a single line, searching for the right word, working and rewording his own verse. Yet he did not even criticize his Héra's work. The impairment of his judgment or of his voice (I wasn't sure which) seems to have stemmed solely from his love for Jeanne. It was clear that he would do anything for her without complaint or criticism. He regularly gave her priceless gifts—gifts of himself—original poetry, his manuscripts, letters, and first editions.

Paul Valéry believed in the power and significance of his love for Jeanne Loviton. As he grew older, his philosophy began to mirror the thoughts of Jeanne's former husband, Pierre Frondaie. His former interests—abstraction, thinking, science, mathematics—were nothing now compared to the love he felt for his mistress. For Valéry, love, pure love, was really all that mattered . . . the centerpiece of life, even a way of glimpsing the divine. It didn't even matter to Valéry if the object of his love was not worthy or did not fully return that love—or even if she was a monster. He decided that true love blinds the lover to all faults of the loved one. It was the love itself that counted.

He started having premonitions in the late fall of 1942. Dark thoughts of losing Jeanne were never far from the surface of his consciousness. Sometimes he dreamed that she was just floating away. Frantically, he would try to catch hold of her, but his outstretched hands grasped nothing as she became ephemeral, smiling and drifting farther and farther away from him. His love for Héra then became even more obsessive. And the more possessive and needy he became, the more elusive and distracted Jeanne appeared.

"He is so needy," she confided to her friend Marion Delbo. "Sometimes I wish he loved someone else. He is tired and sick all the time, whines and broods. And that cough! He could wake the dead with it."

Then Jeanne's father, Fernand Loviton, died. Fernand had been a lawyer himself and lived in a rustic old chateau in central France. Jeanne and Paul had frequently gone there to get away. In addition, Fernand owned a small publishing house in Paris dedicated largely to legal publications. The funeral was held near Vichy. Although he knew and liked Jeanne's father, Paul did not attend. Following the funeral, Jeanne had several pressing problems dealing with her inheritance and the settling of the estate. She had little time for her poet, and he sorely missed her. When she did return to him, he was still in poor health and unable to provide her with much amusement.

Shortly after her return to Paris, Jeanne received a phone call from her friend Marion Delbo. Jeanne enumerated all of the dreary duties she had just performed. "You need some diversion," Marion decided. "I'm giving a party on Saturday night, just a few friends. Please come, won't you?" Marion Delbo was noted for her lively, enjoyable parties. In addition to being a thoughtful and gracious hostess, she was celebrated for her entertaining and amusing stories, her famous *histoires abracadabrantes.* She was, after all, an actress and an able writer herself.

"A small party may be just what I need right now," responded Jeanne. "I wouldn't miss it for the world. Paul will be out of town that day, some lecture he's giving in Lyons, I think. I could use some fun. He's been so dour lately."

I knew all about the party that Marion Delbo had given that Saturday night. Several years after the murder, the police questioned her extensively about that night, and I had her deposition, along with a description of the event in her diary. The police wanted to know when Robert Denoël and Jeanne Loviton first met. Marion recalled that first meeting in some detail. According to Madame Delbo, Jeanne Loviton appeared at the party, arriving fashionably late and very stylishly dressed. She was wearing a soft dark blue and white Schiaparelli dress with broad shoulders, long sleeves, and enormous silver buttons. At her waist was a matching wide silver belt. She was striking, chic. Jeanne knew nearly everyone there, with one exception.

"Who is that tall man over there with his back to us, the one with the dark wavy hair?" she whispered to her hostess.

"That's my publisher, Robert Denoël. Come with me. I want you to meet him." Marion then took her elegant guest by the arm and led her over to Robert and introduced her.

December 1942: Robert Denoël meets Jeanne Loviton. I have done it! I have traced both of them from 1925 until their meeting. I was excited, vaguely pleased with myself—and sad. For in that same month only three years later I knew that Robert Denoël would get into a car with this same woman and he would not return.

I watched them silently. They seemed happy, oblivious to the others at the party, talking about books and publishing. Jeanne was telling him that she, too, had recently become a publisher. It was that statement that made me start to wonder. Was it romantic attraction that drew him to Jeanne Loviton, or did that zebra have another motive? Here was a woman with connections, knowledge of the law— even in these confused legal times—and a little publishing house all her own where Robert might secretly make investments, hide assets, and, if need be, run a clandestine publishing business.

And this brand-new publisher, Jeanne Loviton, might have had other reasons for her attraction to the head of Les Editions Denoël. This intelligent and gregarious woman seemed to be able to attract men who had important influence in her fields of interest. Looking at her background, I noted that her father had been a lawyer, and she became a lawyer. She had dedicated her first book to her father. They must have been close. In addition, although I still had no proof, I had a feeling that the now-famous lawyer Maurice Garçon had been more than just a boss to her. Certainly, her former husband believed that they were having an affair.

Then she had taken up writing, and of course writers entered into her love life: Pierre Frondaie, Paul Valéry, Jean Giraudoux, and Saint-John Perse. Were there more? I wondered. Now she was a publisher, and who should enter her romantic life but one of the foremost publishers in France. Coincidence? It was very difficult at the time for a woman to enter any one of those fields alone. A woman often needed connections and powerful, successful men to help smooth the way for her. Jeanne Loviton was handsome and knowledgeable. And within her outwardly patrician façade, I believed that she must have had a strong animal sexual allure. Men found her fascinating. And long ago she had learned to enhance their enchantment, both in and out of the boudoir. She wore elegant, expensive clothes and kept herself readily informed about the major topics of the day. She was good at conversation, often able to add juicy tidbits to discussions because of her wide circle of friends and connections. She was glamorous in spite of her large legs and long nose. She took pains to diminish her flaws. A lawyer, a novelist with three published books to her credit (one of them illustrated by the most famous poet of France), a publisher of legal works, the owner of a beautiful home in Paris and now a castle in central France, wealthy, intelligent, elegant, Jeanne Loviton was a woman of power and significance at a time when most French women were powerless. Certainly, it could not have been easy for any woman or man to have achieved so much. And here was this handsome, successful young publisher attracted to her and apparently ready for an affair. Why not? And why not use his experience and influence to aggrandize her own publishing house?

Although Jeanne and Robert may have had other motives for this liaison, both were clearly attracted to each other, interested, and ready for a love affair. I remembered that Robert had not been faithful to Cécile following her affair with Antonin Artaud. As for the large circle of famous writers who had romanced Jeanne, Robert was aware only of her former husband, Pierre Frondaie. The others Jeanne described as "some of my dear friends and literary associates." And now Jeanne was ready for a liaison with someone her own age. Robert was only one year older than she. Why not have an affair with this intriguing man?

By January 1943 Jeanne and Robert were romantically involved. Yet both privately decided not to end their other ties—at least not yet. Robert continued to be a dutiful, if often absent, husband to Cécile. He saw his son, Robert, often, taking him on some of his trips, playing with him in the park, and taking him to lunch, the office, or on special Paris outings. Concerned by the influence of Cécile's temperamental tantrums and theatrical scenes, Robert tried to be a stable force in his son's life. And Jeanne saw no need to inform her poet of her new romance. After all, it was fairly simple for her to find the time to be with Robert without the knowledge of the old and ailing Official Poet of France. Quietly, Jeanne became Robert's mistress. While Robert told Jeanne frankly about his relationship with his wife, Jeanne described Paul Valéry simply as a "very good friend," nothing more. And more than anything else, this particular lie would prove most egregious to her.

10

Love and Work

I believe that I am able to understand, as no one else can,
the extraordinary role that **absolute love** can play in the
creations of mind and spirit.

Paul Valéry

*D*uring the war, Denoël ignored the Nazi/Vichy rules for publishers.
While he continued to publish and defend Céline, he also published,
in 1942, a collection of short stories called *A Thousand Regrets (Mille
regrets)*. The author of this work, Elsa Triolet, was a Russian Jew with
well-known links to the Communist Party. She also had secret ties
to the French Resistance. *A Thousand Regrets* was an apt title, embodying
the Forbidden Trinity of French publishing: no Jews, no Communists, no resisters. Publishing this work could certainly have resulted
in a thousand regrets for Denoël. He could have lost his company
for this act or gone to that "Dental Institute" on the Villa Saïd or
faced a firing squad.

In the same year, 1942, Robert Denoël also published *The Rubble
(Les Décombres)*, which chronicled that period in France before Germany seized it. It was written by the actively committed Fascist and
anti-Semite Lucien Rebatet. Among other things, Rebatet has been
described as a Fascist with a gangster mentality, in the guise and
demeanor of a cultured dilettante. Filled with hate and cynicism, this
book also contained a kind of savage lyricism and innovation that

attracted Denoël. Fearful of the implications of such a book, especially if the Allies won, Grasset, Gallimard, and Plon had already turned it down. Aware of Denoël's financial difficulties, Rebatet turned to him as a last resort. With the same speed he had previously used to get Céline under contract, Denoël immediately signed Rebatet, with quite favorable terms for this author.

The Rubble became the largest publishing success of the Occupation. The first printing of twenty thousand copies sold out in two weeks. Even Jean Galtier-Boissière, a diarist and journalist who detested this writer and referred to him as a "little joker," admitted that Rebatet had written an astonishing book "with an extraordinary eloquence."

Céline, Rebatet, and Elsa Triolet—it didn't seem possible that one man could be publishing all three writers at the same time, and in such dangerous circumstances. Céline certainly knew Triolet, knew who she was. He probably suspected her of ties to the Resistance, too. Why didn't he denounce his publisher? And certainly Rebatet could not be trusted with such knowledge. Other people also knew who Elsa Triolet really was—important people, even some who might benefit by reporting Denoël to their Nazi occupiers.

"Close your eyes, don't see. Don't look too closely at who is sitting next to you or walking down that hallway. Don't hear, and do not rock the boat, and we shall publish—all together." That philosophy seems to have been paramount not only at Les Editions Denoël, but also at Les Editions Gallimard. While Céline, Rebatet, and Triolet played their triple bill for Robert Denoël (he even brazenly advertised Triolet in anti-Semitic newspapers), Les Editions Gallimard had an even more bizarre situation in its midst. At the location of Gallimard's *New French Review (N.R.F.)*, there were two offices facing each other in a Janus-like structure. In one of these offices was that ardent pro-Nazi Drieu La Rochelle, now heading the *N.R.F.* and attempting to make this journal the French showpiece for Franco-German collaboration. But in the other office sat the former head of the *N.R.F.* Jean Paulhan. He was at that time an ardent member of the French Resistance and, in addition, the founder of the clandestine Resistance newspaper, *French Letters (Les Lettres françaises)*. Each man could see who was entering and exiting the other's office. And each man knew the other's political leanings. They worked in those two offices in outward perfect harmony, always polite and courteous. There is no evidence that either man ever reported the other's activities to officials. And both received their paychecks from Gaston Gallimard. It is no wonder that Gaston Gallimard was called "the ace player of the double game."

More than a zebra, Denoël was becoming a chameleon. He hid those who were wanted by the Gestapo in his home—writers, friends, Jews, sometimes even relative strangers who found themselves in need of a safe hiding place. Other publishers were not so daring; they refused to help their Jewish writers or others sought by the Nazis. These blacklisted writers were often deported to German concentration camps and frequently to their deaths.

Elsa Triolet was married to the noted writer Louis Aragon. I remembered that Aragon was the writer Denoël had so fondly cited in his farewell to Belgium in 1926. In the early 1930s Denoël had managed to steal Aragon from Gaston Gallimard. Aragon and Gallimard had had several arguments and artistic disputes. Denoël had waited for the right time (following a particularly heated battle between Aragon and Gallimard) and had made Aragon a better offer. Gallimard hated Aragon's defection. In addition to being an important member of the Communist Party, Aragon was now an active member of the Resistance. In 1942 Robert Denoël regularly helped both Aragon and Triolet, enabling them to see each other and helping them to remain out of the hands of the Gestapo. At the same time, Denoël was in partnership with the German publisher Andermann and cooperating with the Germans.

In 1942 Elsa Triolet heard several rumors that Robert was a collaborator. One afternoon he appeared in the doorway of the small room where she was staying. He greeted her warmly. "I have a message for you from Louis," he said handing her a slim unopened envelope.

She took the message, thanked him, and opened the letter. In it were several sensitive coded instructions concerning future Resistance activities. After reading the message, she took out a match and burned it over a large plate on her table, making certain that every piece of the paper was charred. Then she asked her publisher, who had silently looked out the window as she read the message, to sit and talk for a few minutes. Robert liked Elsa and sat happily near her in one of the small chairs by the table. She quickly came to the point. "Robert, I have been warned that you are a collaborator. Is it true?"

"Yes, it's true," he said. He made no effort at evasion or a lengthy defense or explanation.

She was shocked, horrified by his admission. Trying to gain control over her emotions, she finally said, "Then we can no longer be friends."

Both of them sat motionless for several minutes. Finally Robert spoke. "I have a choice. I can collaborate and keep my business open. Or I can refuse to collaborate and lose my business and possibly get shot. I choose the former. Besides, I have others to think about too—my family, my employees, my writers—even you, Elsa."

"I am not sure I want to hear this," she admitted.

"Handing my entire business over to the Germans because I refuse to cooperate with them seems to me a futile protest," he continued. "They certainly wouldn't publish you." He smiled.

It did not occur to her to ask if he was loyal and could be trusted. He had already proven that a hundred times. Denoël and his wife had sheltered Aragon and Triolet in their home on several occasions. He had often served as a liaison between Triolet and Aragon. He had published her work, advertised it, and defended it, just as he defended the work of Céline. When their other "friends" turned their backs on this dangerous couple, Denoël had not deserted them, even in spite of their bitter arguments over a work by Triolet that he published in 1938, *Bonsoir, Thérèse*. At that time she had castigated him because she believed he had not done enough to advertise this book, and it had not sold well. No, the fact remained that in spite of everything, even his collaboration with the Nazis, they were still friends.

She later wrote about Robert Denoël, "Had he been the worst of the collaborators, we would have trusted in him with the same peace of mind: whatever happened, he was for his friends a man to be trusted." Sometimes Denoël would even seek out Triolet and take her in his car to Aragon's hiding places. And this was at a time when gasoline was almost unobtainable, when his actions involved great personal risk, and when Triolet's other friends and acquaintances had abandoned her, refusing even to recognize her if she passed them on the street.

It is no wonder that his employees were loyal to him. Most of Denoël's initial employees remained for years at Les Editions Denoël. Even Bernard Steele kept his friendship with his former partner. Following his return to the States, Steele joined the armed forces. He distinguished himself for his courageous actions as an officer of the United States Navy during the Liberation. Steele returned to France following the war, his friendship with Robert still intact. As for that longtime accountant, Auguste Picq, he too remained with his collaborationist publisher, earnestly trying to keep the books for this business in spite of the fact that most of its assets were now carefully hidden.

It was Picq who helped Robert with some of his more confusing financial difficulties. And with Vichy rules, German rules, and ever-changing political climates, fiscal matters were never clear or easy. Added to these financial difficulties was the fact that many of the supplies so necessary to publishing could only be obtained on the black market. Robert Denoël, collaborator and black marketeer. And just how does one note into an account book the illegal payment of twelve thousand francs to an unnamed man in an unnamed alley for large quantities of paper? Robert left such problems up to Picq. Both men knew that Les Editions Denoël could be in legal difficulties from just about any side. The most recent difficulty concerned that Andermann loan and partnership. The Vichy government was suspicious of it.

Robert asked Picq to come to a meeting in his office. The publisher had just received some bad news. The Vichy government had just decided that the Andermann loan and partnership were illegal. Robert was deeply angry.

"I tried to get a loan from Vichy first, didn't I," he reminded Picq. "But Vichy had so many strings attached and so much damned bureaucratic mumbo jumbo they would have allowed my business to go bankrupt before granting me a loan." Robert paced back and forth in his office, his hands closed into fists. Then he looked at Picq and continued, "And the only reason I needed the money in the first place was because the Nazis robbed me of one-third of my company. Damn them! Damn them all!" The older man nodded in agreement. Robert sat down behind his desk. "I am trying to run a business here," he said. Picq remained silent. Pale, frowning, his boss continued. "First I get sued and fined for an error in Céline's book. Then the Nazis close my entire business while I am off to war in Belgium. Then they rob me for publishing patriotic works. Then Vichy refuses me a loan. And now they decide I can't get a loan from a German publisher, either. Must I be in the wrong in every case?" He looked at Picq, then added, "Must I pay everyone, just for the privilege of keeping my business running?" He was silent for a few moments. Picq still said nothing. Then Robert began to punctuate his remarks by pounding on the desk with his fist. "And every time someone decides I am wrong, I am fined. Big fines! I have more fines than writers these days."

It was true. Commenting decades later on Denoël's unique predicament, famed French publishing historian Pascal Fouché states, "One gets the impression that Robert Denoël paid for everyone." Only Jewish publishers, who lost their businesses entirely during this period, found themselves in more difficult straits than the "outsider," Robert Denoël. Not only did he have to pay the Andermann loan back with interest, he was fined an additional 100,000 francs for taking the loan in the first place. With Drieu La Rochelle and his powerful German friend Otto Abetz protecting him, Gallimard avoided such predicaments. Besides, Gallimard never lost part of his company. And, always wealthy, he never found himself in such urgent financial difficulties as his younger competitor.

I returned to Robert Denoël in 1943 and entered his office on rue Amélie. Although I expected to find the usual drab, sparse furniture, I was surprised to discover that he had gone upscale, bought new plush furnishings, tastefully redecorated, giving Les Editions Denoël a prominent and established look that the former hosiery factory and chapel had never known before. I was impressed—so were Céline and Rebatet, both of whom suspected that *their* money had gone into this investment. As Rebatet later said, "His dark hole on rue Amélie was transformed into a suite of bright, spacious, elegant offices, all newly furnished. Céline and I, his two successful authors, bore the expense of this new luxury."

By 1943 Robert Denoël had managed once again to avoid bankruptcy and turn things around. He was doing well—very well. In spite of the difficulties of war, shortages, rations, Occupation, the black market, and ever-changing rules, his business was thriving. And partially Rebatet was right. Céline and Rebatet, popular both with the French and Germans, brought significant money into this publishing house. But Robert's other writers sold well, too. Denoël's novelist Paul Vialar was hugely popular with readers. In 1943 Denoël published Vialar's *The Big Mob (La Grande Meute)*, which was very successful. He also supported and published the first works by Jean Genet. At that time, even new and unknown writers were snatched up by a public eager to escape the ever-darkening realities of the Occupation and the atrocities of war. Denoël himself admitted with satisfaction, "It used to take a year to liquidate three thousand copies by an unknown author. Everything now is sold out in a week."

That same year Robert published another work by Elsa Triolet, a novel entitled *The White Charger (Le Cheval blanc)*. He had first become acquainted with this work in 1942 when he visited Elsa in Nice. There she read the first part of this novel to her publisher, and he was deeply moved by it. Triolet intended to design this particular novel to circumvent German censorship while at the same time providing aid and comfort to French prisoners of war as well as those in the French Resistance. *The White Charger* was filled with code words and secret phrases that only French resisters and prisoners of war would recognize. Denoël knew this. In fact, they had discussed the clandestine purpose of this novel at length. "You simply cannot change one word, Robert," she insisted. "If you do, you might lose the secret codes. And that would destroy the entire purpose of the book. This book will provide hope to those who have no hope. That's why you can't change it. Don't you see, Robert?" He looked at her and sighed heavily. Did she know what she was asking? Did she realize that if the true nature of this work were even suspected by the Nazis, both she and her publisher could face a firing squad? And in addition, Elsa Triolet was a Jew.

"Let me go over this novel again tonight," he said. "I will give you my answer tomorrow."

The next day Robert and Elsa met and discussed, argued heatedly about the dangers this novel posed to both of them. They went over lines together that worried this publisher. Finally Robert decided. "I will publish everything in *The White Charger* exactly as you have written it. I will make absolutely no cuts except for the very last sentence. That last sentence could get us both killed, my dear."

She read the last sentence aloud. "Stanislas Bielenki did not receive that letter; he had been in the Gurs concentration camp for one year and was forbidden mail there." She thought a moment, then asked, "How would you change it?"

Robert said, "I would end the book with 'Stanislas Bielenki did not receive that letter.' "

Elsa Triolet saw his point and agreed to the change. And so the 1943 edition of *The White Charger* ends with the only cut Robert Denoël made in the entire work. There was no mention of where Stanislas was when he did not receive that letter. It passed the censors and was smuggled into German prison camps, passed from hand to hand by French resisters and, just as Elsa had intended, provided support and encouragement to those in greatest need.

As he had done before, Robert advertised *The White Charger* in anti-Semitic and pro-Nazi newspapers and journals.

If 1943 was a great year for this contradictory publisher, it was proving to be very difficult for Parisian cats and pigeons. Food was becoming very scarce, even on the black market. With many Frenchmen in German labor or prison camps, almost no fuel for farm equipment, and few farm animals (either slaughtered to feed German soldiers, or pressed into service for the German army), French farm production plummeted. Cats and pigeons began to disappear at an alarming rate in Paris, in spite of dire warnings in French newspapers, often carrying the headline "Cat Eaters! Beware!" But no matter that these cats ate rats, and that cats and pigeons might, according to the newspapers, carry disease to their hungry recipients, they continued to be the main entrée (often the only entrée) on some Parisian plates.

Other substitutions, too, were becoming common: coffee from ground chestnuts or wild-rose petals; the juice of licorice sticks for sugar; beet leaves dried and used for tobacco; potatoes instead of meat; and turnips instead of almost anything else. The black market thrived on the selling of foodstuffs—for those who could afford it. Prices continued to climb steeply throughout the Occupation. Another new business arose in the counterfeiting of ration cards. Farmers who hid some of their produce from Vichy inspections grew wealthy by selling it at exorbitant prices to hungry city dwellers, who had to dodge further Vichy inspections (and severe reprisals if caught) to get that food back to their homes.

Wooden soles were nailed onto dilapidated shoes. Shop girls drew "nylon lines" up the backs of their bare legs. Foraging for food became a constant pastime for some. Barter was commonly accepted. With almost no fuel, cars and taxis disappeared from Paris streets; the price of bicycles skyrocketed. Sometimes the black market was the only place where one could obtain necessary food or clothing. As legal commodities became harder to find, and often unobtainable, the Catholic Church decreed that it was no sin to deal on the black market. The Church realized by then that to depend upon legal rations might lead to starvation. "Here kitty, kitty. Nice kitty" became the Parisian hunter's call.

Any form of escapism was welcome to the French at this time. In addition to books, movies served that purpose well. One movie in particular entranced its audience, causing moviegoers to return again and again and watch in adoration one scene in particular. It wasn't a great dramatic scene or sex or a glamorous star they were admiring. It was food. There was a feast in *The Night Visitors* (*Les Visiteurs du Soir*) that left its hungry audiences spellbound. Tray upon tray of food, roast pig, swan, huge piles of amazing delicacies were brought to the table on enormous silver trays. *The Night Visitors* was one of the most successful movies of the Occupation.

But clearly Robert Denoël was not reduced to stalking cats or drooling over films with feasting actors during this period. He simply needed a safe place to hide some of his assets. Right from the start, his affair with Jeanne Loviton also included the use of her publishing house. Shortly after the beginning of their liaison, a shift of money occurred. The sum of 200,000 francs was transferred from Robert Denoël to Jeanne Loviton. The official reason for this transfer was later stated to be a loan to her publishing company. The real reason was probably a clandestine attempt on the part of Denoël to buy an interest in her publishing house, Domat-Montchrestien. Denoël also moved elegant furniture worth 75,000 francs to Loviton's publishing house. He even moved his secretary, Madame Tardieu, to Les Editions Domat-Montchrestien. Two of his most significant writers, Blaise Cendrars and Paul Vialar, quietly slipped from the roster of Les Editions Denoël and began to be published by his other publishing house, Les Editions de la Tour, and by Les Editions Domat-Montchrestien. Soon other former writers from Les Editions Denoël also appeared as part of these other publishing houses.

By 1943 Denoël and most others under the Occupation began to realize that the tide of war was turning. It was no longer assumed, as it had been in earlier years, that Hitler was invincible. America's entry into the war in December 1941 changed the power balance and had a profound impact on the attitudes of most Europeans. Germany held 1.9 million French prisoners of war. France was paying ten million dollars per day as the cost of the Occupation. Then in 1943 came the stunning German defeat at Stalingrad. The Allies were making inroads into North Africa; Italy was collapsing, and Allied bombers were repeatedly and successfully attacking industrial cities in France and Germany. An Allied invasion seemed not only possible, but probable. Anticipating this invasion, the French reacted by joining the Resistance, or taking precautions to hide and/or defend themselves against possible future charges of collaboration—or by shooting each other. As food and commodities became more expensive and difficult to find, life became cheap. Murder was a common way to solve things. Civil war in France was not unthinkable. In fact, as the French continued to threaten and murder each other, some claimed that civil war had already begun.

Those French supporting Hitler joined a French army of Nazi support, established by Germany and called the Militia (Milice). The French Militia and the French Resistance then killed each other, and anyone else who stood in their way. And for each murder, there were other killings, more murders done in reprisal. And to top it off, the Germans automatically killed one hundred French prisoners of war if one German was killed in France by terrorist attack. No matter. As the war continued, more and more Germans found themselves targets of such assassinations, and more and more prisoners held by Germany faced the firing squad. The motto of the French Resistance, having faced horrible torture and murder and now sensing a possible victory for the first time, became "For an eye, both eyes; for a tooth, the whole jaw!" Always divided, France now became a wretched place of murder and bloodletting.

Robert Denoël did not seem to take notice of the tumultuous events around him. He was working hard, publishing, making money, expanding, and providing the reading public with what it wanted. He was, after all, a publisher . . . a Belgian at that, not a resister or

Militia member. He had killed no one, physically harmed no one. He was not political. He simply published books.

Céline, on the other hand, was far more concerned about the situation in France, especially as it related to his own skin. Clearly, some of his writings could be damned as collaborationist and certainly anti-Semitic, and there was no way for him to conceal his published words since everyone in France had read or heard of him. But it would be wrong to assume that the Germans loved him—or even liked him. The irascible Céline had not endeared himself to either side. In fact, he had gone out of his way to insult the Germans. As early as 1941 Céline proved himself to be a supreme annoyance to the Nazis. The Germans invited him to attend an anti-Semitic meeting. Although Céline was incognito, another invitee, Rebatet, recognized him and later recounted what happened:

> While the chairman hemmed and hawed, from Ferdinand's corner I heard grumblings, the tones of which could not be mistaken. As the lecture droned on endlessly, Céline's bass-baritone grew ever more distinct.
>
> ". . . Judeo . . . judeo-marxist . . . tyra . . . tyranny . . ."
>
> "Hey, why don't you talk about Aryan stupidity?"
>
> Fifty pairs of amateur detectives' eyes, darting every which way, tried to identify the source of the sacrilege.
>
> . . . I made for the door through a hopeless uproar. Céline hadn't moved. In the lobby, the fattest of the Krauts was moaning: "Ve vill neffer be able to built anytink vit dees French!"

Céline was always quick to irritate his German occupiers. He dressed so shabbily he was often mistaken for a beggar. At one German party, a headwaiter ordered the dirty and disheveled Céline out of the room, to the embarrassment of everyone, except possibly Céline himself. At another significant German event, he asked an important German official how long he thought it would be before Germany was defeated. Another man at one of these German functions commented about Céline's clothes. Céline responded by calling this man "a scumbag collaborator."

In 1942 Céline further infuriated the Germans when they invited him to go to Berlin. There he was asked to speak at the French Workers' Club. In his speech, Céline said, "These guys [the Germans] are *lousy*. They say they're going to win the war. Maybe so. I don't know. The others, the Russians, on the other side, are no better. They may even be worse. It's a question of choosing between cholera and the plague. Not much fun. So long!" The Germans were angry, amazed, insulted. There was allegedly even talk of putting Céline in prison for his remarks.

I wanted to visit Céline at his Paris apartment, but he did not receive visitors. So I began to look for his friends, hoping I would soon find him with one of them. In 1943 I found him with the poet Théophile Briant. I located a picture of their meeting. Céline looked like a withered old bum, lean and bent. His clothes were dirty; he had not shaved for three or four days and sported a sprouting gray stubble. He wore bedraggled old sandals and kept his pants up with a piece of rope. His hair was long and greasy; his eyes hollow, with deep, dark circles. Others noted that his language was shocking— sometimes explosive—punctuated by bits of spittle that flew out of his mouth as he talked. He was filled with hatred. His laugh was harsh, crazy. I took out a picture of Denoël in 1943—urbane, not a hair out of place, smiling, impeccably dressed, vigorous, healthy, polite. I placed the two men side by side and studied them. But my eyes always turned toward Céline. I could see how this haggard, disheveled anti-Semite inspired fear and mistrust in others, no matter what their political views.

One of Céline's best (worst?) performances was given at a dinner hosted by Otto Abetz. After listening to Abetz and several friends discuss at some length the bright future of Germany, Céline loudly announced that Hitler was dead, and that German defeat was at hand. There was shock, profound silence in the room as Céline continued. He claimed that the real Hitler had been replaced by a double, a

Jew. And this Jew was preparing for a Jewish, not a Nazi, triumph. Then Céline's friend, Gen Paul, who had illustrated several of Céline's works, rose and began imitating Hitler, gesturing wildly, and shouting Nazi slogans and parts of Hitler's speeches, while Céline continued his grotesque and ever-expanding tirade. Abetz was appalled, frightened, for he believed some of his servants to be spies who regularly reported his activities to the Gestapo. Finally in desperation, Abetz got an inspired idea. He began to treat Céline as a madman, sick, reminding others of Céline's disabilities and severe war wounds in World War I. Carefully, tenderly, Abetz and others escorted Céline out of the party, then back to his home.

As Robert Denoël once admitted in a newspaper article, "Céline is not a likable man." Those words, uttered by the publisher whom Céline called a thief, pimp, and incompetent ignoramus, were an understatement. Even the most ardent anti-Semites often recoiled at Céline. This profoundly angry man, prone to exaggeration, contradiction, and surprise, was dangerous. He was also growing fearful. When the war ended, who would defend him? Who would keep him out of jail? Who could prevent his assassination? Would he possibly face a firing squad? Would Denoël? Death had been this writer's first subject of conversation with Robert Denoël. Now thoughts of death obsessed him, dogging him as much as those constant buzzings in his ears. Céline deposited money outside France. He carefully protected his large gray cat, Bébert, from those Parisian hunters. He foresaw that he and Bébert, along with his wife, Lucette, might have to leave France one day.

While Céline was contemplating his possible assassination, another man too was thinking of his own death, not by murder or political necessity, but cruel just the same. Paul Valéry was consumed both by his work and by his lover in 1943. For when he was not absorbed in either work or love, he became increasingly aware of his own mortality. He wrote to Jeanne Loviton more frequently in 1943, perhaps sensing that she was not as concerned with him as she had once been. Looking forward to one of her visits, he wrote to her, "I hope that we will be fine together, that we will be alone together, that we will be WE together; by that I mean the monster with two heads. Love is perhaps a living vestige of mythology." Sometimes he even wrote her twice a day, admitting, "Time is so long without you, like the tail of the Devil." Although Jeanne responded to his letters, clearly her own desires were different from Valéry's. More and more she found herself in the strong young arms of Robert Denoël. They were beginning to plan their future.

As Jeanne's letters became more infrequent, Valéry became more exuberant upon receiving one. "If you only knew what it does to me to receive a good letter from you! . . . suddenly the mystical wind appears." He worried about everything regarding his mistress: her health, her happiness, her troubles, and especially his separations from her. He believed she gave him all that he had ever wanted. He wished he could give her everything. Her voice, her eyes, her laugh, her touch, enchanted him. He admitted to her, "You have given me the most entirely tender, the most perfect hours of my life."

Paul told his love all about his life, his work, his thoughts, his dreams, especially that "strange dream" about his own death. He also attributed great powers to her. He told her she was perfect, wrote of her being, her spirit . . . her bedroom. He praised her mind, told her she could write the best of verses. "I admire you at least as much as I love you. In the final analysis, I am jealous of your astonishing faculties." He despaired that he had so little time with her. He did not know that she was quite well occupied in his absence. He wondered, "if ever lovers tell each other everything which can be told when they encounter that which is most tender, most profound in the other—something which is **like the nakedness of the soul offered to the only Other who is worthy of it . . . That is the only thing, you understand, the only** which I have asked of that which one calls 'life.' "

Robert Denoël took Paul Valéry's "Other" into his arms and kissed her repeatedly upon her lips, her neck, her hair. He did not guess that he had a rival. He held her close to him, encircling her body with his arms, then said, "It's time to tell my wife the truth about us."

"Are you sure, Robert? What about your son?" she asked.

"My son is very important to me. I shall continue to see him regularly, as I have always tried to do. I want to be a good father. As for Cécile, she has to know there is another woman. And I already know she has another lover—another young man who works for me. This news should not come as such a great shock to her."

I followed him back to his home and to Cécile. Robert Jr. was spending the night with a friend. It was the maid's night off. This was the perfect time to tell her. I had hoped to walk into the room with Robert, to find accounts, witnesses, perhaps even Robert's own description of what happened. But the door was quickly locked before I could enter. I scoured journals, papers, notes from Robert's every friend and acquaintance, every possible clue in libraries in France and the United States, but try as I might, I could not witness, even secondhand, what happened between them that night. I stood silently beneath their window, but it was early December 1943 and their window was tightly closed. I heard nothing for several minutes. Suddenly I detected a wail. Then loud moans, followed by piercing screams, sobbing, the crashing of glass, thumps. The crying, thumping, and crashing continued for quite some time. Then I heard footsteps quickly coming toward me, then past me. It was Robert. The wails continued, becoming now almost gasps, and the sobbing—deep, shuddering. Soon I saw Robert returning with another man with a small black bag. A doctor? Both hurried into the home. I knew from that police dossier that Robert did not ask her for a divorce that night. Instead, she had fallen "gravely ill."

Because of his wife's fragile condition, Robert decided to move more slowly. He would stay with Cécile, for the time being. But he wanted to get Cécile used to the idea that he had a mistress and that he was very fond of her. Then, proceeding slowly, he would later move out of the house, and later still, ask her for a divorce. He would move by increments, not all at once. It would be better for

his son this way, too, Robert decided. He had no desire to do something that might send his wife over the edge. As for Jeanne, he was
happy to learn that she seemed to understand. "There is no need to
rush things," she told him. He did not realize that taking their romance more slowly suited her needs, too.

By the close of 1943 Paris was in turmoil, the economy was drained,
and necessary goods were becoming impossible to obtain even on the
black market. Jews continued to be arrested, sent first to Drancy,
then deported to Germany and death. Murder and terrorist attacks
increased. Germany was losing. Those beyond redemption began to
plan for their departure from France. Others chose prudence and
preparations for a good defense. While Denoël continued to publish
both sides, his chief writer, Céline, admitted that he dared not "look
to the future."

With the decline of German power and prestige came more criticism of Denoël and other publishers. In November 1943 the National Writers' Committee denounced collaborationist publishers,
including Denoël, in "Warnings to the Publishers," which appeared
in the clandestine journal *French Letters (Les Lettres françaises)*. The following month the clandestine newspaper *Résistance* excoriated Denoël
for his collaboration. This condemnation of publishers perceived to
have collaborated increased in 1944. Starting in May of that year and
greatly intensifying following the Allied invasion in Normandy on 6
June, denunciations and condemnations of publishers and other col-
laborationists grew bolder and more frequent.

Yet in spite of these denouncements, Robert Denoël did not significantly change his publishing practices. On 13 January 1944 he
obtained the contract from Céline for the first volume of *Guignol's
Band*, a nostalgic and often lascivious look at London in 1916. Denoël
obtained two tons of paper from the Germans. Céline's preface
proved prophetic. Speaking of this book, he said, "It had to be
printed fast because with things so serious you don't know who's
going to be alive and who dead! Denoël? you? me?" Then on the

other side the zebra, Denoël, published in May 1944 René Château's *In Search of Future Time (A la recherche du temps futur)*. Following its publication, the book was banned by the Germans as contrary to German goals and ideals.

In addition, as he had done in 1942 and again in 1943, Robert published another book by Elsa Triolet in 1944. This time he published a book of four novellas *(nouvelles)*. Robert liked this work, particularly the fourth story, for which the book was entitled: *A Fine of 200 Francs (Le Premier accroc coûte 200 francs)*. Amazingly, this book passed the censors.

Robert had always had certain premonitions about his own death. Most of the time he simply brushed off these dark feelings. But now thoughts of his own premature death began to haunt him. He turned to books, which from childhood had always provided escape and solace. But this time even his books turned on him, seemingly predicting his future violent death. One night he went to a bar with a friend of his, a journalist, and a few others. After a few drinks, he confided to this friend his feelings that he might die prematurely, violently. When the journalist asked him why he felt that way, Denoël simply stated, "Each time I randomly open a book or a manuscript, I open it to the most dramatic or the most sinister passage." Intrigued by this "strange confidence," the journalist and others present at the time put him to the test. Someone had on hand a copy of Zola's *L'Argent* (meaning money or silver). They handed the book to him. He looked at it, turned it in his hands, looked briefly up, then opened it randomly. He shut his eyes and pointed at the page. Then he looked, grimaced, smiled, and read, "Under the red reflection of the fire, Marzaud was knocked over on the edge of the sofa, his head smashed by a bullet." I found an account of this incident in Denoël's obituary in *The Literary News (Les Nouvelles litéraires)*.

One day while sitting in his office at Les Editions Denoël, he received a letter. It was unusual in that it had no return address. Invariably, letters to publishers carried return addresses. Curious, Robert opened it. Inside there was simply a picture of a coffin. No signature, no words, just the drawing of a coffin—with his name on it. He pretended that this ominous threat had not disturbed him, smiling and casually showing it to others. But in truth it did disturb him greatly. The drawing was a known practice of the ever more vocal and increasingly bold French Resistance. Designated collaborators were sent anonymous drawings, such as Robert had received, or sometimes a package containing a real miniature coffin or noose. Everyone knew the meanings of these drawings or small packages. They indicated that the recipient had been condemned to death in a Resistance court-martial. Although these court-martials were illegal, they were quite real and greatly feared, especially since the sentence was often swiftly carried out. Usually the recipient was later found dead, his body dumped on a lane or deserted road or in a ditch, a note denouncing him as a collaborator or informer pinned to his lapel. No, receiving such a letter was certainly not something to be taken lightly. Céline also received a few of these threatening anonymous letters. He took them quite seriously.

Then one night at about 3:00 A.M. the phone rang. Robert immediately awakened and ran downstairs to answer it. "Hello?" he said.

There was a brief silence, then a deep rasping voice said, "Prepare to die, you stinking shitty sellout! You will die slowly, you miserable scum collabo. You will writhe in pain, you shit, and cry for death before it gets—"

Robert hung up. Shaken, nervous, he returned to his bed.

Cécile, drowsy, asked, "Who was it?"

"No one," he said. "Just a wrong number." He did not sleep for the rest of the night. More and more he kept away from his home at night, preferring to stay with his mistress or even at Les Editions Denoël to receiving such calls. But in spite of his precautions, those vulgar, frightening, threatening calls still sometimes found him.

Although Jeanne and Robert had many romantic evenings together, they also had a great many serious discussions about Robert's business future. His affair with Jeanne was going well, and more and more he took her into his confidence. Although he had not yet officially separated from his wife, his slow detachment from his marriage was intensifying. Always helpful and encouraging, Jeanne suggested courses of action that he might take in his marriage and business and strongly recommended certain lawyers who might be able to help him with both situations. Robert listened and heeded her counsel. He also selected the lawyers that she recommended. In May 1944, one month before the Allied invasion in Normandy, Robert began to take serious steps to defend himself and his publishing house against possible charges of collaboration.

He decided to sell his other publishing house, where he had first started his business, then called Les Trois Magots, and now called Les Editions de la Bourdonnais. This sale was necessary because la Bourdonnais officially housed the NEF, which published his anti-Semitic literature. Then on 16 May he dissolved the entire NEF.

Just as he had relied on friends and friendship (particularly that of the clairvoyant Irène Champigny) to help him establish his publishing business in the first place, so now he relied upon his friends (and particularly his lover, Jeanne Loviton) to help him hide not only part of his business, but his assets as well. With Jeanne's help, he created "paper" companies and used straw men to serve as figureheads or fictive directors for those businesses. Secretly, however, it would be Denoël who would direct the businesses from behind the scenes. That way even if the worst happened and he were banned from publishing in liberated France, he could still secretly conduct his business through these dummy companies, and through Jeanne Loviton's own publishing house (Les Editions Domat-Montchrestien) as well.

The Liberation of France came officially in August of 1944. When he first occupied Paris in 1940, Hitler had several good reasons for not destroying the city. He hoped that by sparing Paris, he would ensure Parisian cooperation. Besides, Hitler needed the city's enormous wealth and resources. If he controlled the city, bombing it would serve no constructive purpose. In addition, "decadent" Paris served as a great place for R and R for German troops. So Paris was spared in 1940. German officers had certain restaurants and night-clubs (most notably, Maxim's) reserved especially for them, as well as certain cinemas where only German films were shown. In addition, all German soldiers rode the metro anywhere in the city for free. And there were so many beautiful museums to loot, supposedly to add money to the German coffers, but more often than not to become part of the private art collections of Hermann Göring and other German officers. Occupied Paris intact was a prize for any German soldier.

As the Liberation became imminent, Hitler had different ideas about the future of Paris. On 23 August he ordered that all Paris bridges and important installations be destroyed, "even if artistic monuments are destroyed thereby." He gave these orders to General Hans Speidel and to General Dietrich von Choltitz. But both men refused to carry out their orders (Choltitz was later tried for treason *in absentia* for this act). Then, when it became apparent that Hitler would lose Paris entirely, he ordered the total destruction of that city. "Use all the heavy artillery available, along with our V-1 flying bombs," he commanded. "Let the French retrieve their precious city in ruins!" But again both generals turned a deaf ear to the demands of their Führer. Paris was spared . . . twice.

With the Liberation came an ardent desire on the part of many Frenchmen to purge the entire nation of any who had collaborated during the Occupation. Hatred and the desire for revenge fueled the feeling that those who had cooperated with Germany in any way should be made to pay and pay dearly. Many believed that all factions of French society should be purged from top to bottom. One of the first targets of this purge was any woman who had served, fraternized with, or had sex with any German soldier. Such a woman, or even one who was only suspected of being friendly toward a German soldier, faced swift retaliation. Often referred to as a "horizontal collaborator," she was forced to have her head shaved. Then a swastika was often painted on her forehead, and she was paraded through town through jeering crowds and publicly taunted and humiliated.

Other perceived collaborators were summarily shot as the simmering fear and hatred of the Occupation poured forth into a French bloodbath. No one knows exactly how many French people were executed at that time. Some estimates place the number at between thirty and forty thousand, while others place that figure much higher. Most historians agree that more French people were killed under charges of collaboration in the fall of 1944 than were killed in the entire bloody French Revolution. One of Charles de Gaulle's first priorities was to set in place a legal and official court system to deal with those charged with collaboration and thereby put an end to the rampant vigilantism and murder which constituted "justice" in France before the courts were reestablished.

Writers, entertainers, and the publishing establishment itself were chief targets of both the official and unofficial purge. Their collaborationist activities were there for all to see, either on film, in print, or on the radio. Denoël was now in more trouble than he had ever been in occupied France. Only one week after the Liberation, there was a demand by the Resistance press that certain collaborationist publishers, particularly Gaston Gallimard, Robert Denoël, and Bernard Grasset, be blacklisted. Shortly after this announcement, Bernard Grasset, whose pro-German leanings were well known, was arrested and sent to prison. The editor of the collaborationist journal, *Today (Aujourd'hui)*, Georges Suarez, was one of the first to be executed "legally" in October 1944. His entire trial took only four hours . . . with jury deliberation taking only twenty minutes. He refused to be blindfolded, saying, "Oh, no! Let me see this farce to the very end." Two rounds fired by a firing squad composed of new and jittery recruits failed to kill him, and two more pistol shots to his head were required.

De Gaulle made it even more difficult for publishers by announcing that two types of traitors deserved absolutely no mercy: army officers and writers of genius. Although he did not mention the publishers of great writers, it had already become clear that they, too, would be shown no clemency. Apparently, Céline had been right to pack his bags, and, along with his wife and cat, leave France. In fact, he was one of the first to leave the country, shortly after the Allied landing. He was not going to wait and see, as others did. He had received too many anonymous letters with pictures of coffins and nooses to believe that he was not a major target of the purge. But Denoël decided he would not leave France as others were doing. He wanted to stay and defend both his business and himself. He began to take serious steps to protect his family, his business, and his assets. Considering the threats against him and the danger to his life, it was a perfect time for Robert to separate officially from his wife and move out of the house. He did both, and this time his wife seemed resigned to their separation. He changed living quarters several times, staying briefly with various friends, then moving to avoid any general knowledge of his whereabouts. He sometimes used a fictitious name, one in particular that he had once used in Liège in his early writings: Robert Marin (meaning sailor). Perhaps he retook that name because he was once again on the move.

As a further precaution, Cécile Denoël placed her apartment in the name of Maurice Bruyneel, a mutual friend and Denoël's business associate. She and Robert Jr. then moved into the home of Bruyneel's father, Gustave Bruyneel, at 5, rue Pigalle. Her relationship with her husband remained cordial, with the latter often visiting the Bruyneel household and eating lunch there. Jeanne Loviton was also careful. She rented in her name a small bachelor's quarters for Robert at 39, boulevard des Capucines. Denoël finally settled there, telling very few people of his new address.

Denoël also hid his business records with various friends. Just as he had feared, a purge committee for publishers was soon set in place to ferret out any collaboration. The Purge Committee for Publishing suspended him in the fall, banning him from publishing at Les Editions Denoël until his actions during the war were fully investigated. On 20 October 1944 one of Loviton's good friends, Samuel Monod, also called Maximilien Vox, was appointed to take Denoël's place as provisional director of Les Editions Denoël. Monod and Denoël had known each other for some fifteen years. Undoubtedly, Robert believed that having a friend take over his position at Les Editions Denoël would be beneficial for him. In spite of the official decree, which supposedly prevented Denoël from entering his own publishing house, Monod allowed him to retain his keys. Robert often went to his publishing house after hours. He sneaked in and was kept abreast of events by his longtime accountant, Auguste Picq; his new literary director, Guy Tosi; writer and longtime employee René Barjavel; and other loyal employees. Robert then gave his employees his advice and instructions. So clandestinely, Robert Denoël still ran his own company. However, he did not receive his own salary anymore. Monod received Denoël's pay (fifteen thousand francs [over $7,500] per month plus travel and other expenses), a very large salary for those times.

With the help of his mistress, Jeanne Loviton, Robert Denoël created a secret financial and publishing labyrinth. He conducted his clandestine businesses from the offices of his mistress's publishing house. He also began to prepare his court defense in August 1944, having already decided exactly what that defense should be. In short: "Everyone collaborated. Every publisher collaborated in much the same way that I did." But he would also point out that his collaboration was not voluntary. He had done what the Germans demanded in order to keep his business open—just like every other French publisher whose company remained open during the Occupation. There was no choice but to cooperate. In fact, according to Denoël, not having all of French publishing run by the Nazis was far better than total Nazi control. French publishers simply had to publish a few books that the Germans wanted published. By publishing some pro-German books along with other great French works, these publishers had preserved all of French publishing. They had prevented it from becoming a Nazi business with all Nazi publications.

It was a good argument. Now all that Robert had to do was to prove that all of the other French publishers had collaborated, too. As he told one of his writers, René Barjavel, "If I am going to take it in the neck, at least I won't be the only one." Jeanne and Robert then set out to prove this thesis. To accomplish that feat, Robert decided to compile a dossier, based upon the enormous *Bibliographie de France*, which listed everything that had been published and by whom in France during the Occupation. After extensive research he discovered that he could prove that all major publishing houses, with only one possible exception, had cooperated with the Germans by (among other things) publishing pro-German or pro-Vichy books. In the case of French publishing, that tired and tawdry phrase "Everybody collaborated" was true. Faced with closure or cooperation, French publishers had chosen cooperation, i.e., collaboration.

Denoël was particularly criticized for having published Hitler's speeches. Yet the zebra had also published works by Franklin D. Roosevelt. He defended himself for having published both men by saying that both works served to illuminate history. In the course of his research, he also discovered that the publishing establishments of Fayard and Grasset had also published Hitler. In fact, Gallimard, Emile-Paul, Albin Michel, Stock, and others had all published either Fascist, anti-English, pro-German, pro-Vichy, anti-democratic, and anti-Semitic books or works that could be deemed collaborationist. Robert Denoël could implicate them all.

And working side by side with Denoël in all of this research was Jeanne Loviton, his faithful mistress—faithful if you discounted Paul Valéry. They spent months working together, pouring over documents relating to other Parisian publishers. Soon they had amassed a pile of deeply incriminating evidence—books, advertisements, documents, and statements made by publishers promoting collaboration.

While implicating other Parisian publishers might be a logical way of defending Les Editions Denoël, it hardly endeared him to French publishers. There is ample evidence that nearly all Parisian publishers were worried about saving their own skins. They did not need one of their own helping the Purge Committee to find evidence against them. And punishments were severe. The Purge Committee had seen to that. Conviction of a French publisher on charges of collaboration generally included one or more of the following: reprimands, sanctions, fines, the banning of the publisher's imprint on the books he published, total seizure of his business and assets, total liquidation of the firm, banning the publisher from publishing for a certain period or for life, imprisonment, or possibly even death. The cry of those who wanted every collaborator punished was, after all, "A dozen bullets in his hide." It was clear to everyone that the Purge Committee meant business.

In the midst of the preparation of that massive defense dossier, and the secret channeling of funds and writers into dummy companies, Robert Denoël asked Jeanne Loviton to marry him. It was not his official proposal, of course. He was not yet divorced. It happened in the course of a long working night pouring over that giant French bibliography in Jeanne's study. She had just discovered another collaborationist book, this time published by Gaston Gallimard. Excited, she carried the book over to Robert, who was reading in a chair. Proudly, she showed him the offending Gallimard book. But at that moment, he was more interested in her than in Gaston Gallimard's misdeeds. He asked her quite simply. And just as simply, she said yes. He reached into his pocket and took out a small box. "Open it," he said. Inside was a necklace, a large single blue star sapphire surrounded by diamonds. It was exquisite. "Here, let me put it on," he said. She turned her back to him while he closed the clasp and gently kissed the nape of her neck.

"Robert, it's wonderful. That star shines so beautifully. And it changes with the light, doesn't it? I love it," she said and kissed him. Then smiling, busy, triumphant, both returned to their work. But always after that evening Robert referred to Jeanne as his fiancée.

Robert was also making significant progress with his wife regarding their future divorce. He made it clear to her that he did not believe they made a good couple anymore. One of Robert's complaints about Cécile (in addition to her many infidelities with men in Robert's employ) was that while she enjoyed her position as the wife of an important Parisian publisher, she did nothing at all to aid or morally support him. This failure was underlined in view of the immense work and support that Jeanne was providing. He thought of his wonderful mistress and all of the invaluable help she had given him. She recommended lawyers, both for his court disputes and for his divorce as well. She provided able legal advice and helped him establish his fictitious companies. She let him use her own publishing house for his business. She assisted him in preparing his defense. She used her connections to get someone they both knew and could deal with to run Les Editions Denoël in his absence. She gave him her moral support. Cécile had never done any of those things. How lucky he was to have found Jeanne! And she had agreed to become his wife—after his divorce, of course.

Even after Robert had proposed, Jeanne still waited for the right moment to inform Paul Valéry that she planned to marry another man. It would not be easy to admit the truth to her old poet. Paul Valéry was, if anything, even more in love with Jeanne than ever. And certainly he needed her. As for Robert, she still believed that he certainly did not need to know the true nature of her relationship with the Official Poet of France. Robert knew that they were good friends. That was enough.

Paul Valéry's 1944 letters and poems to his Héra reveal a man tortured by love, aloneness, fear, and sorrow. He described his love for Jeanne as an unquenchable, even physical thirst. He wrote of his constant thoughts of her, "In your absence, your memory is king." The days without her were horrible to him. In one poem he is waiting for her to telephone him. The phone rings. He runs to it. "Hello . . . No, sir. Ha . . . I thought!" It is not Jeanne. More and more, it is not Jeanne who phones or writes or visits him. He sits upon days that have become "ruins" to him, as will be the ruin of tomorrow without Jeanne.

When their rendezvous became less frequent, Paul complained bitterly. "It is a sin, a crime of a lifetime, I feel it every day a little more, that we can only be together so rarely. We are very rich, you and I, and yet we live as paupers."

When they were together, he was profoundly happy. He did not complain then about the increasing lengths of their separations, but instead praised her, reveled in his love for her, and delighted in her presence. The war, his work, his ill health all vanished at the thought of her. In one letter to her he wrote, "When the body betrays you, when the epoch is frightful, when an entire life's very laborious work does not even assure you a tomorrow, or if it is going to exist—then destiny all naked presents itself as it is—and I close my eyes and see you."

After her visits, he wrote poetry to her describing his joy at seeing her again and describing her in sublime adjectives. If she hinted that there might be someone else, he did not receive the message. If she told him about her love affair with Robert Denoël, he did not hear her. For Valéry, Jeanne was his and his alone, in a place "where no lies are told" and love is absolute and confirming. In fact, at about that same time he wrote, "I believe that I am able to understand, as no one else can, the extraordinary role that **absolute love** can play in the creations of mind and spirit."

Nearing the end of his life, Paul Valéry decided that there were really only two reasons for living: love and work. Robert Denoël might well have agreed with him. Both men were consumed by love and work in 1944. But what neither man realized at the time was that for both of them their all-important love was for the same woman: Jeanne Loviton.

11

Love Lost

My darling, it's my fault.
Jeanne Loviton

January 1945: France had been liberated, but the war in other parts of Europe raged on. Although Céline had left France in July 1944, he could not manage to escape that war. In fact, his voyage led him right back into the middle of it. He traveled for months, but the war kept thwarting his efforts to reach a safe haven. He proceeded through Germany's bombed-out cities, turmoil, attacks, and confusion, making very slow progress. At all times he had to have the right papers (even his cat, Bébert, had a special passport) and additional German bureaucratic permissions to go anywhere in this tumultuous time. Sometimes the war demanded a detour; sometimes the train tracks no longer existed; sometimes even the train stations and towns had vanished in this bullet-ridden landscape. His descriptions of his voyage across war-torn Germany seemed apocalyptic.

For example, Céline waited for a train in Germany, which was one week late. He tried to get tickets but was told there were no tickets anymore; passengers just got in; they paid later. Then to his joy, he saw the train, "all wood . . . five six cars . . . bristling with all the stuff that's sticking out the windows . . . caterpillars bristle

like that . . . now you can see what's sticking out . . . a hundred
arms, a hundred legs . . . and heads! . . . and guns! . . . I've seen
jampacked Metro trains, cars so full you couldn't get a finger in, but
that train was so crammed, so bristling with legs, arms, and heads
you couldn't help laughing . . ." Then Céline took a closer look at
some of the crowded passengers: "I've said it was full . . . not just
arms and legs . . . heads, I told you that too . . . another . . . another . . . looks like they were asleep . . . one with its eyes wide-open
staring . . . this train must have been riddled from the air, I
guess . . ." The train was so crowded and cramped nothing could
move; the corpses could not be disentangled from the wounded and
living. Céline got on that train. How he managed to find room forms
only a tiny part of his saga.

On another trip Céline's always jam-packed train is trapped in a
tunnel while airplanes bomb from above: ". . . nothing compared to
this tunnel all full of brats and Baltavians and suffocation . . . and
total darkness, had you thought of that? from the entrance, I'm not
exaggerating, all the way to the other end, the exit, tremendous hur-
ricane blasts that made the rock up above us throb . . . a typhoon in
the tunnel . . . I could see this was going to end in a smash . . ."
The train seems human as Céline describes it, groaning, convulsing.
Then ". . . ah something new! . . . down at the end I see a river of
flame. . . . I know what that is . . . yellow! . . . phosphorus . . ."
Céline, the soldier, had described the horrors of World War I. Now
Céline, the civilian, painted the nightmare of ordinary people caught
in the embers of World War II.

Slowly, painstakingly, Céline proceeded through Germany by way
of Baden-Baden, Berlin, and Kränzlin to the most unusual and bizarre exile of all: Sigmaringen. This ancient town, with its enormous
Hohenzollern castle overlooking the Danube, had become the location, designated by Hitler, of France's exiled collaborationist government. These former Vichy French officials, still unwilling to
recognize their defeat, preferred to call themselves the French Governmental Commission for the Defense of National Interests. Technically, the Vichy commission was headed by Marshal Pétain himself,

but the old head of state never recognized its existence. The Germans brought him to Sigmaringen against his will. Although his accommodations were quite luxurious, occupying the entire top floor of the castle, he was held in Sigmaringen as a virtual prisoner. For Pétain the game (or even the double game) was over. He would no longer cooperate with his German "hosts" or participate in the works of a phony French Governmental Commission, preferring to sleep and dream within the elegant confines of his castle.

In addition to housing government officials who had collaborated with Germany during the war, this location also became the place of exile for many others who, for one reason or another, might be imprisoned or executed for collaboration by liberated France. Céline certainly met the qualifications for membership in this community. On 4 September 1944 the National Writers' Committee had placed his name, as one of twelve writers, on their blacklist. And publishers, journalists, and writers were already facing imprisonment and possible execution by hastily established tribunals. Céline was not the only writer in the Denoël stable to find himself in Sigmaringen. Lucien Rebatet was there, too.

Céline was welcomed to Sigmaringen primarily because he was a doctor. This town of French exiles badly needed more medical aid. Throughout his literary career Céline continued to practice medicine, most often treating the poor. Although he loudly and constantly demanded money from his publisher, it seems that this same man seldom even presented a bill to his patients, often willingly treating them without any thought of recompense. He seemed to be most thoughtful and considerate to the elderly, the seriously infirm, the alcoholic—those who could least afford to pay him. Like his publisher, Céline was a man of contradiction.

Along with his wife, Lucette, his friend, the actor Robert Le Vigan, and his big cat, Bébert, whom he carried in a game pouch slung around his neck, Céline left for Sigmaringen in the fall of 1944. Rebatet described Céline's arrival: "He wore a bluish canvas cap, like a locomotive engineer's circa 1905, two or three of his lumber jackets overlapping, filthy and ragged, a pair of moth-eaten mittens hanging from his neck, and under the mittens, in a haversack on his belly, Bébert the cat, presenting the phlegmatic face of a native Parisian who's seen it all before." Those who watched his entrance into this town were aghast. Surely this disreputable-looking man in filthy, tattered clothes could not be that famous French writer, Céline. Rebatet concludes, "I was speechless myself."

Céline immortalized Sigmaringen in his book *Castle to Castle (D'un château l'autre)*, the first part of his haunting trilogy recounting his travels and exile from 1944 to 1945. *North (Nord)* and *Rigadoon* would complete his description of the death throes of Germany and his own exile. Many scholars believe these three books to be among Céline's best, combining his unique, halting, hallucinatory style with the last gasping struggles of a Europe at war. This time the style and subject matter fused to form a dark, disturbing masterpiece. Sigmaringen, particularly the enormous castle itself, with secret passageways, strange winding hallways, and endless rooms, provided the perfect setting for the plots and ruminations of the once powerful and now lost. Céline said of the castle, "I knew the place well . . . the corridors and the hangings, the real doors and false doors . . . the corkscrew stairways, cutting across wainscoting and beams . . . enough dark corners to be knifed in a thousand times over . . . and be left there to dry for centuries . . . the Hohenzollerns didn't deprive themselves . . . experts in traps and tipping corridors . . . and down into the void . . . plunging into the Danube!" He would remain at Sigmaringen until 24 March 1945.

The Paris press continued to castigate Céline, his publisher, and all those who had once collaborated with the Germans. As Céline put it, "the hunt for collaborators . . . the total house-cleaning frenzy was at its height . . . the Circus of Europe." The press, the radio, even the government encouraged denunciations. Céline concluded, "I'm lucky if they don't chop me into little pieces! 'Stinker! Stalinist! . . . Nazi . . . pornographer! . . . charlatan! . . . menace! . . . ' and these kind words aren't whispered! . . . they're written in black and white!"

Those who desired the purge to be a "total house-cleaning," as Céline put it, were in charge. And they wanted vengeance on all those who had cooperated in any way with the Germans. Céline noted that "people made careers for themselves in the Purge, burying collaborators . . . people who were pure shit got to be great big avengers . . . big shots . . . with enormous privileges!" He concluded that "the collaborators' worst bad luck was having been such a windfall for the rottenest horde of stinking, good-for-nothings." Even stuck as he was in Sigmaringen, Céline was glad, grateful to be out of France. But in spite of his absence, his denunciation in France continued.

Then came the morning of 6 February 1945. Only a few hours before Robert Denoël would slowly, deliberately climb the steps of the Court of Justice in Paris, the writer Robert Brasillach was tied to a post at Fresnes prison. Twelve soldiers carefully took aim as Brasillach's horrified lawyer, Jacques Isorni, who would soon defend Pétain, stood by. Now there was nothing more that Isorni could do but silently bear witness as his client was ripped apart by bullets. French soldiers had not executed an assassin or a military traitor; they had killed a poet. He was a writer and editor of a newspaper. His crime? He was shot not for his actions, but rather for his ideas. He had supported Fascism as a way to overcome France's decadence. He considered himself a patriot. Much of what he wrote about, Céline, too, had written. As Denoël later climbed those long stairs to his own inevitable indictment, he stopped for a moment. An almost unspeakable sadness overwhelmed him. He winced. He could not have known that at that very same moment Brasillach's body entered the ground. Les Editions Plon had lost a writer.

On 19 February 1945 Robert Denoël was personally indicted "for infraction of Articles 75." Articles 75 listed crimes against the state and various punishments for those crimes, including death. Acts that might adversely affect "the security of the State" were placed under these articles. Céline explained Articles 75 more colorfully: "All they want is to put Article 75 on your ass, the master permit to skin you alive, to steal everything you've got and sell you for stew meat."

Unfortunately, one of those responsible for judging the case of Robert Denoël would have personally enjoyed skinning this publisher alive. His name was Raymond Durand-Auzias, and he was also a French publisher. Durand-Auzias hated the handsome Belgian who had once stolen one of his best writers away from him. He hated his attitude, his self-assurance—his success. "Devious, underhanded crook," Durand-Auzias muttered to himself as he looked at the charges against Denoël. Now Durand-Auzias could pay him back for that author theft, for now it was Durand-Auzias who was in charge. He had been named president of the Consulting Commission for the Purge of Publishing. No, there would be no leniency toward this Belgian publisher. Durand-Auzias sent to the National Purge Commission a list of compromising books that Denoël had published during the Occupation. And included with that list was his personal recommendation. According to Durand-Auzias, Robert Denoël merited a "definitive exclusion from the profession."

Noted scholars of French publishing have recently uncovered facts proving that Raymond Durand-Auzias was hardly without sin himself when it came to collaboration. Like nearly all other publishers, he had cooperated with his German occupiers and published works pleasing to the Nazis. But now he was on the other side, ferreting out publishing collaborators—and he did his job with great zeal, possibly enjoyment. Now he could dispense with some of his competitors and enemies alike.

One evening toward the end of February, Robert went to Les Editions Denoël, as he often did, to give instructions to his employees. But this particular evening Denoël's supposed replacement, the titular head of Les Editions Denoël, was there: Samuel Monod. The two men smiled and greeted each other. Then Monod invited Robert into his office (Robert's former office). "Sit down, Robert," Samuel said. "You look tired."

Robert sat down, not at his former desk, but in a comfortable chair reserved for visitors. Samuel sat behind the desk. "I am tired," Robert confessed.

"Can I get you anything?" Monod asked. "I have some rum, some wine . . ."

"No thanks. I don't think a drink would help me right now."

"Can I help you, Robert?"

"You know, it's a strange world we live in, Samuel." Robert slumped in his chair. "When the Germans took over, they tried to arrest me . . . said I published forty-one books contrary to the Nazi cause. They took one-third of my company as punishment."

"I didn't know that, Robert. Cigarette?"

Robert took the cigarette Monod offered him, lit it, and smoked, saying nothing. He tapped his ashes into the ashtray on the desk, a gift he had once received from a writer. Then he continued. "Now the reverse is true. I am indicted for having published books the Nazis liked. There's no winning, Sam."

Monod sighed deeply. "I hear that Durand-Auzias is out to get you."

"That old fraud," said Robert. "He has always been out to get me. But now I guess he just might. I'm not sure what to do, Sam." He inhaled deeply, holding the smoke in his lungs. Then slowly he exhaled and added, "They are also investigating me for that damned Andermann loan again. It doesn't make any difference that I have already paid a hefty fine for that transaction . . . already paid one half of the loan back, too."

"You don't mind if I make myself a drink, do you?" Sam asked.

"No, no," Denoël said. "Please do." Sam took out a bottle from his desk and poured himself a short drink.

Both men were silent for a few moments, then Robert continued, "You know, Sam, I think these French need scapegoats and avengers. And it doesn't really matter anymore who plays either part—who is right or wrong. And old Durand-Auzias drew the avenger part, and I got stuck with the goat."

"Have you hidden your assets?"

"As best as I can. But then there is this building—this entire publishing house—Les Editions Denoël. God, I don't want to lose all of it. I don't want to lose any of it. I've worked too hard just to hand it over. And I could, Sam. I could lose the whole thing."

Sam played with the pens on his desk, sipped his drink, then said, "Could you possibly put this place in someone else's name? Supposedly cede it to someone else . . . someone like Jeanne Loviton, for example? Then the company could be yours in every respect but legal title."

Robert thought for a moment, then said, "You know, Sam, that's not such a bad idea. I could run it entirely, behind the scenes, but have it in her name. Then no one could take it from me, not even the courts. And I don't think Jeanne would mind," said Robert.

And Jeanne didn't mind. In fact, she thought it was a terrific idea. She suggested they take their proposal to a lawyer, a man named Jean Streichenberger. This lawyer informed them that the scheme would not work, at least not at the moment, because technically Robert Denoël was not the legal owner of Les Editions Denoël. Legally, it was presently part of the state, and run by Monod. Jean and Robert sadly left their lawyer. But both remembered the idea that Monod had first presented. Perhaps Robert would be able to cede his company to Jeanne at some time in the future.

"Care to join me for dinner tonight?" Robert asked his fiancée. "I could use the company."

"Robert, I would love to, but I can't tonight. I have some errands to run, and I promised to visit Marion tonight. She has been so lonely lately. I am afraid she is drinking too much."

Robert understood.

But Jeanne had no intention of seeing Marion Delbo that evening. She planned instead to pay a visit to her poet. As she became more engrossed with the legal and romantic demands of Robert Denoël, Paul Valéry became more desperately in need of her. She had set several dates with her poet only to break them. She was determined to see him tonight.

Their meeting was to be at the home of a mutual friend who was conveniently out of town on business. As usual, Paul arrived early, and Jeanne was late. As she rushed up the walk, she could see Paul pacing back and forth in front of the window, his face deeply furrowed with worry. Almost immediately following her knock, Paul thrust the door open and, delighted, grabbed her and held her close to him, his large wrinkled hands encircling her waist. "I was afraid something had happened, that you weren't coming," he said as he held her tightly. She kissed him lightly on the cheek, then warmly embraced him. His joy at seeing his Héra was so complete, so profound, it was contagious. She was glad to be with him, to sit quietly and talk and laugh and, for the moment at least, not to worry about courts, indictments, and legal maneuvers. As Valéry once said, they were really "WE together," that night, alone and at peace.

When she wasn't there, he wrote to her, wrote poems about her, included her in his literary creations, drew pictures, symbols, of her. I examined his sketches. In one detailed drawing, he depicted her as an entrancing mermaid, and he was the enchanted sailor leaving his boat and plunging into the sea to seek her. I read his poetry to her. Obviously written in the spring of 1945, one poem eloquently describes a day that is too long, because he is without her; his spirit, which is exhausted because she is not there; and death, his own death, which creeps into him, taking hold of him. He even claims that it is Jeanne Loviton who stands between death and him. Yes, for Valéry only the love of Jeanne Loviton saves him from death. Ominously, he also warns, "That I could die by the one I so love."

Whether Paul Valéry knew there was another man in his lover's life or not, he was not making it easy for Jeanne Loviton to leave him. And she didn't—at least not then. She continued to see her poet, to show him the love and devotion he so ardently sought and needed from her. And he continued to praise her, love her, and give her original poems and first manuscripts.

Yet she was unofficially engaged to be married. She was deeply involved in Robert's legal defense. And worse, she had not told Robert about her true relationship with Paul Valéry. "You will have the best defense possible, Robert," she assured him. "For now, we must concentrate all our attentions on that." And he agreed. They continued to work together. And more and more, Robert listened to the counsel of his mistress and selected the lawyers she recommended.

By spring 1945 it was clear to Jeanne that she had to tell Paul Valéry about her new lover. Denoël's trial was set for July. She had been working with him day and night. More important, others, even some who knew Valéry, were becoming aware of her affair with Robert. She did not want someone else to inform Valéry of her relationship. In addition, the coming trial was certain to be covered by the newspapers. Her name could easily be linked with that of Robert Denoël in some of these journalistic accounts. It was time to tell Paul.

Many Valéry scholars have simply ignored Jeanne Loviton. To this day her name is anathema to the Valéry family. In fact, some Valéry descendants have warned scholars that they could be denied access to the huge and very private Jacques Doucet Library in Paris, with its enormous Valéry holdings, its so-called Valéryanum, if they dare to explore the romantic life of Paul Valéry in his later years. And the Valéry family is still powerful enough to carry out its threats. After all, Valéry had a devoted wife and family during all the time that he was courting Jeanne. And many scholars, finding Valéry's poetry much more interesting than his love life and having no desire to be cut off from primary sources, have acquiesced to the demands of the Valéry family. Those few who have mentioned Jeanne Loviton have done so briefly and often with considerable contradictions. Although the definitive biography of Paul Valéry has yet to be written, two able biographers have briefly described the fateful day when Jeanne Loviton informed Paul Valéry that she was in love with another man. Benoît Peeters simply states, "it was not until April 1945 that he [Valéry] would describe in his *Notebooks* the ending of that relationship." Another biographer, Denis Bertholet, describes a series of incremental losses for Valéry regarding Jeanne Loviton. Speaking of the Valéry/Loviton breakup, Bertholet states, "The months of April and May were nothing but a succession of blows for him, each one more severe than the previous, painful moments of a breaking-off whose merciless progression he endured, immobile and despairing." Then came the coup de grâce. According to Bertholet, Jeanne Loviton told Paul Valéry on 22 May 1945 that she was living with another man.

Tenter. Tenter is a French verb whose first meaning is "to try or attempt." Its second meaning is "to tempt." Paul Valéry was fond of the verb *tenter*. He had used it in one of his most famous poems, "The Cemetery by the Sea" *("Le Cimetière marin")*, which he had written as a young man. In the first line of the last stanza he said, "The wind is rising! . . . We must try to live!" *("Le vent se lève! . . . Il faut tenter de vivre!")* Was it simply an accident that in one of his last letters to Jeanne Loviton this man of words, so fond of le mot juste, would return to the verb *tenter*, this time using its second meaning? "The window tempts me; have pity on me in distress" *("La fenêtre me tente; aie pitié de moi en détresse")*.

After that final blow delivered by Jeanne Loviton on 22 May, Paul Valéry did not leave his residence again. On 30 May he wrote, "I have the feeling that my life is finished—which means that I can no longer see anything at present which demands a tomorrow. What remains for me from now on is simply wasted time." He revised some of his earlier thoughts to Jeanne. Now, for example, he said, "You well know that you stood between death and me. But alas, it seems that I stood between life and you."

Without his muse, his precious Héra, he simply gave up. He took to his bed on 31 May 1945. He did not even try to get up. He was attended by his family and by doctors, particularly Dr. René Gutmann. His friends often visited him. Then on 20 July 1945, Jeanne received her last letter from Paul Valéry: "Dear friend, I am trying to write you. I would like to do better than this scribbling. I have never suffered like this. I am broken. This morning Gide gently came by to see me . . . These lines are the first that I have written for ten days. They are for you, of course . . ." The same day that Jeanne Loviton received this last letter, Paul Valéry died. He was seventy-three.

Dr. Gutmann later described Valéry's death in *The New Medical Press (La Nouvelle Presse médicale)*: "I would like to finish by recounting an episode which at the time greatly moved me; but I ask that you believe that this is not a rigged account, embellished by some sort of romanticism. That fatal morning of 20 July, there was a great storm in Paris. At the same moment, 9:15, when in the arms of his wife Valéry breathed his last, the window of the room opened with a great rush, the curtains whirled, the nurse ran to close the window, and I had the overwhelming and immediate sensation that this powerful spirit had just flown into the tempest."

Following the horrors of the Occupation and the Liberation purges, France badly needed a hero. Charles de Gaulle decided to give Paul Valéry a hero's burial, a national funeral no one would soon forget. Valéry's enormous memorial service took place on 24 July, just one day after the start of the trial of Pétain at the High Court in Paris. That evening his coffin was carried through Paris to the sound of muted drums, escorted by the Republican Guards. After the coffin was placed on the catafalque, draped in French colors, at the palace of Chaillot, the entire city was plunged into total darkness. Only the lights of the faraway Pantheon remained illuminated. Then two giant searchlights placed in front of the Eiffel Tower joined to form an enormous V in the sky, as tall as the tower itself. Parisians silently filed past Valéry's bier all night . . . and all of the following morning. It seems that everyone filed past his coffin . . . except for the one person he most wanted there, Jeanne Loviton. She was at a small restaurant, dining with Robert, when all the lights went out. Quietly they both moved to the window, along with others in the room. And there, they saw the giant V in the sky. Robert stood behind her and placed his hands around her waist. "My darling, it's my fault," she whispered to the window.

"What?" he asked her.

"Nothing," she replied. "Let's go home."

"Are you sure you don't want to take any part in the funeral?" Robert asked. "After all, he was your dear friend."

"I told you before, Robert, I would prefer to remember him alive" was all that she replied.

Paul Valéry was buried in the family plot in that same cemetery by the sea that he had immortalized in his poetry. In spite of the great honors that Valéry was paid at the time of his death, he kept his own personal secret epitaph hidden in one of his private journals. There he stated, "I finish this life in vulgarity, a ridiculous victim in my own eyes, after having believed I would finish it in a twilight of love absolute and incorruptible and of spiritual power recognized by all as rigorously and justly acquired."

July 1945 proved to be a momentous month for Robert Denoël. In the first part of that month he went on trial for infraction of Articles 75, "collusion with the enemy." In addition to his defense that he had simply collaborated as all other French publishers had done, there were other specific charges he needed to counter. The court wanted to know why he had republished Céline's anti-Semitic literature during the Occupation. Denoël's response was that he reissued these works at the author's insistence. Since the author was now safely out of the country, Denoël decided to implicate Céline in this decision. "I had no right to refuse my author's demand," Robert said. He was further questioned about Céline's *A Fine Mess*. Robert argued that this work contained nothing new or different and was, in fact, banned by the Vichy government. He defended his publication of Hitler's speeches by citing their historical interest and by noting that he had published anti-Hitler, anti-Fascist works before the war. As for Lucien Rebatet's *The Rubble*, he claimed that this work was primarily a portrait of France's political parties. In addition, the Andermann loan had been dealt with before and was no longer pertinent.

Many witnesses came forward to defend this beleaguered publisher: members of the Resistance, Jews, and others whom Robert had hidden (often in his own home) and protected. Elsa Triolet and Louis Aragon also defended Denoël. "Now it's our turn to help you," said Elsa. In addition to hiding and aiding Triolet and Aragon during the war, Robert had also advanced them 374,000 francs, knowing full well that this money would probably be sent to the Resistance.

Finally, Robert asked the court to examine the books he had published during the Occupation. He argued that while he had published some pro-Nazi and anti-Semitic works during this period, he also continued to publish and sell a great many forbidden works, including Elsa Triolet, Sigmund Freud, Jean Malaquais, Louis Aragon, and Tristan Tzara. And sometimes he had published these works at great personal danger to himself.

With Jeanne Loviton helping him at every turn, Denoël convinced the court of his innocence. On 13 July Robert joyfully called his wife, Cécile, "We have won!" he announced. "Won on all counts." But his real gratitude was for his mistress. She had helped him select his lawyers, provided invaluable advice, and doggedly helped him to prepare his defense. They celebrated that evening at 11, rue de l'Assomption, Jeanne's home—outside in the secret garden that Paul Valéry had so loved. It was filled with blossoms now, fragrant in the night. Although they enjoyed their champagne and caviar, mostly they simply loved the moment, the fresh evening and the wonderful knowledge that Robert was finally free of his legal problems. Although Robert had kept his small bachelor's apartment, he really lived with Jeanne now at her home. They were happy living together and looked forward to a bright and wonderful future. They had no way of knowing that on that very same night some anonymous person in some anonymous abode was busy composing a letter that would lead directly to Robert's assassination less than five months from that starry warm night.

July 1945—the month marking Robert Denoël's acquittal, Paul Valéry's demise, and the beginning of Pétain's trial for treason—was also the month of absolute contradiction regarding France's treatment of Denoël. In the very same month that Denoël went on trial for personal collusion with the enemy, he won the only literary prize that still eluded him, that most coveted prize of all, the Goncourt, the prize that Céline should have won in 1932. Because of the war and the Liberation, this prize for 1944 had been delayed until July 1945. But it was announced with great fanfare. The winner of the Goncourt Prize for 1944 was Elsa Triolet, for her excellent book, *A Fine of 200 Francs*. It was the first time in French history that a woman had ever won the Goncourt. Robert Denoël was beside himself with joy.

As was true of Goncourt awards in previous years, and in the case of Céline, other considerations may have played a part in the selection of this deserving book. Awarding the Goncourt to Triolet just might have served to aid the cause of some of the right-wing, previously Fascist-leaning Goncourt jury members. As journalist Jean Galtier-Boissière wryly noted, "The Goncourt jury scored a triple coup: Madame Triolet is Russian, Jewish, and Communist." He had neglected to point out that she had also played a part in the Resistance. There was no other choice that could possibly have been more politically correct for the times—and for the members of the jury (The Ten) themselves. The irony was not lost on Triolet's publisher.

While Robert Denoël celebrated, that anonymous informant finished his letter, sealed it, walked to the post office, and mailed it. Informing had become an integral part of the Occupation. Unfortunately, it continued and was even encouraged after the Liberation. This anonymous letter accused Les Editions Denoël of collaborating with the Nazis. To his great astonishment and chagrin, Robert soon learned that his publishing house was scheduled to be formally charged in October for collaboration. Now his company would face the very same charges that Denoël had faced and won: infraction of Articles 75, collaboration with the enemy. His company would be scheduled for court in December.

"Someone certainly does not want me to publish, not now or ever!" Robert shouted to his accountant, Picq. Once again Robert had secretly entered Les Editions Denoël and had gone to Picq's office.

Picq, also stunned, replied, "Do you know who this informant could be?"

"I seem to have acquired a great many enemies these days," Robert said, scowling. "The publishing business itself seems to grow enemies . . . spontaneous generation! Boom, another enemy! A better question might be to decide who might most benefit from this attack."

"And who do you think that would that be?" asked Picq.

"I have narrowed it down to three names. First, although I thought he was my friend, Samuel Monod certainly would profit from this case. Then, he could continue to collect my salary at Les Editions Denoël—for doing absolutely nothing, I might add. Money has certainly corrupted before."

"You do have a point," said Picq.

"Second, dear old Durand-Auzias just might be behind all of this. Since he failed to get me in that first trial, he just may have decided to give it another go. It would be just like him to be an anonymous informant."

"Frankly, Durand-Auzias sounds more plausible to me," Picq responded.

"Third, my old buddy, old pal, Gaston Gallimard has always wanted to see me hang. I'm sure my winning the Goncourt was not something he ever wanted to see. And since I am probably his biggest rival, he might have written that letter just to get rid of me. I certainly wouldn't put it past him."

But speculating about the identity of this informer got Denoël nowhere. He was still forced to use his straw men to run his fictitious companies. He was the clandestine publisher . . . winner of the Goncourt. Monod remained at the helm of Les Editions Denoël, not making the publishing decisions but sitting in Denoël's office, at Denoël's desk, and still collecting Denoël's salary. Robert thought of that defense dossier that he and Jeanne had so carefully prepared. He would use part of that defense again. He would demonstrate once and for all that all publishing companies had collaborated with the Nazis. And just in case Gallimard had written that anonymous letter, he would use Les Editions Gallimard as his prime example. Now it was payback time in this ruthless game of publishing. Even if Gallimard didn't write that letter, in Robert's mind he deserved to be implicated.

"I am tired of being the scapegoat," Robert told Picq at another meeting. "If I go down, I promise you, I will not be alone."

And so Robert and Jeanne worked harder together developing a lengthy and detailed defense demonstrating that collaboration was the hallmark of French publishing during the Occupation and using Gaston Gallimard as their primary example. Gaston Gallimard was not unafraid at this time. Even without the possible presentation of Denoël's defense, he knew he could be in serious trouble. The Resistance press had accused him, too, seeking to blacklist him because of his cooperation with the Germans. He had gone along with the demands of the now-infamous Otto List. He had censored some of his own publications and published other pro-German and anti-Semitic works. Worse, he had permitted a pro-Nazi and anti-Semite, Drieu La Rochelle, to head the *New French Review* (*N.R.F.*). He had accepted invitations from Otto Abetz, and he had attended various receptions at the Deutsche Institut. While he could defend some of his pro-German publications during the Occupation (such as Goethe) on the grounds that he was publishing great German literature, he hardly needed someone informing the Purge Committee about all of his other collaborative publications, including such pseudo-scientific works as Herman Lommel's *The Ancient Aryans* (*Die alten Arier*). He didn't need anyone pointing out that he had also issued advertisements in his firm's name that promoted collaboration, as the Germans had requested. Furthermore, he did not need anyone to explain how closely allied the *N.R.F.* was with his publishing firm, that the *N.R.F.* was an important extension of Les Editions Gallimard. It was not long before Gaston Gallimard learned for himself exactly what Robert Denoël intended to do in that December trial. Robert made no secret of his intentions. Gaston Gallimard was in serious trouble.

On the stand, Pierre Drieu La Rochelle could have destroyed Gallimard. But this Fascist was no longer a problem. In March 1945 Drieu La Rochelle, who had been in hiding in Paris since the Liberation, committed suicide by using gas and drugs. It was his third attempt. Both Jean Paulhan and Gaston Gallimard, along with many other notables, attended his funeral. In a letter to Drieu's first wife, Jean Paulhan suggested that this suicide may have been a sacrifice that Drieu had made so that others would not be dragged into this trial or otherwise troubled by their association with him. Although Paulhan did not say it, the person who stood to gain the most by this "sacrifice" was Gaston Gallimard. Had Drieu and Gallimard discussed this? Whatever the case, there is no doubt that with Drieu La Rochelle gone, Gaston Gallimard could breathe more easily . . . until Robert Denoël decided to implicate him.

The only thing that seemed to be proceeding as Robert had planned was his divorce. Going along with her husband's wishes, Cécile had initiated proceedings for an amicable divorce in June 1945. She was in no rush to accomplish this legal action, hoping that if she drew things out, the situation might become different—her husband might change his mind. But she was cooperating, taking her time to fill out papers and see her lawyer. At least the process was moving.

Robert was determined to regain control of his entire publishing establishment. Since he had now been cleared of all personal charges of collusion with the enemy, his legal situation changed. He could now legally sell Les Editions Denoël. Of course, he didn't want to sell it. But the suggestion that Monod had made to him months ago, that he cede his company to someone else in case he lost his trial, still lingered in his mind. On 25 October 1945 Robert had a legal document drawn up that would do just that. But there was a catch. This document was deliberately left unfinished. Not all of the spaces were filled in. Most important, the space designated for the name of the person receiving the company was left blank. In addition, the document was not dated. And, of course, no actual money changed hands. However, Robert Denoël did sign this incomplete document. He believed that if he lost his December trial, he could quickly fill in the necessary blanks and date the document before the final trial decree, thereby turning his company over to someone else, probably to Jeanne Loviton. Then he could still, in effect, have his company and run it covertly.

November 1945, one month before his trial (so Robert thought), but in reality one month before his murder, was quite busy for this publisher. In addition to his covert publishing duties, he was still occupied with his defense and with various maneuvers that would enable him to take over his own business as quickly as possible if the case was decided in his favor. In all of this work, Jeanne Loviton had been at his side, tirelessly working on his behalf. Then something happened.

Someone told Robert Denoël the truth about Jeanne Loviton and Paul Valéry. I know that this event happened around the middle of November 1945. I know that Robert was acquainted with several people who knew the exact nature of the Valéry/Loviton relationship. I realized that several journalists whom Robert might have encountered also knew the truth. But after having spent weeks, then months in research, I was unable to determine who that person was. Research, no matter how diligent, cannot always find everything.

I was able, however, to watch Robert's reaction. He became much like he was that night when he sat silently in the back of the Folies-Wagram theater so many years ago and watched Antonin Artaud carry on with his wife. He grew cold, silent, reserved. Robert was not like Cécile, who threw tantrums, screamed, and cried at bad news. He seemed to keep everything in. In fact, there was not even a huge scene with his fiancée. Jeanne knew that something was wrong. She made several attempts to talk about it, but he brushed her off.

Finally, one morning as Robert was preparing to go to work, she said, "Robert, something is bothering you. I want to know what it is. Have I done something to offend you?"

Robert, stuffing papers into his briefcase, did not bother to look up.

"Please answer me," she said.

He closed the briefcase, picked it up, and headed toward the door. "Let's just say I have learned a few things about you and your 'dear friend' Paul Valéry."

He gave her no chance to respond. He shut the door behind him.

Very late that evening he returned to 11, rue de l'Assomption. Jeanne was waiting up for him. "Robert," she said as soon as he entered the door, "I don't know what you heard, but Paul Valéry and I were only good friends, nothing more. There was never any romance between us. You have to believe me!"

Again Robert said nothing.

The following morning Robert found Jeanne drinking tea in the kitchen. She was wearing the same clothes she had worn the night before. Her eyes were red. Robert looked briefly at her, then said, "Look, we both need more time to sort things out. My entire career goes on trial in less than three weeks. Let's put this matter aside until after the trial. Until then, let's go on as if nothing has happened. Then after the trial, when things have calmed down, we can discuss things sensibly."

"Robert, I was not ever romantically involved with Paul Valéry," she insisted.

"We can talk about that later," he said. Then he bent over and kissed her on the cheek. "Right now, we have a big trial ahead of us."

It was over. Both of them knew it, although neither acknowledged it to the other at the time. Outwardly, they acted as if nothing had happened. But both of their goals and actions changed. A few days later Robert called his wife. He told her she didn't need to pursue that divorce proceeding if she did not want to. He explained that his situation had changed. A chambermaid overheard Cécile's part of that conversation. Apparently Cécile was not the only one to whom Robert confided his change of heart. He also told his old friend, Catherine Mengelle, that things had changed. She later testified, "When I asked him how his divorce was coming along, he answered me with an evasive air, saying that after all there was no need to hurry."

The telephone rang at 11, rue de l'Assomption. Jeanne answered. There was a long discussion. Then Jeanne went out to meet someone. After the meeting she did something quite unusual. On 21 November she went to a doctor who was a good friend of hers and obtained a medical certificate that allowed her priority in getting a taxi. Because there were still few private automobiles in Paris, and very few taxis, those with serious maladies could go to the nearest police station or post, present this medical certificate, and call a cab. That person with the medical certificate would then get the very next available taxi. But why would Jeanne want this medical certificate? In the first place, she had no malady or disability to warrant such a certificate. In the second place, she never took taxis. She had her own automobile, a wonderful automobile, the Peugeot 302. In addition to the car, she had a capable chauffeur. She could go anywhere she wanted, at anytime, and even be driven there. Yet she would use this medical certificate to call a cab for the first and only time eleven days later.

Part 2

How to Steal a

Publishing House—

With Murder on the Side

12

2 December 1945

My darling, it's my fault.
Jeanne Loviton (again)

I had reached the last full month in the life of Robert Denoël. If he had further premonitions, he was ignoring them. Clearly, he had every expectation of resuming complete control of his publishing business. He took steps to assure the smooth transition of power, read manuscripts, and contacted his authors. He polished his own court defense, which now included a huge pile of damning evidence against other publishers, particularly Gaston Gallimard. In addition, he converted some of his assets into pure gold. In November he showed several of his friends his small suitcase filled to the top with gold. They would later testify to that fact, adding that he asked some of his friends where he might obtain even more. The gold could serve to pay for his defense—either legally or, if necessary, under the table. There were many times during the Occupation when Robert had been required to resort to *le système D*. That *D* referred to the French verb *se débrouiller*, which means "getting out of a problem by any means possible."

Le système D became an accepted way of life during the Occupation. For example, if the store had no vegetables, you got them on the black market or covertly from a farmer—and if you had no money, you traded something, used barter. That was how *le système D* worked for meat, produce, clothing, tools, problems, almost anything, even that most desired object for publishers, paper. Unfortunately, in the purges of the Liberation, *le système D* still applied.

Robert wanted to win his battle in court and legally assume his rightful place as head of his publishing firm. However, grim reality and experience had taught him that the courts could do anything. He could lose his case or be required to deal with legal matters and lawsuits well into the future. He was willing to resort to other, less legal ways to solve his problems. Selecting someone in every profession to pay for the sins of collaboration seems to have been the custom of the times. It was a better solution than dragging one-quarter of the French population (a rough estimate of those who had collaborated) into court on charges of some sort of collusion with the enemy.

The results were often ironic. I already knew that Paul Valéry held many anti-Semitic views, had allowed himself to be entertained by his German occupiers, and had made anti-Semitic statements. Furthermore, he had illustrated Jeanne Loviton's deeply collaborationist book, *The Open City*. Yet he died a hero and was given an extravagant state funeral. As for Robert Denoël, he did not help his own cause, either. He refused to keep his opinions and intentions to himself. It was well known, for example, that the French Communist Maurice Thorez deserted the French army in the fall of 1939. Yet he returned to France from Moscow in 1945 and became a minister in de Gaulle's government. Why was his desertion overlooked? Because Charles de Gaulle wanted him in his government. Commenting ironically upon Thorez, Denoël stated publicly, "General de Gaulle did not pardon me, but instead he pardoned M. Maurice Thorez for his desertion." His words hardly endeared him to General de Gaulle or to others.

Robert Denoël noted with obvious disgust that the rules were applied differently for different people. While Denoël was tried for personal collusion with the enemy and then faced another court trial for collaboration by his entire company, the head of the Publishers'

Association who had circulated the lists of books banned by the Germans now circulated the lists of books banned by liberated France. He was under no indictment. Contradictions were sometimes even worse in industry. Does one dismantle a major company because it had produced goods for the Germans during the war? Even guns and ammunition? The sad fact was that those industrial companies that had collaborated with the Nazis were often the best equipped and managed, and therefore the most sought after following the war. Companies that had refused to cooperate with their German occupiers were either wiped out or left in a badly weakened condition. As for the couture industry, it hardly faced any purge at all, not because it had not collaborated, but because rich women the world over wanted Paris fashion and were willing to pay a great deal for it. And France desperately needed that money. True justice seemed to be something found in fairy tales.

Robert Denoël recognized what his role as "designated scapegoat" in this new France might imply. He knew that if he played by the rules, he might never become disentangled from litigation, might always be the object of some anonymous informant or some new charge requiring all of his efforts—and all of his money. He had already spent so much of his time in court battles, the thought of endless future litigation was anathema.

But possibly there was another way. In this post-Liberation period it was not always clear exactly who was in control. Because of their active role in the Resistance, French Communists had considerable influence in this era. Nearly everyone knew of their bravery in the Resistance. It was by now common knowledge that during the Occupation, whenever a German soldier was assassinated by a French terrorist (often a Communist), German reprisal would result in the executions of many French prisoners of war. A great number of those shot were French Communists. Their martyrdom and heroic actions during the Occupation gave them a new power, prestige, and influence following the war. In addition, the Occupation had provided for no real French government, except, of course, the puppet government of Pétain and the Germans. Following the Liberation, there was no French government set in place to take charge. The country was still divided; loyalties were fractured. A full-blown civil war or national insurrection was clearly a possibility. Although General de Gaulle seemed to have unchallenged power and glory on the day that he marched into Paris, in reality he faced formidable obstacles within the provisional government itself, and from the French Communists and the Resistance. France still had no common vision.

In this atmosphere many Stalin-supported French Communists, who were at the height of their power in France in 1945, dedicated themselves to making France a Communist state. To amass more money for this Communist effort, it was sometimes possible for a person accused of collaboration to "purchase innocence." In other words, if the accused provided enough money to the Communist cause, his legal problems could go away. His trial would be "fixed."

Always a connoisseur of *le système D,* Robert decided to see if he could better his legal situation and put an end to his scapegoat role by making a significant contribution to the Communist cause. Some (or all) of the gold in that suitcase could become his donation. Jeanne Loviton, of course, knew of Robert's plans. In fact, she allegedly helped him prepare for and set up a meeting with those who might be able to influence the court in his favor. Although in late November neither Robert nor Jeanne knew the exact date or time of this meeting, they believed it would surely take place before his trial, scheduled to begin on 8 December 1945.

The seriousness of the situation that writers, journalists, and publishers faced cannot be underestimated. Publisher Bernard Grasset had already been arrested and sent to prison at Drancy, then to a convalescent home. He frantically tried to summon the help of his writers and friends. "But all the writers seemed suddenly to suffer amnesia; they forgot the publisher he had been to them before the war and even under the Occupation. The man was suddenly a social leper." The dissolution of his publishing house was ordered in 1948, with 99 percent of its assets confiscated. Those pro-Nazi managers who had taken over the Jewish-owned publishing house Ferenczi were banned from publishing for life. Gilbert Baudinière, publisher of Les Editions Baudinière, also faced in 1945 a possible ban from publishing for life. Journalist and publisher Horace de Carbuccia had already fled to Switzerland.

The following writers and journalists were sentenced to death and executed, primarily for their ideas and words: Georges Suarez (1944), Robert Brasillach (1944), Paul Chack (1945), Paul Ferdonnet (1945), Philippe Henriot (killed by the Resistance in 1944), Jean Hérold-Paquis (1945), and Jean Luchaire (1946). Henri Béraud (winner of the 1922 Goncourt Prize), Charles Maurras, Raymond Abellio, Maurice-Yvan Sicard, and Robert Denoël's writer, Lucien Rebatet, were initially sentenced to death, but later received a lesser sentence.

Countless other writers, journalists, academics, actors, and entertainers received lengthy jail sentences, not because they had taken up guns, but rather because they had put down in writing, acted, or otherwise communicated their ideas. For the most part, shooting and imprisoning writers and intellectuals was much more a French than a German pastime. Defeated Germany generally did not try to kill its writers, publishers, and entertainers. The Nuremberg trials began on 20 November 1945. The judges at Nuremberg, not Germany itself, decided the fate of German leaders. France, on the other hand, wanted to purge itself—quickly and thoroughly. Many viewed the purge as necessary before France could begin again. As Céline put it, "Purges are quick . . . half a second, they cut your throat and help themselves . . . you go back and it's all over! . . . your successor is reading his paper, smoking his pipe, Madame is busy doing something with her brassiere, sewing, farting, and discussing vacation plans . . . the little girl is playing the piano, out of tune . . . you've got no more business there . . ." Those who had once espoused the Fascist cause had "no more business" in France. The purge saw to that. But Gaston Gallimard and Robert Denoël were right in the middle of the purge, both of them. Both men had been on various blacklists and were excoriated by several newspapers of the time. Both

were deeply worried, and with good reason. Both men were willing
to take drastic action, if necessary, to save their publishing houses
and to save themselves.

If either publisher had faith in the French justice system after the
Liberation, he had only to look at the postwar trials of the two top
men within the Vichy government to become disillusioned. Pétain's
trial lasted from 23 July to 15 August 1945. Pétain was eighty-nine.
Twelve of his jurors were members of the former anti-Pétain par-
liament and twelve were members of the Resistance. As avowed enemies of Pétain throughout the war, these jurors could hardly have
been impartial. In front of the High Court, his jurors, and the
French people, Pétain rose to defend himself, reading a speech that
had been written for him by his lawyers. He began by citing his
glorious war record in World War I. "I have spent my life in the
service of France. . . . I led her armies to victory in 1918. . . . On
the most tragic day of her history, again it was to me that she
turned. . . . I asked for and desired nothing. They begged me to
come: I came. Thus I inherited a catastrophe that I did not cause."

Under those appalling circumstances Pétain contended that he
had done his best to serve and protect France from its German occupiers. "Every day, a knife at my throat, I fought against the enemy's
demands. History will tell of everything that I protected you from,
while my adversaries think only of reproaching me for what was inevitable."

He maintained that, under the circumstances, he had done everything possible to protect France's interests. "If I could not be your
sword, I tried to be your shield." He had done his best to preserve
France for posterity, and to end any further destruction. "What good
would it have done to liberate ruins and cemeteries?" He then proclaimed his innocence of all wrongdoing and said, "I put my trust
in France."

That, in effect, was all that he said. He paid little attention to the
rest of the trial. In fact, he may not have been deeply aware of that
trial and its meaning. He was very old, finished, probably senile.
"His chief diversion was ogling the breasts of a well-endowed young

lady at the reporters' table and the day that she was absent he pouted. Most of the time, he dozed." Then came his verdict. He was found guilty of crimes listed in Articles 75 and 87. The verdict: "The High Court condemns Pétain to the penalty of death, to national indignity, and to the confiscation of his goods." Because of his advanced age, his sentence was commuted to life. He was banished to an island off France's western coast, the Ile d'Yeu. He died there on 23 July 1951.

If Pétain's trial lacked a certain objectivity, the trial of Vichy's second in command, Pierre Laval, was even worse. That trial was a mockery of justice. The jurors were Laval's avowed enemies, and they taunted and cursed the man during the proceedings. His judge and prosecutor had even served in the Vichy government. During the trial, jurors shouted, "Bastard!" "Twelve bullets in his hide!" and "He hasn't changed a bit!" In October 1945 (two months before Denoël's scheduled trial) Laval was sentenced to death, national degradation, and confiscation of all of his wealth. Laval attempted to cheat the executioners by taking poison shortly before his execution. Heroic efforts, including the pumping of his stomach, were made to restore the gasping and vomiting half-conscious Laval to enough life so that he could be given the French death decreed by the High Court. Their efforts to "save" Laval succeeded, and he was rushed, staggering and half-dead, before the firing squad.

It was generally believed that such trials and executions were necessary to provide legitimacy to France's new government. Punishment and purge were needed, especially for those who represented the old regime or who might not be essential to the French economy. Céline urged Denoël to leave France. "Two days before he was murdered I wrote him from Copenhagen: 'Clear out . . . damn it! . . . make tracks . . . the rue Amélie is no place for you . . .' He didn't split, people never do what I say . . . they think they're guaranteed . . . amulets rubbed with onion . . . okay . . ." Refusing to leave his company, Denoël prepared to fight, and if the cards were stacked against him, he would resort to other means to win his trial. He had the money. He decided to meet with the Communists to see what they could do.

Among other things, that box held captive in the French archives for more than four decades, then unceremoniously released, detailed the day of Robert Denoël's murder. The morning of 2 December 1945, the last day of Robert's life, he paid a visit to his son, Robert Jr., then age twelve. He remained a devoted father in spite of his separation from his wife, and he saw his son often. That particular morning they talked about school, books, and atom splitting. "How can splitting an atom get such a big bomb?" young Robert had asked his father. He was trying to understand what had happened to Hiroshima and Nagasaki the previous August.

"I'm not sure myself," Robert admitted. Then they discussed the pictures of these two cities his son had seen in the newspapers. They spent the entire morning talking, neither remotely suspecting that this would be their last time together. Then Robert checked his watch. "I have to get ready for a little party," he told his son, "and it looks like I'm going to be late."

"Not too late to give me a spin around the block on your motorcycle," Robert pleaded.

"Next time I will take you for a long ride. You'll see. I promise," said his father. Then he turned and went out, got on his motorcycle, and returned to 11, rue de l'Assomption.

Jeanne and he were invited to a luncheon at the home of Marion Delbo, who lived about half an hour away. The luncheon would be part pleasure, part business. Marion had asked Robert, who was still her publisher, to give his reaction to a collection of *nouvelles* (long stories) she had just completed. She had already achieved some distinction as a novelist, especially with *Monsieur Durey*, which one critic had called *"délicieux."* Marion considered herself a good friend of both Robert and Jeanne. After all, it was she who had first introduced them. In the past few months, however, Jeanne had been more aloof toward Marion, often refusing her social invitations. Marion would later tell the police that right from the moment that Jeanne met Robert Denoël, "she made our relationship more distant; I don't know her reason for this." Marion was glad they both could come that day.

Jeanne and Robert were not the only guests invited to this luncheon. Marion's mother, a charming older couple recently back from the French West Indies, and music critic Claude Rostand were also invited. "Would you mind picking up that couple from the West Indies?" Marion had asked Robert on the phone. She knew they would be driving Jeanne's car, a Peugeot 302, which seated four comfortably. "They're right on your way, and they don't have a car yet. You'll like them. Their names are Monsieur and Madame Charles-François Baron. Monsieur Baron was once Governor of the French West Indies. He has a formidable memory and loves to talk about his experiences."

"Fine, Marion. Tell them we'll pick them up around 12:30."

They arrived at the Baron residence as planned, picked up the couple, and drove to their destination, arriving at Marion's about 1:00. By all accounts they spent an agreeable afternoon at the Delbo home. The talk was lively, pleasant, and general in nature. Always the gracious hostess, Marion invited them all to stay for supper, and Jeanne and Robert agreed. Then Monsieur Baron distinctly remembered that the phone rang. It was for either Robert or Jeanne, he wasn't sure which one. Following that phone call, Jeanne told her hostess that they would be unable to accept her invitation. They had to return to Paris, meet a friend (or some friends), then go to the Agnès Capri Theater. Although Marion tried to insist, even suggesting that Jeanne call the friend back to say they had other plans, she refused. She said there was a special performance at the theater that night. Marion Delbo later told the police that she believed that Jeanne was simply being polite, using both the friend and the theater as an excuse.

On 2 December 1945, the last day of his life, the two of them arrived at her elegant Paris home at about 6:45 P.M. He was driving her car, a shiny black Peugeot 302. He stopped the car in the drive, and silently they entered the house and took off their coats. She rang for the maid, Mademoiselle Sidonie Zupaneck, and told her that they would like to have supper. After a few minutes, Sidonie served the soup, a consommé brunoise, in the dining room, followed by a cold

ham braised in Madeira and a salade aixoise. Both ate rapidly, looking down, with little conversation. Neither wanted the dessert Sidonie
had prepared for them. Following their meal, he finished his wine
and smoked a cigarette, while she excused herself to freshen up and
change into evening attire. At about 7:45 he got up from the table
and went to the phone in the library, calling a business colleague.
They had a long conversation, lasting more than twenty minutes.
When he hung up, she was still not ready. He went to the hall mirror,
straightened his elegant burgundy tie, adjusted his blue pin-striped
suit and vest, and combed his hair. Then he took out his wallet,
looked into it, and verified its contents: twelve thousand francs (more
than six thousand dollars). When he heard the sounds of her high
heels descending the staircase, he went to the closet, took out her
black mink coat, and helped her on with it. While she adjusted her
matching mink hat in that same hall mirror, he put on his own
overcoat. The maid watched them as they left the house. Then she
looked up at the grandfather clock. It was exactly 8:30.

Both seemed determined, tense, that night. They walked to the
Peugeot, and he opened the door for her, then quickly walked to the
driver's side, adjusted his overcoat, and got in. The maid could still
see them from the window. The woman in the fur smiled briefly at
him, then looked straight ahead, serious, as he started the engine
and backed out of the drive. Quickly he turned the car into the street,
and they roared off into that cold, rainy Paris night. Traffic was very
light. They did not take a direct route. Instead, they went by (or very
near) his publishing house. At 8:50 they stopped the car at a deserted
area on the boulevard des Invalides, close to the corner of the rue
de Grenelle. They both got out of the car. He had about twenty-six
minutes before the bullet.

Seated alone in my office I slammed shut the top of the box
holding my copy of the police and court dossier. It made a loud,
satisfying thud. "Don't do it!" I shouted. "Just don't go. I am tired
of watching you go. Tired of tracing your steps, counting the
minutes." Rupert, my large black cat who had been dozing on my
papers, awoke with a start and jumped off my desk, taking some of

my research with him. Then, once again, I sadly reached for the box and reopened it.

I imagined that Jeanne and Robert said very little in the car, since I knew their relations continued to be strained. They were gracious and polite in front of others, but alone together there was a stiff silence between them. It had been raining that Sunday night. There was little traffic on the road—no reports of traffic jams or accidents. Why then did they not proceed directly to the theater? Why did they head for 19, rue Amélie, the location of Les Editions Denoël? Did they stop there for something (the defense dossier? the suitcase filled with gold?)—or pick someone up?

I noticed that their unusual route also took them very near or right by the residence of Guillaume Hanoteau. This man, too, was a lawyer, working for the Court of Paris. Hanoteau had known Jeanne for a long time. In fact, like Jeanne, he had once worked for Maurice Garçon. He was that second person I should have looked for when I first discovered Jeanne. He had seen Jeanne several times after she stopped working in Garçon's law office, and had even dined with her on at least one occasion. He lived at 13, rue de Verneuil. Robert and Jeanne could have picked him up that night. Then they turned toward what would become the scene of the crime and stopped.

Directly across the street from Robert's parked car was a large building, the Ministry of Work. Inside that entire building on that particular Sunday night were the night watchman, André Ré, and Pierre Roland-Lévy, who, like Hanoteau, was also a lawyer at the Court of Paris and who also knew Jeanne Loviton. In fact, Roland-Lévy worked for Jeanne's own principal lawyer, Monsieur Rosenmarck. Roland-Lévy could see Jeanne's parked Peugeot 302 from his office window. According to the night watchman, Roland-Lévy entered the Ministry of Work at around 8:30, the same time Jeanne and Robert left their home. Pierre Roland-Lévy was a Communist. Guards and watchmen were given strict instructions to note in particular the comings, goings, and associates of all Communists. Ré followed his orders. He wrote down the time that Roland-Lévy entered the building. Although he did not specify that he was alone, he entered no other name, just Pierre Roland-Lévy. Roland-Lévy had been assigned to the Ministry of Work for only four days. What was he doing there, alone, on a Sunday night?

Guillaume Hanoteau and Pierre Roland-Lévy knew each other well. In fact, they were good friends. And both men were well acquainted with Jeanne Loviton. Both even had professional links with her. Roland-Lévy was also a very good friend of the son of Samuel Monod. Until all legal claims could be satisfactorily solved, Monod still remained at the helm of Les Editions Denoël. Monod's son, Flavien Monod, was a journalist who also knew Denoël very well.

There were even more connections. I learned from the police report that at the time of the murder Roland-Lévy was deeply involved in a love affair with Simone Pénaud-Angelelli. I already knew that she was the lawyer Denoël had chosen, on Jeanne's advice, to represent him in his divorce with Cécile. So there were three lawyers (all acquainted) at or near the deserted intersection of the boulevard des Invalides and the rue de Grenelle where Robert Denoël stopped his car on a Sunday night: Pierre Roland-Lévy, Guillaume Hanoteau, and Jeanne Loviton.

It was six days before the trial of Les Editions Denoël. I had read a great deal about the Liberation, and both Roland-Lévy and Hanoteau had turned up in these readings . . . but not as respectable, upright citizens. Both men seemed to specialize in secrets, clandestine transactions, with several historical hints at trial fixing. No proof, just circumstantial evidence. I therefore knew even before I looked at the Denoël police reports that both men had secret, sometimes unsavory pasts. And here was Roland-Lévy again—an important Communist and lawyer, apparently knowledgeable in that fine art of buying innocence.

At around 9:10 P.M., according to the written record of the night watchman, André Ré, Pierre Roland-Lévy left the building alone. Ré later testified that he did not hear the gunshot, or gunshots (were there two?) about five minutes later. Nor did he hear that long, agonizing male scream. The walls of the building were too thick.

Others heard it. Others went to the window to look. Pierre Roland-Lévy returned to the Ministry of Work about eight minutes later, at 9:18, again according to Ré. And this time, he was not alone. Monsieur Hanoteau accompanied him. Ré opened the door for both men and dutifully wrote down both of their names in that record he kept. As the two men entered the Ministry of Work, Roland-Lévy told Ré that he had forgotten his cigarettes and that he was going back to his office to get them.

At that point Roland-Lévy said to the guard, "This must be a strange place, your section of town; there has just been an assassination attempt at the corner of the boulevard." Roland-Lévy then told the guard about a man he saw trying to repair a tire on his car. Then he added as an aside to Hanoteau, "There must have been a romantic entanglement." Or, depending upon the English translation, "There must be a woman involved." [*"Ça doit être une histoire de bonne femme."*] Because the hallway was dark, André Ré offered to accompany them with a flashlight. But Roland-Lévy told him not to bother. They remained in the building for four or five minutes, then Ré once again opened the door for both men and recorded their exit.

And Jeanne Loviton, where was she in all of this? She had been in the car as Robert drove to the boulevard des Invalides. Then either very shortly before or immediately following the shooting, she left. She walked to the nearby police station, a four- or five-minute walk, and ordered a taxi, using that medical certificate she had obtained only eleven days before. During her walk she saw a policeman (Guardian of the Peace) named Testud and asked him directions. Testud was a rookie and late for his post. During the time it took Jeanne Loviton to walk to the police station, Roland-Lévy and Hanoteau were probably in the Ministry of Work. I would later read in the court records, "The stop in the office on the pretext of looking for a package of cigarettes lasted four to five minutes. Exactly, and timed by a watch, the time needed to go on foot from 127, rue de Grenelle [the location of the shooting] to the police station." After these four or five minutes, both men left the ministry, saw Testud, and informed him of the shooting. By the time Testud made his call to the police station, Jeanne Loviton was there, with the perfect alibi.

The two lawyers then accompanied Testud to the scene of the crime. By this time several onlookers had gathered around Denoël. Robert was lying on his back on the sidewalk in front of 127, rue de Grenelle. There was no blood or sign of a bullet wound. He had been shot in the back. His arms were stretched out, strangely pointing in opposite directions. After looking briefly at Robert, Testud ran to a nearby call box, reported the shooting, and asked for a police ambulance. According to police records, that call came into the police station at around 9:25. Jeanne Loviton was at the police station by that time and heard the call. According to the police blotter for that night, she then ordered a taxi at 9:30 P.M.

The taxi arrived promptly. The police did not interrogate Monsieur Desprèz, the taxi driver, until 1950. However, even nearly five years after the fact, he did remember Jeanne Loviton and some of the events of that evening. He testified that she had asked him to take her to Agnès Capri Theater, and to go by way of the corner of the rue de Grenelle and the boulevard des Invalides. Desprèz said she "seemed very nervous and turned around all the time to look out the rear window. Her attitude seemed suspicious."

She arrived at the crime scene just in time to see the policemen loading Denoël into the police ambulance. She seemed "completely panic-stricken." According to the taxi driver, she got out of the taxi and immediately shouted, "They have killed him for me . . . They have killed him for me." The taxi driver, speaking to Testud and others, told them that he believed that this woman was expecting to find this scene. He also stated, "In effect, I had the impression she thought she was being followed, always looking behind her." Although Roland-Lévy and Hanoteau both knew Jeanne Loviton well and were still present at the scene, they gave her no sign of recognition. And she ignored them both as if they were strangers.

At this point, no one knew the exact condition of Robert Denoël.

He was not pronounced dead at the scene and may not yet have expired. Jeanne got into the back of the police ambulance with Robert. They then proceeded to the Necker Hospital. Others present in that ambulance later testified that they found her behavior then to be strange. Although she later testified that she did not know Robert's condition as they rode in that ambulance, she said absolutely nothing to him during the entire trip. She offered her lover no words of comfort, strength, or hope. She did not even cry out in despair. At the hospital, when she received word that Robert Denoël was dead, she had only a brief period of emotion. According to the Guardian of the Peace, Monsieur Lefevre, who was with Jeanne at the time, she simply knelt near the body, looked intently at Robert's face, and said very quietly, "My darling, it's my fault." Two police officers then confirmed that she seemed to have entirely recovered from the shock only half an hour after the news of Robert's death. How strange, I thought.

Reading on in the police report, I learned that Jeanne made at least one phone call from the Necker Hospital that night. Following that call, two of her friends appeared at the hospital. The first was Yvonne Dornès, her friend, business associate, and friend of Suzanne Bidault. Madame Bidault was the wife of Georges Bidault, who was the minister of foreign affairs in General de Gaulle's provisional government. Yvonne Dornès was the daughter of Pierre Dornès, a very powerful and influential member of the court overseeing government spending. In addition, she herself had quite important contacts within the police department. The second woman to appear on Jeanne's behalf at the Necker Hospital that night was Mademoiselle Pagès du Port, who also had significant police connections, particularly with the Prefect of Police.

On the very night of the murder, then, Jeanne Loviton appeared to have the help, protection, and influence of Hanoteau, Roland-Lévy, Dornès, and Pagès du Port, all of whom had important court and/or police connections. It was clear from reading their initial report that the police that night could not possibly have done more to satisfy the needs and desires of Jeanne Loviton. They relied entirely upon her "good faith" and took as absolute truth her version of events.

According to Jeanne Loviton, there was no meeting. Absolutely no meeting! Robert and she were on the way to the theater when, at the intersection of the boulevard des Invalides and the rue de Grenelle, they had a flat tire at around 9:00 P.M. or a little earlier. Both of them got out of the car. She then claimed that since they were already late for the theater, Denoël, knowing she had a medical certificate, advised her to walk alone to the police station, get a taxi, and proceed to the theater. He told her that after he had changed the tire, he would meet her at the theater. She further noted that when she left him, he was wearing his overcoat and getting ready to get the tools out of the rear trunk. That was all.

The police did almost nothing to attempt to corroborate her story. She was, after all, an important and influential woman with very significant contacts. They accepted her story entirely. Based upon her version of events, the police declared that the murder of Robert Denoël was a random crime of violence, *"crime crapuleux."*

⤳ *13* ⤳

Not Only Murder
but Theft

Finally, I will prove that certain people have profited
beyond belief from this reprehensible crime.
Cécile Denoël

*C*écile had not been home the night of 2 December 1945. She had
been visiting friends. She returned to her domicile around 11:00
P.M. Almost immediately after her arrival, a neighbor knocked at her
door. "Cécile, I'm afraid there has been an accident involving Robert. The police have been looking for you. They left a message that
you should go immediately to the Necker Hospital."

"What!" Cécile exclaimed. "What's happened?"

"That's all they said. You'd better hurry. They said it was urgent."

Cécile did hurry. At the Necker Hospital she was informed of the
shooting, and her husband's demise. The police asked her to come
back tomorrow and give them a statement. Dazed, Cécile returned
home. She knew so little of what had happened. She decided to call
Jeanne to ask for more information. She dialed her number. There
was no answer. She waited a few minutes, then tried again. Again
there was no answer. She spent hours trying to call Jeanne Loviton.
Where was she?

Then Cécile tried to call a friend who had known both Robert
and her for many years, Dr. Maurice Percheron, a medical doctor

and biologist. Robert had published some of his books. The Denoëls liked this man, trusted him, and even designated him as legal guardian of their son, should both parents die or become incapacitated. Robert also made him one of his straw men, a titular head of part of his business. But Dr. Percheron was also Jeanne Loviton's good friend. Although it was quite late, he did not answer Cécile's call, either. She tried again and again, but failed to reach him until 7:00 A.M. Where had he been all night? And where was Jeanne Loviton? Dr. Percheron simply said that he had not heard the phone.

On 3 December Cécile went to the police station, where she was interrogated. She told the police that her husband had lately been preoccupied with the defense of his company, which faced charges of collaboration. She also said that the trial was scheduled for 8 December.

"Did your husband have any enemies, Madame?" the police officer asked.

"Yes," she affirmed. Then she told the police about those menacing letters and the drawings of coffins that he had received while he still lived with her.

"Has he ever been assaulted?" the officer asked.

"No, not that I know of," she responded.

"And when was the last time you saw him?"

"About two months ago," she admitted. "He phoned me regularly, asked about Robert Jr., and kept me informed. But we rarely saw each other."

"And where was he living at the time of his death?"

"He had a small bachelor's apartment at 39, boulevard des Capucines, but in reality, he lived at the home of his mistress, Jeanne Loviton."

"And her address is 11, rue de l'Assomption?"

"I believe so, yes."

Her official statement took up only one page. After it was typed, she signed it. Then Cécile returned home. Shortly after her arrival, she received a telephone call. It was from Jeanne Loviton. Under the circumstances, Cécile could not be aloof or mean. She did not even ask where she had been all last night. Jeanne was no longer her rival, not in the face of such a catastrophe. It was time, she believed, for mutual sympathy and politeness. Then on the phone Jeanne made a special request of this new widow. "Everything happened so quickly last night, I didn't feel that I had a proper chance to say good-bye to Robert. I wonder if you would permit me to see him one last time at the Necker Hospital sometime today." By now, administrators at the Necker Hospital realized that Robert Denoël had a wife, and that she, as next of kin, should oversee all things concerning her husband's body and effects, not his mistress. The Necker Hospital had, in fact, already made a mistake by giving Robert's overcoat to Jeanne. So now, if Jeanne wanted to see the body of Robert Denoël again, she had to ask permission of his widow.

Caught off guard, Cécile did not know what to say at first. Then she replied, "Of course, you can. I do not hold any grudges, certainly not under these circumstances."

"Thank you," Jeanne said softly.

They set up a time late in the afternoon for Jeanne's visit to the Necker Hospital. Because Cécile had to give her personal permission for this visit, she would also be at the hospital. She arrived early, accompanied by a few of her close friends, and waited. Jeanne arrived, looking pale and as if she were about to faint, leaning heavily on the arm of Dr. Percheron. Cécile was surprised to see Dr. Percheron with Jeanne. In fact, she had expected him to be one of those standing firmly at her own side. At first Cécile did not know what to do. Should she shake Jeanne's hand? Should she just stand there and not offer her hand to this woman? After a brief moment of confusion, Cécile, overcome with emotion, took Jeanne in both of her arms, hugged her briefly, then said, "You have my permission to embrace Robert's body. You have the right, you loved him enough."

Jeanne entered the hospital morgue accompanied only by Dr. Percheron. There they discovered that Robert's clothes and personal effects were gone, taken by the hospital officials. All that was left of the vibrant determined publisher was his cold, still body, lying on an examining table, partially covered by a white sheet. Jeanne did not stay long.

The following day, 4 December, Cécile received a condolence call from her half-brother, Guillaume Ritchie-Fallon. He was an eccentric man, a bit odd. He and Cécile had never been close. In fact, Guillaume was much closer to Jeanne Loviton than he was to his own half-sister. He admired this handsome, powerful woman; he may have been in awe of her. And when Jeanne asked him to pay a visit to Cécile on her behalf, and to make a simple small request, he was more than happy to do so. He greeted Cécile warmly and presented the usual condolences. Cécile invited him in for tea. After they had settled into two comfortable chairs with a pot of tea, some biscuits, and two cups on a small table between them, he broached the subject.

"I saw Jeanne Loviton this morning," he said simply.

"Yes?"

"She is quite distraught. She doesn't seem to be handling this whole affair very well at all. I am worried about her health. When I told her of my intention to visit you today, she asked me to make a very small request on her behalf."

"I am afraid I am not handling all of this very well, either," Cécile admitted. "What more could she want of me?"

"Nothing much at all, I assure you," he said. "All that she wants is some small memento—oh, nothing big, just something small to remember Robert by."

"What sort of memento?" she asked, puzzled.

"Well, something inconsequential, without monetary value. She suggested to me that Robert's Hermès [a brand name] notebook would serve the purpose."

Cécile's eyes widened. Her mouth opened slightly as she took an intake of breath. She straightened in her chair. Suddenly everything clicked; she understood. Although it was true that Cécile was not very familiar with her husband's business activities, she did know what was in that Hermès notebook. Robert carried that notebook with him at all times. During those periods of hiding assets and building phony companies, that notebook was the only true account of Robert's finances. Some memento! she thought, but she said nothing. Quickly she began to play a role, acting as if what her half-brother had just requested had not registered in her mind. She told him she would think about Jeanne's request. Then, feigning exhaustion, she asked if their meeting could possibly be cut short. She needed to rest. Guillaume said he understood completely. "No, no, please don't get up," he said. "You needn't show me out. Rest, dear Cécile, I can find the door myself."

As soon as he left, Cécile rushed to the phone. She called the Necker Hospital and ordered a total block of all items once belonging to Robert Denoël. From now on, all of the remaining personal effects of Robert Denoël should be sent directly to Madame Cécile Denoël—and to no one else. So that's why she wanted to see the body of my husband "one last time" at the Necker Hospital, she thought. She didn't want to say good-bye to him. She was looking for that notebook. Cécile Denoël did ultimately receive the Hermès notebook from the Necker Hospital. She was right. Her husband always carried that notebook with him, for it did contain, in her husband's small, clear handwriting, the only account of most of his secret financial transactions. Although she did not yet fully realize it, this notebook would become invaluable to her in the private war she had not yet declared.

Almost immediately after she hung up the phone, her friend Maurice Bruyneel knocked at her door. "Come in," she said. "Have I got something to tell you!" Then she told Maurice the story of Jeanne Loviton's request.

"She actually wanted his personal financial record as her memento?" he asked, incredulous.

"She probably didn't think I would know what the Hermès notebook really was," Cécile explained. "Maurice, I don't like this. I don't like this at all."

"Then maybe I shouldn't tell you what my father saw yesterday," Maurice responded. "It's probably not important anyway."

"What?" she asked.

"Well, the police said they impounded Jeanne's car, right?"

"Right."

"Guess who my father saw the morning after the murder, and guess what she was driving."

"No!" Cécile exclaimed. "Jeanne Loviton was driving her own car the morning after Robert's murder?"

"That's what he said he saw," Maurice told her. "In fact, he said he was sure it was her; he recognized the car."

Cécile did not have much time to discuss Maurice's revelations or even think about the "memento" that Jeanne had requested. She had a funeral to plan and a huge number of people to greet, important people who were Robert's writers and associates, Robert's friends. So many people, flowers, exclamations of sorrow. It was almost a haze of duties and events. Then Jeanne called Cécile and offered to pay for the funeral. This can't be happening, Cécile thought to herself. "No, Jeanne. Thank you, but no. It's my duty to pay for the funeral arrangements," Cécile told her. And Cécile did pay for the funeral and greet Robert's friends and console her confused and despairing son.

In the midst of the police investigation, the funeral arrangements, and Jeanne's strange requests came the media. This murder made the headlines in nearly every newspaper in Paris and was also given some attention across France. And nearly always those words, or variations of those words, were written: "He died under very mysterious circumstances." If the French did not at first recognize the name of this publisher, they certainly knew his authors, especially Céline. Everyone had an opinion about this murder. "He got what he deserved!" was often said in bars and cafés. It was not long before the news of this crime even reached Denmark, where Robert's principal writer was now residing.

Céline, his wife, Lili (Lucette), and their cat, Bébert, had left Sigmaringen for Denmark on 22 March 1945. The trip was not easy. They walked, rode trains, sought destinations that no longer existed due to the bombings, were bombed themselves, and lost every possession they had taken . . . except for the clothes on their back and that cat. Describing Bébert, Céline later wrote, ". . . he crossed all

Germany twice, Constance to Flensburg, under a hail of machine-gun bullets and bombs! In and out of five writhing armies! . . . the finish! . . . phosphorus armored trains! . . . never an inch from Lili! A cat that never obeyed anybody . . . *Komm mit!* that did it, the only German words that appealed to him, the only ones Lili ever learned . . ."

On 19 April a warrant for Céline's arrest was issued in France. He was charged with treason, according to Articles 75 and 76. Had he remained in France, he would probably have been condemned to death. But getting him extradited from Denmark, that was a much slower matter. It was not until 23 November 1945 that Georges Bidault decided to begin the process to extradite Céline. Then came two additional blows for this writer. On 1 December, Jean-Paul Sartre attacked Céline in the journal *Modern Times (Les Temps modernes)*. In his "Portrait of an Anti-Semite" Sartre said, "If Céline supported the social theories of the Nazis, it was because he was being paid." Céline was outraged by the lie. Using the thinly disguised name Tartre, Céline would castigate Sartre in his later novels.

And then on the following day his publisher was murdered.

Céline, the man who had called Robert Denoël stupid, a grocer, pimp, and thief, did not take the news well. "Many things are buried with that unfortunate man . . . so many things that life itself has come to a halt . . . that it has ceased to beat . . . that the heart beats to a new rhythm. . . . A very bitter, very demoralizing weight has been added to our bag of sorrows."

He wrote to his friend, Marie Canavaggia, who attended Denoël's funeral, "The poor man's fate has caught him as if in a net. . . . I can't get my mind off that horrible moment. I feel as if I've left a double in France who's being wantonly flayed . . . first one thing then another . . . a slow and vicious curse wantonly mauling me. And so powerless. No one." Robert Denoël had served this writer well. He had shielded him from public criticism and defended him. He had recognized his genius and skillfully promoted it. In spite of all of his previous diatribes and name-calling, Céline knew that he had lost a friend. Only fifteen days after the assassination of his publisher, Céline would be locked up in a Danish jail, his wife locked in another cell, and his cat, Bébert, locked in a cage in a Danish pound.

It was not long before the news of Denoël's murder even reached the inner wards of insane asylums. Antonin Artaud, locked up since 1937, soon incorporated Robert Denoël's murder into his rantings. Briefly, I looked into the treatment of the mentally ill during the Occupation . . . and was horrified. If Parisians were reduced to eating cats and pigeons at that time, the privation within insane asylums was even worse. Patients often starved to death. In addition, many patients, like Artaud, who were deemed incurable, were sent to Nazi concentration camps. Rightfully fearful, always hungry, and still having violent hallucinations, Artaud's writings became desperate cries for food, for drugs, for help, for freedom. Those patients who had friends on the outside often relied upon them to bring their only food. Robert Denoël and others supplemented the severely restricted rations of the badly emaciated Artaud. They sent him little packages of food and gifts during these impossible times and tried to see to his needs.

As part of his illness, Artaud was convinced that someone or something was out to kill his friends. In a letter written to Henri Parisol on 4 December 1945, Artaud complained bitterly that someone was casting spells and that these bewitchments were causing evil to befall anyone who came to help him. As examples, he cited his friends Anie Besnard and Catherine Chilé, who (in Artaud's mind) were prevented from seeing him and had horrible things happen to them because of these spells. Then he wrote, "Raymond Queneau wanted to see me at Christmas in 1943, with food, sugar, rice, butter, jams, bread; someone made him fall ill, *to force him to forget me,* and I haven't heard from him since. Did he also become by magic someone else who no longer cares about me and renounces me when he was once one of my best friends? And the day before yesterday evening, 2 December at 10:00 P.M., is that not another striking example?— Would you please shed light on all of this? Thank you with all my heart, Antonin Artaud"

Perhaps Artaud was right, I thought, as I examined once again Jeanne Loviton's initial deposition. Perhaps someone was casting spells—it was as good an explanation as the police had given. They were still saying that Denoël's murder was a "random crime of violence." It didn't make sense. None of it made sense, and especially Jeanne's deposition. She had summed up her entire knowledge of the murder of Robert Denoël in one and a half pages. Even at face value, her story was strange, and right from the first lines I realized that she had lied. She insisted, for example, that although they were engaged to be married, she had never slept with Robert. "I never lived in a marital sense with him." And according to Jeanne, he never lived with her at her home. Instead, he lived in that little carriage house on her property, listed as 9, rue de l'Assomption. And furthermore, according to her, he had only lived there for eight days. Certainly this information directly contradicted Cécile's deposition.

While she did mention that luncheon at the home of Marion Delbo, she left Monsieur and Madame Baron entirely out, not mentioning picking them up or taking them home, and certainly not ever mentioning that phone call that Monsieur Baron would later so distinctly remember. At least one-third of her deposition dealt with events that occurred after she left Robert Denoël the night of his murder.

Immediately following the funeral, Cécile Denoël began the process of recovering her husband's papers and personal possessions. At every turn she was thwarted. First, she tried to get the properties that she believed to contain his possessions put under police seals. To her dismay, she learned that Jeanne Loviton had already stated before le juge de paix (judge of the peace) that Robert Denoël had not left anything at his bachelor's quarters, the bungalow next to Jeanne's residence, or at her home. The case was decided. There would be no seals. Cécile soon discovered that all that remained of Robert's possessions were his dressing gown, his slippers, and some underwear. Jeanne did admit that she had given a few small items, without monetary value, to various loyal servants and friends of the publisher. Cécile was confused, frustrated, enraged. She had hired a lawyer to help her settle the estate. She decided to make an appointment with him. Perhaps he could help her locate all of Robert's possessions.

As she entered his office, her lawyer warmly greeted her. He was a thin, balding, middle-aged Frenchman with dark hair, kind brown eyes, a pencil mustache, and angular features . . . a polite man, distinguished but unassuming. No one would guess just by looking at him that he had the stubborn tenacity of a bulldog. His name was Armand Rozelaar. Cécile asked him if he could find out what happened to her husband's belongings and find out exactly what the police had discovered about the murder of her husband. Rozelaar promised to do what he could.

The following day, Armand Rozelaar went to the police station, talked with the police and read Jeanne Loviton's deposition. So this Jeanne Loviton claims that they stopped where they did because they had a flat tire, Armand Rozelaar said to himself. That should be easy enough to verify. First, I need to check that tire. But there was a problem with examining the tire. There was no tire. He asked the police. They didn't have it. He questioned the men on duty the night of the murder. No one remembered a flat tire or Jeanne Loviton having mentioned a flat. Rozelaar also questioned that rookie policeman, Testud, the one Jeanne had asked for directions to the police station, "Did Jeanne Loviton say anything to you about having a flat tire?"

Testud thought a moment, then replied, "No, Monsieur, she didn't."

He later asked the taxi driver who took her back to the scene of the crime, and again he received the same negative response. If she needed a taxi because of a flat tire, why hadn't she mentioned it to anyone?

Then Armand asked the police who had impounded the car about that flat tire. To his astonishment, no one could verify that there actually *was* a flat tire. In fact, the police had driven the car to the police station without changing the tire. How could they drive the Peugeot five hundred meters with a flat?

Armand then decided to question Jeanne's chauffeur. Apparently, he was assigned to retrieve the car and repair the tire. But his story (stories) was even more bewildering. At first he stated that he had repaired the tire himself. But he claimed that he did not have the tire. Later, he stated that he had had the tire repaired at a local garage. Then he said he never picked up the tire.

"Strange, very strange. Why would the chauffeur be allowed to handle such a key piece of evidence in the first place?" Armand muttered to himself. "And then he changes his story!"

Then Armand returned to the scene of the crime. According to the police report, Robert Denoël was lying on his back with his arms spread out. He had a car jack near one hand and an automobile crank near the other. Would not that prove that he was getting ready to change a tire? But when and how did the flat occur? Did he stop because he had a flat tire, as Jeanne Loviton continued to claim, or did Denoël's attackers flatten the tire to prevent his escape? Did someone puncture the tire with a knife, or possibly shoot it flat? One witness even claimed to have heard not one, but two shots. Or was there no flat at all? Could Denoël have used some of the tools in the car to try to defend himself? Rozelaar paced back and forth, thinking. Robert was shot in the back. While it had first been thought that Denoël was probably fleeing, closer examination clearly allowed for the possibility that he might have been pursuing one or more of his attackers. "Strange . . . very strange," Armand continued to mutter.

Rozelaar remembered that Cécile had told him that she was unable to obtain any of Robert's keys. "Did he have many keys?" he had asked her.

"A great many keys, Monsieur," she had responded. "Keys to his apartment, to his own publishing houses, keys to their coffers, keys to Loviton's publishing house, and to her home, I believe. I remember laughing at the big bulge those keys made when he put them in his pocket. And, of course, he must have had the keys to her car that night, too. After all, he was driving."

Where were those keys now? Madame Denoël could not find them. All of his keys were missing. When the police found Denoël's overcoat, they immediately turned it over to Jeanne. This was the same overcoat that she claimed he was wearing the last time she saw him alive. Rozelaar soon learned that, upon receipt of the overcoat, Jeanne had immediately searched all the pockets. He found that action to be very unusual for a grieving lover. What was she looking for? His keys? Had she found them? Kept them? Used them?

Rozelaar believed that the keys were vital to solving the crime. Whoever had those keys had apparently used them to dispose of nearly everything that Denoël had ever owned: his personal correspondence, his business papers, his books, manuscripts, clothing, jewelry, his pictures, his contracts, his personal belongings, and items he kept in his apartment, Jeanne's home, his businesses, and Jeanne's publishing house. Everything had disappeared! Jeanne explained that he had no keys, at least not to his publishing houses, and certainly not to those strongboxes. It was almost as if Robert Denoël had never even existed. Jeanne's explanation for all those missing articles was that none of those items had ever been there in the first place. She suggested that perhaps he kept all of his papers and belongings in his wife's residence.

Virtually all of Robert's money was gone, too. That suitcase filled with gold—gone! The only remainder of Denoël's money was discovered on his body the night of the murder: twelve thousand francs (more than six thousand dollars) in his pockets. More astonishing still was Madame Loviton's explanation. She claimed that Denoël had no money at all. He was a pauper. He didn't have any money for his defense. He never had a suitcase filled with gold. And furthermore, she stated that she had been supporting him. In fact, she claimed that the only money he had at all was the money found on his body. She never explained why a man in dire poverty would be carrying all of his money on his person and to the theater. Armand Rozelaar found these explanations to be unbelievable . . . incredible, in fact. He soon learned that other people had seen that suitcase filled with gold. They even testified to that effect. Other witnesses knew and testified that Robert was far from a pauper. Still the police believed this woman. Armand Rozelaar paced slowly back and forth in his office, his hands behind his back, thinking.

Something else was missing . . . something crucial. The defense dossier—which Denoël planned to present at his 8 December trial demonstrating that virtually all publishers (and Gaston Gallimard in particular) had collaborated with the Nazis—was gone. Fearful that something might happen to his defense dossier, Denoël even had a second copy made. That copy was gone, too. "Who would benefit from the loss of that defense dossier?" mused Armand, still slowly pacing, thinking. Then he thought of Jeanne's explanation for that missing dossier. Although versions of her story varied, she generally claimed that the dossier was not missing. It had never existed in the first place . . . just like everything else. Even in 1950, in spite of all of the evidence to the contrary, Jeanne maintained that there was no such dossier. In a sworn statement *(Déclaration)* before Judge Gollety, given on 28 April 1950, she adamantly stated, "For five long years now I have been hearing people speak of a dossier which never existed."

"So Robert Denoël, by all accounts a very intelligent man, was going to present himself before the courts without having prepared any defense at all for his company," mused Armand. "She would have us believe that." And for a very long time the police did believe that.

But Jeanne Loviton, in her statement to the police and the courts, went even further. She denied that it had ever been Robert Denoël's intention to implicate other publishers or to show in any way that they had also collaborated. With such statements she contradicted nearly everyone associated with Robert Denoël. More than a quarter century later, with her testimony safely sealed and the murder investigations forgotten, she would even contradict herself. She did so in an interview that she consented to give to writer Pierre Assouline, who at the time was working on a biography of Gaston Gallimard. Sometime before 1984 Jeanne Loviton stated to him that she and Denoël spent months working together, "day and night, going through piles of books published between 1940 and 1944 by the publishing community, and making notes on those that were apologias for collaboration." She also told Assouline about their collection of pro-collaboration advertisements that Robert and she had gathered. According to Jeanne, the thick dossier that they had amassed proved conclusively that other publishers had done exactly what Denoël had done, and sometimes even more. At least part of that dossier that she discussed with Pierre Assouline was the very same one that Armand Rozelaar was looking for, and the one that she claimed in 1950 had never existed.

The tire had disappeared; his keys were missing; all of Robert's papers and personal belongings had vanished; the gold had disappeared; the dossier was gone—now it was time for the main event, the final disappearance, the most astonishing disappearing act of all. On 8 December 1945, only six days following the murder, the exact date that Robert had been scheduled to defend his company in court, Madame Jeanne Loviton caused the entire company of Les Editions Denoël to disappear from the estate of Robert Denoël. She did it not with a wand, but with the stroke of a pen on a simple piece of paper—that previous hedge against an unfavorable outcome in his December 8 trial. On 25 October Robert Denoël had drawn up a contract that would cede his company to someone else (probably Jeanne Loviton) in case the trial went against him. In that way he believed he could still run his company covertly no matter what the courts decreed. At that time he still intended to marry Jeanne, and she strongly supported him in the creation of this contract. Although certain lines were left blank, Denoël had signed the document. All that Jeanne Loviton had to do following his murder was fill in the blanks ceding his company to her, date the document, and she would become the new owner of Les Editions Denoël. On 8 December 1945 she filled in those lines that Denoël had left blank and dated the document.

This newly filled-out document stated that Robert Denoël ceded 1,515 shares of Les Editions Denoël, at the grossly undervalued price of five hundred francs each (slightly more than $250 each) to

Jeanne's publishing house, Les Editions Domat-Montchrestien. Exactly to whom the shares should be ceded was left blank. On 8 December 1945 Jeanne put her name in that blank. The estimated value of Les Editions Denoël at that time was about nine million francs (more than $4,500,000). At the undervalued price of this business specified on this document, Jeanne would be required to pay only 757,000 francs (close to $380,000) for the entire business. At that price Jeanne may have obtained one of the greatest business deals ever. But she did even better than that. She stated that she had already paid Robert Denoël for the purchase of his company on 30 November, two days before his murder. Was there a receipt for this huge transaction?

No, there was no receipt. Was there a canceled check? No, there was no canceled check. There was, in fact, no record at all—anywhere—of any transaction that might show any payment for Robert's company. There was not even any evidence of money going out of her accounts and into his. There was not one shred of evidence that she had paid even one franc for Les Editions Denoël.

Armand Rozelaar sat quietly at his desk. He studied Jeanne's claims. Jeanne Loviton, a lawyer, had allegedly purchased an entire company without any legal documentation whatsoever. At least that is what she maintained. She claimed that Denoël had used the money she gave him to pay off his creditors. Rozelaar had copies of Robert's bank accounts, and Cécile had given him Robert's Hermès notebook. While it was true that he did pay off some of his creditors shortly before his murder, the sums paid out did not even come close to the amount of 757,000 francs. Far from it! Not to mention the fact that no money at all had gone out of Jeanne Loviton's account or into his. After carefully, meticulously looking at all the documents in front of him, Rozelaar sighed deeply, shook his head, then said aloud to his empty office, "She didn't purchase Les Editions Denoël. She stole it!"

Armand Rozelaar then turned his attention to those two other lawyers who were at the scene of the crime that night, Guillaume

Hanoteau and Pierre Roland-Lévy. He learned that the police had received a letter from Roland-Lévy, dated 3 December 1945, the day after the shooting. It said:

> Yesterday around 9:15 P.M. I left the Ministry of Work, accompanied by a friend, when we heard a violent detonation followed by a cry. The noise came from the direction of the rue des Invalides. We hurried there and discovered, stretched out on the sidewalk, the body of a man who was moaning, a car jack was located several meters from the body, along with the automobile crank.
>
> We returned toward the direction of the rue de Grenelle where we immediately spotted a Guardian of the Peace who returned with us to the location of the crime. Several people were already assembled there at that moment around the body. One of them, a man with a dark hat, declared to the Guardian that he had heard the cry of "Stop, thief" right before the shot. This witness could be found, at that moment, on the other side of the boulevard in the direction of the Esplanade des Invalides.
>
> Regarding what I know, I saw no one fleeing, neither in the rue de Grenelle where I was, nor several seconds later on the boulevard des Invalides.
>
> My friend certainly cannot add anything to these declarations. He saw nothing, and heard no more than I myself.

The letter was signed "Pierre Roland-Lévy." He didn't even say who his friend was. The police didn't ask. This letter directly contradicted the written record of André Ré, that night watchman at the Ministry of Work, on several points. Yet, not only was Ré not questioned at this time, neither were the two key witnesses, Pierre Roland-Lévy and Guillaume Hanoteau. The police decided that Roland-Lévy's brief letter was all that they needed. Why weren't the police investigating?

In fact, six weeks passed before Cécile learned that Jeanne Loviton was supposedly the new owner of Robert's publishing house. When she found out, she was even more astounded and confused. She turned to her lawyer, Armand Rozelaar, for advice and direction.

Rozelaar had even more disturbing things to tell her. Although it had rained the night of Denoël's murder, the police made no attempt to see if the back of Jeanne's Peugeot had muddy footprints, a clear indication that Jeanne and Robert were not alone. Not all of the witnesses were questioned. No one tried to reconstruct the events of that day or immediate events leading up to the murder. No one who worked with or for Denoël was questioned. Cécile admitted that aside from that initial deposition, she was not further questioned either. No one interrogated any of Denoël's friends. Nothing was ever searched or placed under police seals. Jeanne's medical certificate allowing her to obtain a taxi was not examined or questioned. The written and phone threats to Robert's life, along with those drawings of coffins, were never investigated. The police had not even interrogated Jeanne's taxi driver that night or Jeanne's chauffeur, who allegedly picked up the car and repaired the tire. Basically, there was no investigation. Jeanne Loviton's statements were taken as total truth right from the start. Furthermore, no one even bothered to look at the time line of the murder.

Almost from the very beginning, Armand Rozelaar found the time line to be quite amazing. Apparently no one ever asked why, if the Peugeot arrived at the scene of the crime between 8:50 and 9:00 P.M., or even earlier, there was absolutely no progress made toward the changing of a tire. There was a twenty-minute period or more that was unaccounted for. If Robert was not changing that tire, then what was he doing? The police station was only about one-half kilometer away, a four- or five-minute walk. Why, then, did the police blotter show that Madame Loviton ordered a taxi at 9:30? What was she doing during those thirty or more minutes?

Shortly after Cécile hired him, Armand sat at the table in his kitchen. He was supposed to be eating his breakfast, but he wasn't. Instead, he was staring off into space while repeatedly stirring his coffee. His wife, sitting across from him, chuckled. Armand looked at her.

"I think you have that sugar well dissolved by now," she said, in her low, soft voice.

Armand smiled and put down his spoon. "My dear, let's assume that we are going to the theater."

"Lovely," she replied.

"And on the way, we get a flat tire. Now a four- or five-minute walk away there is a police station where you could go to order a taxi to take you on to the theater by yourself. You see, you have a medical certificate."

"Do I?" she said as she placed two big croissants and other assorted breads on the table.

"Yes. What would you do? Stay with me while I fixed the flat or walk to the police station?"

"I would stay with you, of course."

"Why?"

"Well, for one thing, I like being with you." She smiled. "But also it would probably be the fastest and safest thing to do. Why would I want to go out alone to a police station? Is it an evening performance?"

Her husband nodded.

"Then why would I want to go out alone and in the dark to a police station, call a cab, wait until it comes, then go to the theater alone by taxi? It would even be faster to stay with you. What does it take to change a tire? Ten minutes?"

"About that," her husband responded.

"Besides, where would be the fun in going alone?"

"I have even left out a few facts," her husband said, picking up his spoon to stir his coffee again.

"Such as?"

"Such as it's a cold, foggy, dark, damp winter night in a relatively deserted area where random crimes of violence are sometimes reported."

"In that case, you couldn't budge me from the car! Oh dear, we need more jam," she got up and went to the cupboard. Armand put his spoon down and looked down at the coffee.

"Her story just doesn't make sense," he said.

"Whose story, dear?" his wife replied. But her husband didn't answer. He was still lost in thought.

Cécile Denoël waited nearly five months for the police to take some sort of action. But the police continued to do nothing. Then one day she went to Armand Rozelaar's office at 12, rue de Moscou, determined to do something. It was a long meeting. They discussed and considered many options. Armand Rozelaar looked briefly at his client, then glanced down at his notes. He cleared his throat, looked at her again, paused a moment, leaned back in his chair and began:

"I would advise that you take two actions at present," he told Cécile.

"And those actions are?"

"First, I would suggest that you file a civil suit against Jeanne Loviton."

"Good! And what would be my exact charges?"

Rozelaar glanced back at his notes. "Theft, swindle, breach of trust, forgery, use of forgery, and breach of a blank document." He looked up briefly at her. "Does that cover it?" he asked.

"No," she said adamantly. "What about murder?"

"We can't charge her with murder in a civil suit, and we don't know for certain that she did it," he told his client. "To solve that problem we need to do something else. That's where my second recommendation comes in. Do you know what becoming a *partie civile* means?"

"Well, I have heard of it," she said.

"I am not sure if they have the same law in Belgium, but here in France becoming a *partie civile* means that you can legally become part of the official investigation into the murder of your husband. The problem is that you would have to use your own personal resources to conduct your investigation."

"At least if I became a *partie civile,* there would *be* an investigation," she said indignantly.

"It's not an easy thing to do," he replied. "Basically, with my help, of course, you would be asking the questions and conducting research. And that would be expensive. Both actions would, in fact, be expensive," he told her.

"What other choice do I have?" she asked him. "Just fold up? Resign myself to the status quo? Right now, Jeanne Loviton claims she owns Les Editions Denoël. Robert would never have sold that company. He risked everything to stay in France to save that company. He would never have sold it!" She sat straight in her chair, a look of resolve on her face. "He expected our son to inherit Les Editions Denoël. *We* expected our son to inherit it. No, I can't let her get away with this. I shall agree to both of your recommendations."

And so exactly five months to the day after her husband's murder, Cécile Denoël wrote a letter to Judge Gollety, the *juge d'instruction* in this case. In France a *juge d'instruction* is a judge charged with examining all of the evidence in a certain case. Generally, he remains with that case from start to finish. Madame Denoël stated in her letter to the judge, "Permit me to express to you my painful surprise in noting that today, five months after the event, nothing has yet been done to look seriously for the assassin of Robert DENOEL. . . . To my knowledge, no search, no research, no inquest whatsoever has been conducted. You have never summoned me, and yet I would have important things to tell you." She continued by saying that she could not imagine why the police still thought the murder of her husband was a "random crime of violence." She believed that this act was not random at all. She concluded by saying that because of police carelessness and negligence in this case, she now believed it was necessary for her to become a *partie civile.*

On 21 May 1946 Armand Rozelaar wrote another letter to Judge Gollety. Without any preparatory introduction, Monsieur Rozelaar formally declared in his first sentence Madame Denoël's intention to become a *partie civile* in this case. He then underlined the position of Madame Denoël and detailed the situation of her husband before his murder. He challenged the notion that Robert Denoël would have sold his business to anyone. In fact, Denoël had told his wife shortly before his murder that he was prepared to fight anyone for his company, whether friend or enemy. Rozelaar summarized the lack of police action and investigation on all counts; then he began immediately to take a more aggressive role.

Instead of simply saying that this crime was probably not a random theft or murder, he began to point to those who might have benefited from Robert's death. Jeanne Loviton was first on his list. She stood to gain the entire Editions Denoël by highly questionable means; her testimony was suspect; and immediately after this murder, she attempted to obtain Denoël's financial account, that Hermès notebook. Rozelaar also included among his suspects other Parisian publishers who did not want their pro-Nazi and/or anti-Semitic publications brought up in court. As Rozelaar stated in his letter, "Needless to say, this report was not particularly sympathetic toward a certain number of people whose conscience should certainly be more bothered than Denoël's and who held their heads high and continued to conduct their business." And yes, Rozelaar concluded, contrary to Jeanne Loviton's claims, there certainly was a defense dossier, in spite of the fact that "this report disappeared along with all the rest."

He proceeded to suggest that Samuel Monod, who obtained his position as provisional head of Les Editions Denoël with Loviton's help and drew Denoël's considerable salary, should also be investigated. He added that Robert Denoël had, undeniably, many enemies, some of whom clearly wanted him dead either for political, business, or financial reasons. Surely these enemies should also be considered.

He then asked if Jeanne Loviton actually drove that supposedly impounded Peugeot the morning after the murder. He wanted to know where she was all night after she left the Necker Hospital. And in addition, where was Dr. Percheron all night? He added that immediately following Cécile Denoël's legal actions, she became "the object of diverse maneuvers." Madame Denoël was harassed, often by strangers who made bizarre and frightening proposals to her. And one time someone in a car took out a gun and pointed it at Robert Jr. as he played. He screamed and ran inside. Why were these intimidations now happening?

Rozelaar concluded by boldly suggesting that the police should interrogate those two key witnesses, Pierre Roland-Lévy and Guillaume Hanoteau. Important information might be gained from them. In addition, the police should find out once and for all how much money Robert Denoël actually had at the time of his death. He urged the court to question his accountant, Auguste Picq, Denoël's faithful employee for the past sixteen years.

Cécile Denoël was pleased with her lawyer and happy finally to be doing something, taking action in this case. She did not realize that at the very same time that she and her lawyer were taking the offensive, Jeanne Loviton was putting in place powerful and significant actions against this widow. And her defense would nearly destroy Cécile.

14

Closing In on the Truth

Justice Has Reopened the Dossier on the Murder of
Publisher Denoël.

France-Soir headline

*I*t would be difficult to underestimate the impact of two prominent
and distinguished women, fighting in the courts over such juicy items
as theft, swindle, forgery, and even murder, not to mention the
future ownership of a major publishing house. The newspapers loved
it! It seemed that all of Paris discussed this case. Already the battle
had divided Parisians into two camps, some cheering the widow and
others aligning themselves with the mistress. Even the newspapers
started to take sides.

Although Cécile's evidence against Jeanne Loviton grew stronger
with each passing day, she faced a powerful, formidable opponent.
In 1946 Jeanne Loviton had enormous political and social clout and
knew heads of state, businessmen, artists, and other publishers. In
addition, as a lawyer herself, she had friends within the courts and
was familiar with court procedure and key players within the system.
And she was still the friend of the now famous and quite influential
lawyer, Maurice Garçon. She knew everyone: the former Minister of
Finance, Germain Martin; Yvonne Dornès, a socialite with significant police connections; and the very political and powerful Georges

and Suzanne Bidault. It was quite clear that when Jeanne Loviton needed a favor, many important people ran to accommodate her.

Cécile Denoël was not nearly as well connected. Although she had several good friends, they did not have important social, political, or legal ties. Even the writers and employees who had once worked for her husband could not readily align themselves with Cécile without risking their jobs. After all, Jeanne Loviton was now their boss and would remain at the helm of Les Editions Denoël if Cécile lost her case. In addition, Cécile did not have Jeanne's knowledge of the mechanisms of the courts or even of her husband's business. And then there was one other almost insurmountable problem with Cécile.

It was that same problem that had so vexed her husband and had led directly to the breakdown of their marriage. Shortly before her husband's murder, Cécile had once again apparently chosen as her lover someone who was in her husband's employ. This time it was Maurice Bruyneel, the titular head of Denoël's other publishing house, Les Editions de la Tour. And once again her husband had found out. At least, Robert believed she was having this affair. He did not confront his wife directly. Certainly, he was in no position to do so. After all, they were in the process of divorce, and he had his own mistress. But he did decide to sit down and write a long and detailed *brouillon*, a draft. In this draft, he outlined his grievances against his wife. Was it a letter? If so, it was certainly unfinished. He did not address it to Cécile. And he did not sign it. It could simply have been a way that Denoël had devised to vent his own private feelings. In any event, he apparently never mailed this work to his wife. Instead, he put it carefully among his private papers—those same papers that allegedly disappeared after his murder.

In that draft, Robert wrote to Cécile about the man he believed to be her newest conquest, Maurice Bruyneel. He said, "I am certain, especially in the light of all that has happened previously, that you are Maurice's mistress. He is not a bad guy. He has certain qualities of the heart and of devotion. He pleases you. He pleases you more than anyone else, me included, for you can astonish him, dominate him, possess him." Denoël even suggested that following their divorce she should make her relationship with Maurice permanent. "Why don't you marry him? You are used to him; you have the same tastes, the same connections, the same friends. He will work. I will even help him if he needs it." Somehow, this draft appeared one day in the hands of Jeanne Loviton. She turned it over to the courts without comment.

This unmailed, unfinished draft profoundly damned the character of Cécile Denoël. It enumerated all of the lovers, real or imagined, that Robert believed she had had within his publishing house: le petit V, Claude, Artaud, possibly Bernard Steele (although Denoël believed he was only *"un épisode"* and defended him), possibly Billy, and others. And then there was that awful sentence: "I admit that I can scarcely keep my composure when I think of this morbid need that you have always had of choosing your lovers from among the *'familiers'* of the publishing house." In this letter he demonstrated her use of lies, ruse, intrigue, and her love of dramatic scenes. He even claimed that some of her lovers felt guilty. Speaking of a man named Claude, he said, "He suffered because he was receiving my money with one hand while taking my wife with the other." Robert questioned her proclaimed virginity when he first met her. He admitted that what had hurt him the most was that she even carried on her love affairs in front of their son. He claimed that she didn't love him. "In spite of all of your protestations, you have not loved me for a very long time. You haven't loved me for years. But you don't want to lose me."

Throughout the court battle, Cécile claimed to have knowledge of her husband's business. In fact, some of her sworn statements assumed a familiarity with Les Editions Denoël. With this draft, Robert directly contradicted his wife's assertions on that count. He wrote, "I submitted alone to the anguishes and the difficulties of a very hard career. Most often, you aided my efforts, my struggles, from the comfort of your bed. Never did you take an active part. You are really interested only in yourself and in the people who admire you."

Jeanne Loviton wasn't calling her opponent an unstable liar, given

to tantrums and ruses, a wife who had no knowledge of Les Editions
Denoël. Her dead husband was! To turn such a draft over to the
courts, as Jeanne Loviton did, caused more embarrassment and damage to her legal opponent than anything else Jeanne could possibly
have done. Cécile Denoël's reputation was tarnished before the
courts and even in the newspapers. Robert's draft did not just call
into question the character of his wife, but also that of Maurice
Bruyneel, who was often the sole corroborator of many of Cécile
Denoël's claims. It was almost as if Jeanne had summoned Robert
Denoël's ghost to rise up, haunt, and condemn his wife. Worse for
Cécile, it made Robert himself appear to be on the side of Jeanne
Loviton.

Armand Rozelaar was working quietly in his office at 12, rue de
Moscou when there was a knock at the door. *"Entrez,"* Rozelaar said
without looking up.

His secretary appeared and explained that Madame Denoël was
there. She wanted to see him right away. "She says it's urgent, Monsieur."

"Show her in," he said, closing his papers and placing them into
a drawer.

I slipped quietly into the back of the office and watched the two
of them attempt to deal with this ugly new turn of events. I looked
at Cécile. Her eyes were red, her dress rumpled; there were red
splotches on her face and some on the back of her hands. Her lower
lip trembled. Rozelaar smiled at her, rose, and showed her to a chair.
Dispensing with the usual niceties, she began almost at once to defend herself.

"It isn't true!" she claimed. "So much of what he said simply isn't
true or has been exaggerated all out of context." Her eyes welled up.
"How could he do this to me?" Sitting on the edge of her chair, she
took a handkerchief out of her purse, dabbed at her eyes, then began
twisting the handkerchief.

"At this point, my dear, our problem is not to disprove the allegations your husband made in that draft. I am afraid that damage
has been done. Denying all of his charges would only become a side

show in this Loviton circus, a diversion. No, what we need now is to keep our eyes on the issues at hand and to parry."

"And just how do we do that?"

Rozelaar leaned back in his chair, put his hands behind his head, and looked at the ceiling for a few moments. He seemed lost in thought. Then quickly he sat up and said, "You have seen the handwriting. Is it his?"

"Yes," she said. "It's his."

"And you had absolutely no knowledge of the existence of this draft? He never mailed you a copy or spoke to you about it?"

"No, I didn't know anything about it until that wretched woman gave it to the courts," she responded.

Rozelaar paused again. He tapped his pen softly on his desk. Again he looked up and was very quiet for some moments. Then he said, "Tell me about your husband. Did he often talk with others about your personal problems?"

"He did not!" she responded hotly. "Robert would never have talked openly about such things. I know that for certain."

"Do you think it's possible that he would have given a copy of this draft to his mistress?"

"Never!" she said.

"Then how did she get that draft?" Rozelaar asked in a slow, even tone.

Cécile's lips twitched slightly, then formed a brief smile. "Of course," she replied. "She stole it . . . like everything else."

Then Rozelaar looked directly at his client and said softly, "What has happened is indeed unfortunate. But you are not on trial here. We do not need to prove or disprove what your husband once wrote while he was contemplating divorce. What we need to do is refocus the courts—we need them to wonder just how Jeanne Loviton obtained that draft, especially since all of your husband's personal papers have disappeared."

"Do you think it will work?" Cécile asked her lawyer.

"I am an optimist, Madame," Rozelaar replied. "This draft could become serious evidence that Jeanne Loviton did indeed take Robert

Denoël's personal papers following his murder. Yes, it's certainly worth a try."

Rozelaar did try to turn the court's attention to the question of how Jeanne Loviton had come upon that draft. But the accusations that Denoël had leveled against his wife were so charged, so juicy, that Rozelaar failed to make his point. Jeanne Loviton had won on this score. She then placed other papers before the court, ones that might damage Cécile Denoël or throw into doubt some of her statements. Like that unfinished letter, all of them "mysteriously" reappeared at just the appropriate times.

Yet in spite of that draft, other damaging attacks, countercharges, humiliation, accusations, and denial, Cécile Denoël relentlessly pursued Jeanne Loviton in the courts and in her own investigation. This battle began officially in May 1946 and continued with verdicts for and against both women, pronouncements, new police investigations, appeals, and other legal maneuverings, into the summer of 1950—more than four years. Newspapers also continued to inflame the battle with articles supporting one woman or the other, or alleging new evidence, giving opinions, and advancing new charges. Major news stories and articles in gossip columns could be found in most newspapers of the day, including *Aurore, Aux Ecoutes, Carrefour, Combat, Express-Dimanche, La Libération, Le Figaro,* and *France-Soir.*

The first police investigation officially ended with a brief report submitted on 26 January 1946. In this report the police concluded that the murder of Robert Denoël resulted from a random crime of violence or possibly an attempted theft. Virtually all of Jeanne Loviton's statements were taken as truth in this investigation. Thanks to the detailed work of Cécile Denoël and her lawyer, the police were forced to launch a second police investigation. They produced in November 1946 a much more lengthy and thoughtful report. By that time the police found certain discrepancies in Madame Loviton's testimony that clearly demonstrated that too much emphasis had previously been placed upon her word, her "good faith." This report also criticized the lack of police thoroughness and careful examination in the first investigation and questioned its conclusions. Yet the police still were unable or unwilling to make a definitive conclusion.

While the police and journalists were taking a closer look at the murder, so was Cécile's central ally, her lawyer. Slowly, carefully, he began to examine the more personal aspects of the case. Again and again he looked at Jeanne's account of that night. Jeanne had done something else that Rozelaar couldn't understand. She had shown the police her two tickets to the play that she and Robert allegedly planned to attend at the Agnès Capri Theater the night of the murder. But why? Armand Rozelaar knew that neither Robert nor Jeanne needed a ticket to go to the Agnès Capri. Jeanne was a good friend of Agnès Capri. She was always given the best seats in the house, free of charge, whenever she went to that theater. As for Robert, he had a press pass that also allowed him free entrance to the theater. Rozelaar believed that Jeanne's tickets for the play that night were merely a prop used to reinforce her alibi.

Jeanne told Marion Delbo at her luncheon on 2 December 1945 that they were going to a special performance. Rozelaar looked into that matter, too. He learned that the performance that night at the Agnès Capri Theater was *Zig-Zag*, a series of musical sketches, parodies, songs, and poetry. Agnès Capri herself was in the performance. Sometimes celebrities were invited to the dress rehearsal or premiere of such plays. Under those circumstances the dress rehearsal became an important social event. But Armand Rozelaar soon learned that *Zig-Zag* had been running at the Agnès Capri Theater since 15 October 1945. There was no dress rehearsal, first performance, or other celebrity event scheduled for 2 December.

Then Rozelaar repeatedly examined the very last moments that Jeanne spent with Robert Denoël the night of the murder. Here was a woman who claimed to be in love with and engaged to Robert. Her departure from him to obtain a taxi would be the very last time that she ever saw him alive. Armand, again seated with his wife at breakfast, and again slowly stirring his coffee, asked her, "Wouldn't that last picture of Robert Denoël as she left him that night become indelibly engraved on her mind, particularly in light of the violence that would happen to him only minutes later?"

"I would certainly think it would," his wife responded.

"Then why does her memory of that moment change so much? Every single time that she relates her departure that night, her story changes. Once she said that she turned around to see him busy changing the tire, tools in hand. Then she said that when she left him, he was opening the trunk and getting ready to take out the tools. Then she told the police that she had opened the trunk herself so that Denoël could get his tools out. Then she said he had taken out no tools at all when she left him."

"Maybe she didn't leave him then," said his wife.

"That would certainly be a good explanation for all of these discrepancies."

His coffee growing cold, Armand continued to stir. "And that overcoat. Loviton claims Denoël was wearing his overcoat when she left him. But the police found it neatly placed on the back of the car seat. When and why did he remove his coat? And the keys. Who besides Jeanne Loviton would have had access to them that night?"

The following day Rozelaar questioned the maid who served Jeanne and Robert their last meal together. Jeanne kept changing the time of their departure from her house, now saying they left very shortly before nine. The maid, Sidonie Zupaneck, had a different story. "They left right around 8:30," she said. "I watched them leave myself."

"And where was Robert Denoël living then?" Armand asked her.

"Well, right here, of course, Monsieur."

"In the same house with Madame Loviton?"

"Oui, Monsieur, the very same."

"And how long had he resided at 11, rue de l'Assomption?"

"Oh, for some months, Monsieur, some months."

So much for Loviton's sworn testimony that Denoël lived in a small pavilion next to her home and that he had only moved into that pavilion eight days before his murder, Armand thought. He drove past Jeanne Loviton's home and looked at that pavilion next to her sumptuous home. It was little more than a gardening shed.

A few days later something very curious happened. Sidonie Zu-paneck suddenly left Jeanne Loviton's employ. Although the maid had worked for Jeanne Loviton for five years, she left abruptly after she told the police the same story. Jeanne explained that her maid had found a better job. Even the police believed the maid's rapid change of employment following her interview to be suspicious. If the police had interrogated the maid immediately after Denoël's murder, they might have put Jeanne's main house under police seals, thereby preventing anything belonging to Denoël from leaving. Following her change of employment, Sidonie Zupaneck said no more about the events of that evening.

When Rozelaar phoned Cécile and told her about the maid's quick exit, Cécile responded, "She fired her, didn't she?"

"It seems likely," Rozelaar answered. "Actually, I think it may be more than that. I suspect that our Madame Loviton may have told the maid that if she said anything more to me or to the police, she wouldn't be able to work anywhere in Paris. In any event, Mademoiselle Zupaneck is not saying anything more to anyone about the night of the murder."

"Too bad," Cécile murmured.

Then Rozelaar learned that in addition to having Jeanne Loviton as her publisher, Marion Delbo had an even bigger problem. She had had some financial difficulties in 1943, and Robert had bailed her out. In return for his generous loan, she had given him the mortgage on her home as collateral. Now Jeanne Loviton held that mortgage. Marion Delbo could lose her publisher and her home if she displeased Jeanne Loviton.

Armand Rozelaar paid a visit to Marion Delbo. They sat for some time in Marion's parlor, discussing Robert's murder. Most of what she told him was not new. Suddenly the conversation stopped. Marion seemed to be lost in thought, hesitating. Then she told the lawyer, "Please wait a moment, I have something I think you might want to see." She left the room briefly, then returned with a letter from Jeanne:

"Dear Marion, Please recopy the enclosed letter in your own

handwriting, sign it, and return it to me as soon as possible. Thank you. Yours very sincerely, Jeanne Loviton."

Rozelaar then looked at the letter Jeanne had asked Marion to recopy. It said basically that Marion Delbo was greatly pleased to learn that Madame Loviton was now the owner and publisher of Les Editions Denoël. "And did you recopy this letter and mail it to her?" Rozelaar asked.

"I did what I was told. I later learned that Madame Loviton had sent similar letters to many of the authors at Les Editions Denoël. Apparently, these authors also did what they were told." Armand quietly thanked Marion and left.

Rozelaar also visited Robert Beckers, the business associate Robert Denoël had had that long telephone conversation with the night of the murder. Beckers, too, was now the employee of Jeanne Loviton. He told Rozelaar exactly what he had told the police: "He telephoned me on Sunday, 2 December, a little before 8:00 P.M. I don't remember exactly what we talked about during this conversation, which lasted at least twenty minutes." Rozelaar found it difficult to believe that a longtime friend would not remember any of the last words spoken to him by Robert Denoël—unless, of course, the conversation was about that meeting which was allegedly scheduled to take place less than an hour after they hung up.

Then Armand Rozelaar went to the home of Denoël's loyal accountant, Auguste Picq, who resided at 44, avenue de Vendée in Beauchamp (Seine et Oise). He wondered if Picq would bow to the desires of his new employer, as so many of the others had. It was Picq himself who answered the door, ushering the lawyer into his library. He offered Rozelaar a seat at a library table, then sat down next to him. He had a briefcase beside the table, and almost immediately he opened it, took out some papers, and set them on the table. Then Armand said, "I need to know, Monsieur Picq, as much of Robert Denoël's financial situation as possible. I need to know if he was really poor, as Madame Loviton claims."

Picq was straightforward. "Madame Loviton is mistaken," he said. "Robert Denoël made a fortune during the Occupation. And even when he was not collecting his salary from Les Editions Denoël, his other publishing house, Les Editions de la Tour, was very profitable. Denoël paid Maurice Bruyneel a salary to be titular head of that company, but Denoël took all the profits from that publishing house every night. Maurice Bruyneel can verify that for you."

"Maurice Bruyneel already has," said Rozelaar. "How much do you think Les Editions Denoël itself was worth at the time of his death?"

Picq showed him some ledgers, saying, "His business was flourishing with assets that one could evaluate as having a commercial value of around twelve to fifteen million [francs]. Denoël hid most of his assets, you know. I have records of some of them, but not all." Picq then took out more papers, forming a neat pile on the table. "And I believe we have already discussed his investments in Les Editions Domat-Montchrestien. I have some of those papers here, too. He moved some of his best authors to that publishing house. Before he invested in it, Les Editions Domat-Montchrestien published only vulgarizations of scientific works and law books." Sorting through the pile of papers, Picq continued, "Oh yes, here is the receipt for the furniture he purchased for Domat-Montchrestien. Quite a significant sum, wouldn't you say?"

Rozelaar took the receipt and looked at it, then whistled softly under his breath. "Seventy-five thousand francs for office furniture for a publishing house in which Madame Loviton claims he had no interest! *Very* interesting!"

Picq did not seem to be listening, still rustling through his papers. "And here are the records of payment for Denoël's secretary, lovely girl. He moved her over to Madame Loviton's publishing house, too."

Rozelaar spent some time studying Picq's records. "These are hardly the records of a pauper," he concluded. "Denoël was rich!" After several more minutes of silence in which Rozelaar examined Picq's records, he asked, "Are you aware of any other significant assets he might have had?"

Picq thought a moment. "Well, of course, there was the gold," he said.

Rozelaar sat upright, eyes shining. "You saw the gold?"

"Yes," Picq responded matter-of-factly. "He kept it in a little suitcase, and one day he opened it up and showed it to me."

"Do you know how much was in that suitcase?" Rozelaar asked, trying to contain his excitement.

"He must have possessed about 900,000 francs in gold and currency,"

Then, excited, Rozelaar continued, "And the dossier, did you see that, too?"

"Although I never knew exactly what was in it, I knew of its existence. Robert and I had scheduled a meeting for 3 December 1945, the day after his murder. He said he intended to show me the dossier at that time." He paused a moment, then said, "That dossier must actually be in the hands of Madame Loviton."

"It has to be," said Rozelaar.

Picq was silent for a moment, then he added, "She has a Swiss bank account, you know."

"Who?" Armand asked.

"Madame Loviton. She has a Swiss bank account in Geneva. I understand that she also made several trips to Switzerland and Belgium shortly after the murder."

"A Swiss bank account! Of course! How much do you want to bet that Denoël's papers and money are in that account? Do you know anything about her account?" Rozelaar continued, now seated bolt upright.

"I know for certain that she has an account at the Février Tailleur Bank, 15, rue Petitot in Geneva."

The two men sat together, studying the financial records before them and quietly talking. Finally Armand rose to leave. "Your help has been invaluable," he told the older man.

"Monsieur Denoël—Robert—was my friend, my good friend. I want to correct some of the lies that have been told about him," he said.

One week later Jeanne Loviton fired Auguste Picq.

. . .

Armand Rozelaar knew that under certain circumstances, particularly when a crime was suspected to have been committed, Swiss bank accounts could be opened. He informed the police and the courts about this account and recommended that it be investigated. He also looked into Jeanne Loviton's trips. He verified that she had indeed made several trips to Switzerland and Belgium soon after the murder. He also informed the police of these findings. When the police questioned Jeanne Loviton about these trips, she claimed that she made them for medical reasons. She had gone to spas to regain her health following the trauma of the murder. Once again the police did not check her story, taking her word as truth. As for that Swiss bank account, the police did not investigate it further or attempt to have it opened.

By 1949 the newspapers were running out of stories about this unsolved murder and the court battles of the victim's widow and mistress. Journalists began to wonder why nothing seemed to move forward in this case. Some at the newspapers began to notice incidents in which Jeanne Loviton seemed to have used her influence and connections. It was the famous newspaper *Combat,* whose origins stemmed from the days of the Resistance, that first commented upon Jeanne Loviton's seemingly special privileges. In an article published on 3–4 December 1949, *Combat* claimed that undue political influence had been used to sway the judicial system in the case. The article quoted an unnamed judge who said that never before "have we received so many and such diverse kinds of solicitations." This article also claimed that the police may have known what really happened from the very start, and that this information was placed in a secret police dossier that still remained in the hands of the Prefecture of Police. If this document were ever revealed, the author claimed it could cause this case "to jump to a new level, that of obstructing justice."

Turning his attention again to those two other lawyers who were present at the crime scene that night, Guillaume Hanoteau and Pierre Roland-Lévy, Rozelaar made two discoveries. First, although a Communist at the time of Denoël's murder, Roland-Lévy had the dubious distinction of later being ousted from the Communist Party. But why? Armand wondered. In spite of considerable effort on his part, he was unable to find a Communist (or anyone else, for that matter) who would tell him. Second, although Guillaume Hanoteau was a lawyer in 1945, at some point before 1950 he became one of the very few French lawyers ever to be disbarred. Again Armand Rozelaar tried to determine exactly why Hanoteau had been disbarred, but he failed. Why are these facts so covered up? he wondered. "And these two men were 'too important' to be bothered with a police interrogation," Armand said aloud to himself.

Worse, although the police did not interrogate them for several years, even then they did not manage to get their stories straight. When asked why they were at that particular location on a Sunday night, Hanoteau replied that they were going to attend a meeting of the Chamber of Deputies, which was to start at 9:00 P.M. Armand Rozelaar checked his story. That meeting did not require the presence of either man. And furthermore, the meeting ended (not began) at 9:00 P.M. As for Roland-Lévy, he mentioned no meeting at all. He stated that they were at that location because they were going out to dinner together.

Hanoteau's story also contradicted Roland-Lévy's letter to the police, written on 3 December 1945. According to Hanoteau, he and Roland-Lévy had entered the Ministry of Work together, stayed for a short time, and then left together. Then Roland-Lévy remembered that he forgot a dossier and returned alone to the Ministry of Work to get it. Hanoteau swore that he remained outside the building. He heard the shot just as Roland-Lévy exited. Immediately both men hurried to the scene to find Robert Denoël lying on the sidewalk. Then Roland-Lévy returned to find a policeman while Hanoteau checked out the car.

At the time of their testimony, neither man knew of the written record of André Ré. Not only did Hanoteau and Roland-Lévy contradict each other, both directly contradicted Ré's written words jotted down the night of the murder. If they had not returned to the Ministry of Work together after the shooting, why then did Ré record the names of both men, and why did he not only write about this attack in his record book, but record Roland-Lévy's own words, even about the man being attacked while repairing a tire? And where would Ré get Roland-Lévy's theory that there must have been a woman involved? Armand Rozelaar was certain that both men had something to hide about that night.

By 1950 the newspapers had also picked up on some of the blatant contradictions of Hanoteau and Roland-Lévy. The latter then decided to settle the confusion once and for all. He wrote a letter, published in *Express-Dimanche (The Sunday Express)* on 4 June 1950, giving yet another version of events. In this letter he stated that after he and his friend saw Denoël on the sidewalk, he [Roland-Lévy] immediately returned to the Ministry of Work and ordered the night watchman [Ré] to call a police ambulance. Yet Ré stated, and his records clearly showed, that he was never asked to call, nor did he ever make a call for a police ambulance. The words of Hanoteau, Roland-Lévy, and Ré continued to stand in direct contradiction. And with this published letter, Pierre Roland-Lévy even contradicted himself.

Armand sat in a large overstuffed chair in his living room. He was supposedly reading the paper, but his wife noticed that he had not turned a page for several minutes. In fact, he seemed not to have moved his eyes either. He was just staring at the paper . . . silent. Then he said out loud, *"Un rassemblement* [a gathering]."

"What?" his wife asked.

He looked up at her and smiled. Then he repeated, "Of course, *un rassemblement!"*

"My dear, I don't know what you are talking about," his patient wife responded. Armand Rozelaar got up quickly from his chair and headed toward the hallway. He picked up his briefcase, put on his hat, and headed for the door. "Where are you going?"

"Back to the office, don't wait up for me," he told his wife.

"But why?"

"I think I have just solved the murder of Robert Denoël."

As he walked briskly to his law office on the rue de Moscou, I got out all of my information on the murder, the piles of testimony, the police investigations, and my own time line, which I had spent weeks constructing. I knew what Armand Rozelaar was going to do, and this time I was going to do it with him. As I expected, Rozelaar burst into his office and immediately took out his papers regarding the murder, spreading them out into neat piles. Then we were ready.

"Hmm," Rozelaar said. "I think I will start around the middle of November 1945."

"Fine with me," I responded, shuffling my papers to correspond with his.

"Around the middle of November, something happened to cause Robert to change his mind about marrying Jeanne Loviton," mused Rozelaar.

"I know," I said. "He found out about her long and overlapping affair with Paul Valéry. And maybe about her other affairs with prominent literary men."

"Shortly after that," he continued, "she obtained a medical certificate that enabled her to obtain a taxi at a police station."

"Yes," I said. "Did you know that that medical certificate was not even legal?"

"Robert Denoël believed he had become the designated scapegoat for publishing. He believed he was going to be purged as an example to all other publishers and to the public as well. If he were really the designated scapegoat for publishing, then it is likely that he would be found guilty at that trial in December. After all, he had collaborated. And a guilty verdict would most likely lead to his permanent exclusion from the profession of publishing."

"So he had to take covert steps to assure that he could remain in publishing clandestinely," I said.

"That's where the document ceding his company to someone else comes in—the one he signed but on which he left blank spaces. And who knew about that document?" he asked himself.

"Jeanne Loviton," I volunteered.

"Jeanne Loviton," he said aloud. "But Robert Denoël did something in addition to making that document. He decided to try to fix his trial," Rozelaar continued.

"And if enough money were given to the Communists, they could sometimes sway 'justice' the way they wanted," I said. "Just as, for example, those who wanted Denoël to be the scapegoat may have tried to sway 'justice' their way."

"That's where Guillaume Hanoteau and Pierre Roland-Lévy come in," Rozelaar said, talking to himself. "Jeanne Loviton and Robert Denoël set up a meeting with these two lawyers to try to fix his trial in return for gold . . . a great deal of gold."

"But wait a minute," I said. "There's another element here. The publishers, or publisher . . . He or they have to enter into the picture."

"But some publisher, or publishers, interfered with that meeting," Rozelaar continued. "It was a double game. Hanoteau, Roland-Lévy, and Loviton were in the pay of a publisher, or some publishers. They were paid to get rid of the problem, to see that Robert Denoël's defense dossier never came to light. And who was the only one who could have served as go-between for the publisher(s), the lawyers assigned to fix the trial, and Denoël?"

"Jeanne Loviton," I said.

"Jeanne Loviton," he said.

Then we stopped talking and began to study our notes and documents. It was clear to both of us that the phone call for Robert or Jeanne at the Delbo home the afternoon of the murder was probably to set up that meeting. It was also obvious that the meeting was a double game. Robert thought he was fixing his trial. The others wanted to take his defense dossier and do everything possible to see that Robert Denoël did not implicate other publishers.

I proceeded to go over my time line again and compare it with that of Armand Rozelaar. Robert and Jeanne were ready to leave 11, rue de l'Assomption at about 8:30 P.M. They walked to the car together. The maid watched them leave and noted the time. They did not take a direct route to the theater, instead possibly going by 19, rue Amélie, probably to pick up something. In all likelihood Robert put what he had picked up at his publishing house in the trunk, since there would be another passenger for the back seat. Then they picked up Guillaume Hanoteau at 13, rue de Verneuil, which was on their way. They arrived in front of the Ministry of Work a little before 9:00. Pierre Roland-Lévy could see the car from his office window. Robert, Jeanne, and Guillaume Hanoteau then had a discussion in the car. This discussion lasted from about 8:55 until 9:10. It must have been warm in that small car with three people inside. At some point they all got out of the car. It was probably at that time that Robert took off his overcoat, folded it neatly, and put it on the seat.

Their discussion had to deal with how to fix Robert's trial. But the lawyers had something else in mind entirely. They wanted that dossier! In return for their help, they wanted to be assured that Robert Denoël would not implicate any other publisher in his defense. But that was the centerpiece of Robert's whole defense. It is probable that Robert refused to make that promise. How could he?

According to the written record of André Ré, the night watchman at the Ministry of Work, Roland-Lévy left the building alone at about 9:10. Ré signed him out and pushed the button that opened the door. Roland-Lévy walked toward the car. He was gone only seven or eight minutes. But in that time Robert screamed, "Stop, thief!" according to a witness, then one or two shots followed. They took something from Robert—part or all of his gold? His defense dossier? Most likely it came from the trunk. He may have taken out the automobile tools to defend himself, or they may have been thrown out to get at the object in the trunk. Robert may have briefly pursued the thief when he was shot in the back around 9:15.

There were about four witnesses, not counting Hanoteau and Roland-Lévy, who heard the shot (shots), followed by a long, agonizing scream. But Armand Rozelaar noted that not one of them rushed to the scene. Three of those who heard the shot did look out immediately at the scene. All three swore that they saw no one fleeing in any direction. Nor did they see a car or other vehicle leaving the scene. But Robert was not alone when they looked out. As one of the witnesses, Colonel L'Hermite, explained in his testimony, there was *"un rassemblement,"* a gathering, around the body. If no one immediately rushed to the scene following the shooting, and if no one saw anyone fleeing the scene in any direction, just who could that "gathering" be? Armand Rozelaar had spent a great deal of time thinking about that "gathering." He later wrote to Judge Gollety, "It is the term *gathering* pronounced by Colonel L'Hermite, which left me for a moment thoughtful." In his letter of 26 April 1950 to Judge Gollety, Armand Rozelaar stated that by all reasoning, all logic, and objectivity there could be only one conclusion: "that the aforesaid gathering must have actually been composed of three people: Messieurs LEVY and HANOTEAU and Madame LOVITON."

This conclusion explained why no one was seen fleeing the scene. The killer and conspirators didn't run. They waited for Denoël to die. Then Hanoteau and Roland-Lévy walked back into the Ministry of Work, under the pretext of getting a pack of cigarettes. André Ré recorded their entrance and their strange words about the attack of a man on the rue de Grenelle. Hanoteau was probably carrying the briefcase or object that belonged to Robert Denoël. The gold? The dossier? And as previously planned, Jeanne Loviton walked to the nearby police station to use her recently acquired medical certificate and order a taxi. She even asked a policeman for directions to reinforce her alibi. While Hanoteau and Roland-Lévy waited for her to arrive at the station (a four- or five-minute walk) they could easily have stashed the gun and/or whatever they had taken from Robert Denoël in that office. According to Ré, they left about five minutes later. Then the two men returned toward the scene of the crime, reported it to Testud, the Guardian of the Peace, and were on the scene when the police ambulance arrived.

Testud's call came into the police station at about 9:25. We know that Jeanne Loviton was at the police station at that time. She stated that she heard the police call. But according to the police records, she had not already made a call for a taxi at that time. She waited. Perhaps she had been instructed to wait. Although she gave the impression in her testimony that she had already ordered a taxi and had been in the police station about five minutes when she heard the call for an ambulance, the police records of that night clearly show that she did not order a taxi until 9:30, five minutes after the call for a police ambulance.

This time line explained why Jeanne Loviton's description of her last moments with Robert Denoël changed so much. When she left him, he was not occupied with his tools and getting ready to change a tire at all, as she had consistently maintained—although with various other stories. When she left him, he was dying on the sidewalk. This version of events also explained why Jeanne Loviton said absolutely nothing to Robert Denoël in the ambulance. What could she possibly have said to him? If he were still conscious in the ambulance, then he knew that she was his betrayer and part of a conspiracy to murder him. It had to be her fervent hope that he would not be able to say anything in that ambulance . . . or ever again. This scenario also explained why Roland-Lévy, Hanoteau, and Loviton pretended not to recognize each other at the scene of the crime. It also explained why she searched the pockets of his overcoat as soon as the hospital turned it over to her. She was looking for his keys and for that Hermès notebook in which Robert kept his financial records. Although she was unable to obtain that notebook, she clearly got his keys. With the possible help of Dr. Percheron, who already headed one of Robert's fictitious businesses and who had already proven himself to be greedy, and possibly others, Jeanne Loviton took all of Robert Denoël's personal possessions and papers the night and early morning of 2–3 December 1945. And most likely, she hid them in a Swiss bank account (or several bank accounts).

The notion of a double game, the idea that Loviton, Hanoteau, and Roland-Lévy were also paid by and working for another publisher or publishers that night provides the most logical reason why Jeanne Loviton would maintain that Robert had no defense dossier for his 8 December trial. It further explains Loviton's contention that it was never Robert Denoël's intention to implicate other publishers as part of his defense of his company. Every other close Denoël associate knew that she was lying on both counts. And, of course, if Jeanne Loviton took all of Robert's money and personal belongings following his murder, her only reasonable explanation for the missing items was that there was never any money or belongings in the first place.

Rozelaar also learned that following the murder, both Roland-Lévy and Hanoteau received tremendous boosts in their careers. At the time of the murder, Roland-Lévy had only served for a few days as head of the cabinet of the Minister of Work, Monsieur Croizat. It was almost unheard of for Roland-Lévy to become a member of the powerful and significant Superior Council of the Magistrature by 1947. This Superior Council was an influential watchdog committee for all of the magistrates in France. It had the power to remove judges for misconduct while in office. Armand Rozelaar believed that Madame Loviton obtained that position for Roland-Lévy. He stated in a letter to Judge Gollety on 26 April 1950, "You can also determine the relationships common to Monsieur Pierre ROLAND-LEVY and Madame LOVITON by researching the conditions by which Monsieur Pierre ROLAND-LEVY was named Magistrate and designated to fill that exalted post which he still holds."

As for Hanoteau, while it would seem that the future for a disbarred lawyer might appear bleak, he too had "amazing luck." In 1949, at the age of forty-one, he began a career as a playwright, apparently with considerable support, contacts, and influence. Then in 1952, with no journalistic experience or qualifications, he was hired as an important journalist for *Paris-Match*. Rozelaar believed that Jeanne Loviton was also behind this man's amazing rise in the field of journalism and literature.

Yet in spite of Armand's compelling time line and all of his overwhelming circumstantial evidence, Jeanne Loviton appeared untouchable. The litigation seemed endless. Doggedly and at enormous expense, Cécile Denoël refused to give up. Just when it appeared that Jeanne Loviton might win on all counts and that the case against her might finally be closed for good, Madame Denoël managed to persuade the Attorney General to open the case all over again. Cécile charged that her opponent had used undue influence upon the courts by intervening repeatedly and directly into the judicial system, thereby obstructing and falsifying justice. Her evidence and newspaper pressures were so strong the Attorney General decided to reopen the case. Judge Gollety, who by now hoped the case would simply go away, was very annoyed by the Attorney General's decision.

The case was officially reopened for the final time on 28 December 1949, with Madame Denoël again becoming an official investigator, a *partie civile,* on 6 January 1950. In conjunction with this ongoing legal battle, a third and final police investigation into the murder of Robert Denoël was ordered. Although this investigation of the 1945 murder was not conducted until the spring of 1950, it was much more thorough and complete than the two previous police investigations. The seventy-five-page conclusion of this police investigation was submitted to Judge Gollety on 25 May 1950. This time the results of the police investigation corroborated the meticulous work of Armand Rozelaar. Now both the police and Rozelaar were pointing directly at Jeanne Loviton.

In this report the police found that Jeanne Loviton's statement that Robert Denoël was impoverished and relied upon her for moral and financial support could not be substantiated in any way. In fact, there was considerable evidence that Denoël was a wealthy man when he died. In addition, they viewed Jeanne Loviton's takeover of Les Editions Denoël as highly suspect. There was absolutely no evidence to support the notion that Jeanne Loviton had paid for her shares in Les Editions Denoël. To the contrary, there was considerable evidence to suggest that Robert Denoël had invested both his time and money in Jeanne Loviton's publishing house, Les Editions Domat-Montchrestien. The police agreed with the conclusions of several reliable witnesses in this matter who believed that the Domat and Denoël publishing houses were one and the same. They also found it quite credible, and substantiated by three witnesses, that Robert Denoël had changed his mind about marrying Jeanne Loviton shortly before the murder.

The inspectors in this investigation looked at five possible motives for this crime: random street crime, crime of passion, political crime, crime for profit, or settlement of a dispute. They concluded that the last motive seemed most likely. After reviewing all the evidence, these inspectors concluded that Denoël's death probably came "at the end of a discussion at the exact spot of the drama where he reportedly went for a meeting that went badly for him." Such a conclusion clearly made Jeanne Loviton part of a conspiracy. These police inspectors concluded that Jeanne Loviton knew of the meeting. She may have made the arrangements for that meeting. She was there, and she knew who else was there and why. As for her statement that she left Robert Denoël to obtain a taxi because their car had a flat tire, the inspectors in this third police investigation found her explanation to be ludicrous.

The inspectors in 1950 did something else that had not been done in the previous two investigations. They asked, "Who profited from this murder?" One answer was quite clear: Jeanne Loviton. Another answer was equally clear: any other Parisian publisher who might have collaborated in any way at any time with the Nazis. And it was clear to anyone who closely studied Robert Denoël's defense strategy that one publisher in particular benefited by the theft of Denoël's defense dossier: Gaston Gallimard. In this third investigation the police disregarded Jeanne Loviton's claims that there was no defense dossier. It was absurd to assume that Robert Denoël, scheduled to defend his entire company on charges of collaboration just six days after his murder, would not have prepared an elaborate and detailed defense. In fact, the police now gave great importance to that defense dossier. The police postulated that Denoël's aggressive defense of his company might have caused another publisher (or publishers) to seek ways to suppress the defense dossier, either through violence or a payoff. They concluded that Denoël's defense dossier not only existed, but may have been an indirect cause of his murder.

Unlike the previous two police investigations, this one completely discounted Jeanne Loviton's "good faith." The police found countless contradictions in her various versions of what happened the night of the murder. Her word was no longer assumed to be worth anything. In fact, the police described Jeanne Loviton as ambitious, self-serving, and duplicitous. Many of their direct conclusions about the murder suggested that she was involved in a conspiracy. This police report and the conclusions of Armand Rozelaar finally agreed. Jeanne Loviton faced the distinct possibility of standing trial on several charges, including the blatant theft of Les Editions Denoël and conspiracy to murder its owner.

Finally, French newspapers had something new to write about concerning Denoël's murder. From January until July 1950, newspapers and journals entered into a frenzy of sensationalism. The 13 January 1950 edition of *France-Soir* carried this headline: JUSTICE HAS REOPENED THE DOSSIER ON THE MURDER OF PUBLISHER DENOEL. This newspaper cited evidence suggesting that the murder was the result of a "crime of interest." The front-page headline of *Express-Dimanche* on 30 April 1950 read: THE SECRET DOSSIER OF THE DENOEL CASE. SUPPRESSED FOR 5 YEARS THE INVESTIGATION INTO THE ASSASSINATION OF THE FAMOUS PUBLISHER WILL HAVE SENSATIONAL REPERCUSSIONS.

With the newspapers fueling and magnifying the issues of this case, with a new and very thorough police investigation now contradicting most of Jeanne Loviton's claims, and with the detailed, overwhelming evidence brought forth by Armand Rozelaar, it seemed that Guillaume Hanoteau, Pierre Roland-Lévy, Jeanne Loviton—and perhaps even Gaston Gallimard—were in very serious trouble.

15

The Verdict

In the final analysis, Justice was a reflection of the society of the time.

Judge Antonin Besson

I reread all of the testimony given by Jeanne Loviton between 1945 and 1950, found in the police and court records of the Denoël dossier. Throughout those long years of allegations and court battles, Jeanne seemed unflappable. Then I read Cécile Denoël's testimony. Even in those yellowing pages, now more than fifty years old, her emotion and frustration were fresh. I had even seen Cécile fall apart on a few occasions, mostly in the office of her lawyer or with a few close friends. I had felt her emotion in her letters to the court. But I failed to locate any picture or record that even hinted that Jeanne Loviton had ever become overwhelmed with emotion. In fact, although I had looked very closely, I had never seen her with one hair out of place. She wore heavy makeup, giving her face a masklike quality. Throughout this ordeal, even during her lengthy questioning by the police, she seemed . . . well, haughty. She changed her stories as often as she changed her hats, apparently without fear of reprisal. I looked at the transcripts of her police interviews. Her favorite responses were: "I can't remember" or "I don't recall" or even sometimes "I have no idea." She was either the bravest and most brazen liar I had ever encountered, or the most foolhardy—or she knew something I did not.

Cécile was infuriated by her opponent's manner. "She thinks she is untouchable! I would like to wipe that superior, smug look right off her face," she told her lawyer as they sat in his office.

Armand smiled briefly, then said, "You might just get your chance."

Cécile sat upright in her chair. "How?" she asked.

"As a *partie civile* you do have the right to question Madame Loviton." He looked directly at her, then continued, "But let me warn you, it won't be easy. Jeanne Loviton is an experienced lawyer. Trapping her in any significant way would be most difficult."

"I want to try. I can't do any worse than these inspectors and policemen," she said.

And so Armand Rozelaar arranged for a legal confrontation between Jeanne Loviton and Cécile Denoël. Rozelaar spent hours with his client, deciding upon the questions, the procedure, the way they would treat Madame Loviton. Rozelaar had to admit that he had come to like the passionate Cécile Denoël. He admired her tenacity, her spirit. But just the same, he was worried. He knew that she could be emotional and unstable. Could she stand up to her formidable, savvy opponent?

Finally, the day of the questioning arrived. I sat in the back of the courtroom. Cécile entered first. She was wearing a plain black dress with long sleeves and a high collar. Both the collar and the sleeves ended in short black ruffles. She looked nervous. Her eyes were wide and her hands shook as she greeted her lawyer, who had arrived shortly before her.

Then her adversary entered the court. Jeanne didn't even look at Cécile as she entered. She was also wearing black, a wonderful black suit with a white silk blouse, and one string of pearls at the neck. She reminded me of a *Vogue* magazine cover. Her makeup, her hair, her clothing, everything was absolutely perfect, almost as if they had been airbrushed. The flawlessness and straight lines of her attire made the ruffles on Cécile's dress seem somehow girlish. Cécile watched Jeanne's entrance. Clearly, Jeanne would be a confident, difficult defendant.

As the proceedings began, Armand smiled at Cécile and patted the back of her hand. "You will do fine," he said, as she was summoned to begin.

I held my breath. Seated beside her lawyer, Cécile appeared to be a nervous, inexperienced wreck. She fumbled as she gathered her papers together. Rozelaar helped her with her papers. His face seemed frozen in a slight tense smile. Then, as Cécile walked toward her adversary, a transformation occurred. Cécile—Cécile, the actress—deftly undertook her role as prosecutor. She walked with confidence, exhibiting a strength that belied her ruffles. And when she spoke, she did so clearly, with authority. She had some very hard questions to ask Jeanne Loviton. She and her lawyer had seen to that. Listening to his client, Armand sat back in his chair, attentive, encouraging. Robert Denoël would have been proud of her. Everyone was impressed by her preparation and her professionalism—everyone except Jeanne Loviton.

I studied the transcript of the court proceedings of that day. Jeanne seemed hugely annoyed that anyone would dare ask her questions again about the night of the murder. Sitting before the court, she did not remind me of a defendant, but rather of a duchess who, through no fault of her own, was forced to do something very distasteful. As for Cécile's probing questions, she simply avoided them, as if sidestepping a puddle. How could the court let her get away with that?

For example, Cécile asked, "What time did you leave the rue de l'Assomption?"

Jeanne responded, "I don't look at the time when I leave my domicile."

"Then how did you know you were late?"

"One can know one is late without knowing how long one is late."

Cécile continued, "The shortest way [to the theater] was to the right; that's the road one should take when one is late. How do you explain the considerable detour that your car took?"

Without hesitation, Jeanne replied, "I have already responded to that question, and I state that neither Robert Denoël nor I are taxi drivers."

Taxi drivers? Jeanne was treating this court procedure as a game. Here was a lady accused of theft, possibly murder, and her answers were sarcastic, short, deprecating, ludicrous. In fact, all of her responses to Cécile's questions were like that. When Cécile asked her how long it had taken to drive back from the Delbo residence the day of the murder, Jeanne responded, "I am not a living stopwatch."

I looked at her statement again—"a living stopwatch." How could she give such glib answers at such a serious time? Surely the judge would take note of her behavior. I glanced at Judge Gollety. His face revealed nothing. In fact, he didn't even seem to be paying attention.

Of course Cécile asked her about Robert's overcoat. Jeanne had given many versions of the whereabouts of that coat the night of the murder. This time Cécile asked, "When you left Robert Denoël at the boulevard des Invalides, was he wearing his overcoat?"

Wearily, Jeanne replied, "I no longer know anything about it." No one forced her to answer, or to explain her previous versions.

Cécile also asked Jeanne, "How much time elapsed between your arrival at the police station and the police call about the shooting?"

Jeanne gave a strange, unhelpful answer: "I stayed there for what seemed to me like a long time but which was, however, short."

Once again the judge did not attempt to get her to be more specific. How could she get away with this? I sat silent in my office, reading with one hand, and absentmindedly petting my loudly purring black cat with the other, slowly drawing my hand down his sleek coat. After having read the entire transcript and all of Jeanne Loviton's nonsensical, arrogant, flippant answers, it finally dawned on me. Suddenly I knew why Jeanne Loviton was so arrogant. "She didn't fix Robert Denoël's trial; she fixed her own!" I said to myself. It didn't matter how well Cécile did. It didn't matter that Judge Gollety wasn't paying attention. It wouldn't have mattered if Robert Denoël had written the names of the perpetrators of his murder in his own blood! The trial was fixed! The entire thing was a fiasco. Slowly, unwillingly, I reached for the final judgment. And I began to read.

It was up to the French Attorney General *(Le Procureur de la République)*, Antonin Besson, to decide if there was enough evidence to prosecute Madame Jeanne Loviton on any count relating to the murder of Robert Denoël. Besson was considered to be an able and experienced Attorney General. He made his final ruling in this case on 1 July 1950, in his Definitive Charge. After carefully considering all of the evidence in that third police investigation, along with the exhaustive research of Armand Rozelaar, Antonin Besson arbitrarily changed that all-important time line. Based upon no new evidence and with no apparent logic, Besson decided that Robert Denoël and Jeanne Loviton had arrived at the scene of the crime shortly *after* 9:00 P.M. and that Robert Denoël was shot at 9:10 P.M. or even a little earlier. According to Besson's new time line, Robert Denoël was present at the scene of the crime only between five and ten minutes, and Jeanne Loviton spent even less time there, since she was allegedly absent when the shooting occurred. By using this new time line Besson was able to eliminate any notion of a meeting, thereby exonerating Hanoteau, Roland-Lévy, and Loviton. As for the maid, who said they left their house at 8:30, all the witnesses who claimed to have heard the shot much later, and the police blotter showing that Jeanne Loviton had not ordered a taxi until 9:30, they were all completely ignored.

I examined Besson's conclusions closely, as stated in his Definitive Charge. Besson had completely disregarded that third police investigation. Once again, the story asserted by Jeanne Loviton was accepted at face value. Based upon no evidence at all, Antonin Besson decided that Robert Denoël was murdered after he stopped his car because of a flat tire. There was absolutely no other reason for him to be at that particular spot the night of 2 December. Besson also decided that Robert Denoël was indigent at the time of his murder and relied entirely upon the financial support and good will of Madame Loviton. He added that Madame Loviton did indeed purchase

Les Editions Denoël, in spite of the fact that there was no record of payment, and the document giving her ownership was filled out six days after Denoël's murder. She was deemed to be the rightful owner of that company and owed no further payment.

As for Madame Loviton's trips to Switzerland and Belgium, they were made solely for reasons of health. In addition, Robert Denoël had no enemies. There were no threats made against him. Gaston Gallimard and other publishers, the Jewish resistance movement, and the anti-collaborationists were not his enemies. Therefore, any business conflicts occurred as a result of the murder and were certainly not the cause of it. As for Denoël's defense dossier (still missing), it could not possibly have played a part in Denoël's murder.

Besson also decided that Guillaume Hanoteau and Pierre Roland-Lévy were men beyond reproach whose "good faith" ("*bonne foi*") should not be questioned. The contradictions in the stories of Hanoteau and Roland-Lévy, the former's disbarrment and the latter's ousting from the Communist Party, were completely ignored, as were their amazing relationships with others in this case. As for the written record of that night watchman, André Ré, his testimony was not ever considered.

Cécile Denoël lost her legal suit on all counts. She was ordered to pay all court costs—a staggering amount. She was also treated more as an annoyance in this case than a plaintiff. Sometimes in this Definitive Charge she was even blamed for the incompetence of the police. For example, Besson reproached her for not having requested the use of police seals, as if this were somehow her duty and not that of the police. Madame Loviton could not possibly have achieved more success if she had written that Definitive Charge herself. . . . I began to wonder. Did she?

After reading the Definitive Charge, there were only two possible conclusions. Either Antonin Besson was a total incompetent in this case, or Jeanne Loviton had managed to accomplish what she had promised to help Robert Denoël do—sway the court in her favor. In addition to the highly dubious conclusions of this document, I noticed that there were many misspellings, errors, cases of specious reasoning, non sequiturs, and outright omissions. It seemed as if that Definitive Charge had been hastily written. What had happened? To try to find the answer, I returned to the graduate library of the University of Michigan.

There, I learned that when the Nazis and the Vichy government controlled France during World War II, they had neither the time nor the inclination to replace all of the French judges who previously served France before the war. In fact, both the Nazis and their Vichy collaborators desired a swift purge of the existing judges, followed by official declarations of legitimacy for the remaining magistrates. Such actions would be most expedient for a smooth German takeover. Those who would be purged were obvious: all Jews, Freemasons (whose secret societies generally opposed Fascism), Communists, and anyone else who refused to cooperate and bend to the rules of the Nazis.

In total about 5 percent of the magistrates were purged, leaving 95 percent of those judges who had served a free France before 1939 now serving the will of the Nazis in the same positions. All of these remaining judges had to swear allegiance to Pétain, not to France, and had to promise to do whatever else the Nazis required of them in order to keep their jobs. Their sworn oath began with, "I swear fidelity to the person of the Head of State." Therefore, all of the French judges serving during the Occupation technically collaborated. Just as they had previously upheld French law, they later upheld Nazi and Vichy law.

Following the Liberation there was again an immediate need to purge the magistrates. It was believed that such a purging would once again lend legitimacy to the existing judicial system. And legitimate courts were needed right away in order to curb the excesses of vigilante purging that was rampant immediately after the Liberation. Just as had occurred in other areas of government and business at that time, the more prominent and well-known judges were treated much more harshly than lesser-known magistrates. Once again, the purpose of the purge seemed to be to make an example of certain prominent judges rather than to punish everyone who had collaborated. Of all the magistrates, only about 10 percent faced some sort of condemnation, sanction, or court case.

The vast majority of French judges who presided before the war, during the Occupation, and following the Liberation were in fact the same judges. They simply upheld and legitimized different laws—and different powers. It could be argued that just as almost all French publishers collaborated, so too did nearly all the French magistrates who were to judge them. Individual cases of judges were often deeply confusing. For example, during the Occupation a French judge sentenced two French resisters to death by firing squad, as prescribed by law, because they had thrown a bomb that killed two Germans. But following the Liberation, that same judge could be said to have been responsible for the deaths of two patriots. Should he face criminal prosecution for his Occupation ruling?

After considering these disturbing facts, I then turned my attention to that Attorney General who had turned justice upside-down in his Definitive Charge regarding the Denoël case. I strolled over to the library computer. To my amazement, Antonin Besson was there. There were two entries, and one of those entries was entitled, *The Myth of Justice (Le Mythe de la justice)*. Excited, I quickly ordered the book to be brought to the main library from its location in the Buhr Annex and impatiently waited the obligatory twenty-four hours for its arrival. I was not disappointed.

No, Antonin Besson did not confess to having toppled justice in the case of Robert Denoël. He did not even discuss that particular case. But he explained. He demonstrated how such a reversal of justice could have happened at the time. He explained what had occurred to the French justice system as a direct result of World War II. And finally he made one of the most eloquent cases for the true separation of powers that I have ever read. I soon learned that Antonin Besson was deeply critical of the French justice system even at the time of the Denoël case. And he was often in direct conflict with Charles de Gaulle himself over judicial matters. His arguments with De Gaulle led directly to Besson's early retirement in 1962. Still angry and deeply troubled by what he had witnessed within the French justice system, Besson decided to write about his judicial concerns during his retirement. The result was *The Myth of Justice*, published in 1973.

Besson pointed out with exceptional clarity what happened to France during this period. He demonstrated that, in general, the same police, lawyers, and judges who were working in 1939 also presided over the Occupation, then the Liberation and post-Liberation periods. This fact led to many contradictory, deeply ironic situations. For example, the police who rounded up and jailed the Jews in France before their deportation to German concentration camps were the very same police who later rounded up and jailed suspected collaborators and anti-Semites following the Liberation. Besson explained that the police were no longer following the law, but rather serving as the henchmen of those in power. According to Besson, the police were "in the service of Power before being in the service of Law." But there was more. As Besson stated, "Beside those specialized police forces concerned with common law, we find the political police services with multiple implications and the police services for maintenance of public order." With different police services, I reasoned, it becomes easier to understand the possibility of more than one police dossier on Denoël's murder, as many journalists had claimed.

Besson deplored the fact that judges who condemned resisters were the very same judges who later condemned collaborators, completely ignoring the fact that the judges, too, had collaborated. And lawyers also found that the laws had changed; the rules were different as France was occupied and then liberated. And by simply keeping their jobs, following the rules of the day, and swearing an oath to the Head of State (who was Pétain), they were all collaborators. In fact, because of that oath to Pétain taken by every single government official (whether judge, schoolteacher, or janitor), all of them technically had collaborated.

In addition, nearly any activity, whether running a restaurant, a publishing house, or opening a play in Paris during the Occupation, required a license—a German-approved license. Therefore, in the strict eyes of the law following the Liberation, most French people could be accused of collaboration during the Occupation merely because they did their jobs and pursued their professions. One could therefore claim that those who were later held up as model resisters during the Occupation did in fact collaborate: Sartre, Simone de Beauvoir, Camus, and many others.

Besson noted that during the Occupation it was difficult for any Frenchman to know exactly what was the right thing to do. "At any particular moment, and as a result of the coexistence of competing political powers, the French who were not committed had some difficulty in differentiating between the path of obedience and the path of duty." And Pétain himself exacerbated this confusion. He was popular, beloved, a World War I hero, a model. And he was not only collaborating himself, he was urging all other French people to do likewise—for the good of the nation. He had already told the French people how much he hated untruths. However, as Besson pointed out, "Now, the Marshal was called upon to lie during the entire duration of the Occupation, to lie to the Germans, to lie to his ministers, to lie to his entourage, and to lie to himself." But in Antonin Besson's mind Pétain had done something much worse than to lie to the French people and play his double games. He had weakened and corrupted France's court system. Pétain inserted politics into the justice system by directly intervening in certain court cases, as did certain high-ranking Nazi officials. In some court decisions Pétain asserted that he and he alone would be the judge. With Pétain's actions, the political branch of the government became more powerful than the judicial.

Besson noted the strength and independence of the French court system before it became corrupted by politics. He discussed the power of the *juge d'instruction,* that judge who followed a court case from its inception to its conclusion and ultimately made the final judgment. He recounted the story of a professor long ago who asked one of his law students, "Who is the most powerful man in France?"

The student hesitated. "The king?"

"No," his professor replied.

"The prime minister?" the student suggested.

"No," said his professor. "The most powerful man in France is the *juge d'instruction*. No man can counter his decisions." Then Besson quoted Balzac, who described the *juge d'instruction* as "a sovereign uniquely submitted to his conscience and to the law."

But as Besson pointed out, the power of the *juge d'instruction* changed dramatically in France during and following the Occupation. As politics took control of the justice system, the role of the *juge d'instruction* became that of an actor in "a stage setting. Those who were initiates, that is to say, all those jurists who frequent the Palace of Justice, know that it is his impotence that is manifest." During and after the war, the power of the *juge d'instruction* became subordinate to that of the Attorney General, and then to other influences, most particularly to political meddling. By deciding legal cases themselves, Pétain and high-ranking German officials made a sham of the courts.

Following the Liberation, many magistrates believed that the practice of direct intervention by politicians into court cases would finally cease. But they were wrong. Just as Pétain had intervened directly into the legal system, so later did Charles de Gaulle, and so did the head of the provisional government and later Minister of Foreign Affairs, Georges Bidault. I remembered that Bidault and his wife, Suzanne, were great friends with Jeanne Loviton.

Georges Bidault had no real experience when he became France's Minister of Foreign Affairs under Charles de Gaulle. In fact, the British Ambassador in Paris stated upon first meeting Bidault, "He seemed curiously young and somewhat overcome by his responsibilities, admitting himself that he knew nothing, and had had no experience." Bidault also had frequent disagreements with De Gaulle, had problems with his job, and was often apologizing for some of De Gaulle's high-handed tactics, saying, "De Gaulle loves France, even if he doesn't like Frenchmen."

Probably because of the stress of his job, Bidault developed a drinking problem and was sometimes called In Bido Veritas by other diplomats. At the time diplomatic relations with the Soviet Union were considered to be particularly crucial for France. Determined to drink as much vodka as the Russians, Bidault sometimes collapsed into an alcoholic stupor at diplomatic parties. Unfortunately, Robert Brasillach's trial and sentence for having written pro-Nazi and anti-Semitic works became inextricably intermingled with Georges Bidault's foreign policy regarding the Soviet Union.

As one of the first writers to go on trial for his artistic work, Brasillach faced the harshest sentence: death by firing squad. His short trial had an even shorter jury deliberation: twenty minutes. A petition, initiated by François Mauriac and signed by many leading intellectuals and even several resisters, was presented to de Gaulle to try to save this writer's life. And that's when politics once again interfered with justice. It was well known that Robert Brasillach was also anti-Communist. Bidault began to worry. What would the Russians think if France spared the life of Brasillach?

Robert Brasillach had another strike against him. He had witnessed and written about a massacre of around 4,500 Polish army officers at Katyn in western Russia during the war. According to him, the Soviets had been responsible for this atrocity. But the Soviets later blamed the Germans for the massacre. The only other two French witnesses to this act mysteriously disappeared. Only Brasillach, that ardent anti-Communist, remained. Wouldn't it be better just to have him shot? Bidault wondered. His execution would certainly facilitate Bidault's foreign policy with the Russians. As one scholar of that era has noted, "Then it is possible that in order to please the Soviet authorities they executed the only witness of Katyn who had not disappeared." It was not until 1990 that Mikhail Gorbachev admitted Soviet responsibility (as ordered by Joseph Stalin) for the Katyn atrocity, thereby confirming Brasillach's claims. Georges Bidault was heavily involved in the decision to execute Brasillach. He allegedly encouraged Charles de Gaulle to put Brasillach before the firing squad so as not to annoy the Soviets. Politics became the supreme power.

While reading about Brasillach, I came across a very familiar name. Before his trial Brasillach had met a young woman, an actress named Alice Sapritch, who was very taken by him. She and the poet

Brasillach had shared many hours of poetry and conversation. She often recited his poetry. She was clearly falling in love with this charming and romantic man. Then another man, "very engaged in clandestine activities, spoke to her about Brasillach." Long before Brasillach's trial and sentence, this man told Sapritch that her poet was in fact a dead man. He had no hope. He would be executed. The name of the man with this information was Guillaume Hanoteau, one of the lawyers who was present at the murder of Robert Denoël.

All that Hanoteau had told Sapritch came true. Brasillach was shot for writings, which were often much milder than Céline's. And the massacre at Katyn? Since there were no more witnesses to dispute Russian claims, the massacre at Katyn was officially blamed on the Nazis. And as a bonus, the Communists could not accuse Charles de Gaulle or Georges Bidault of being softhearted in their purges. Politics had once again determined justice. As for Alice Sapritch, she later married Guillaume Hanoteau.

Armand Rozelaar and Cécile Denoël both adamantly accused Georges Bidault and his wife, Suzanne, of direct intervention in the course of justice in the Robert Denoël murder. Those good friends of Jeanne Loviton had allegedly stepped in at the last moment to force Antonin Besson to change the course of justice and help Jeanne in her time of need. This last-minute overturning of the Definitive Charge would also explain all the errors and misspellings within the document. It was really no longer the product of the thoughtful, learned man who wrote *The Myth of Justice*. Although in his book Antonin Besson did not directly corroborate the version put forth by Cécile and her lawyer, he did note that such obstructions and thwarting of justice by politicians did happen at the time of the Denoël trial.

This political intervention into the justice system created a class of untouchables within French society. Those with enough important contacts and political clout could get away with anything . . . even murder. Although this unfortunate fact has not yet been fully examined by scholars of this era, it is clear that having some within

French society who were truly above the law was another profoundly disturbing result of World War II for a country already so deeply torn by its effects. It is no wonder that most French people, even today, do not want to discuss this period. Jeanne Loviton had become one of those untouchables within French society. Her political contacts and influence protected her, even against charges of conspiracy to murder and the theft of an entire company. No matter what lies were discovered in her versions of events, no matter what amazing coincidences occurred, no matter how many things conveniently disappeared, no matter who turned up on a deserted street corner on a winter Sunday night, she remained beyond reproach.

16

The Winners Take All

I have lessons to give, reckonings to demand. I am the
accuser, not the accused!

Céline

Once again, I decided to look at Robert Denoël's principal writer.
When I left him, Céline, his wife (Lucette), and even his cat (Bébert)
were all imprisoned. Although his wife and cat were soon released,
Céline spent eighteen long, hard months (from December 1945 until
June 1947) in his Danish prison. Often ill, he lost considerable
weight and was in constant fear for his wife, his cat, and, of course,
for himself. He was in a nightmarish limbo, having had no trial and
not even knowing the Danish charges against him. He was simply
held in prison indefinitely while France slowly began to make official
requests for his return. His cell (number 603) was on death row.
Céline was frantic. Lucette was allowed to visit him every Monday.
Of course, she was not allowed to bring Bébert, but she brought him
anyway. "She comes to see me with Bébert . . . seven minutes . . .
Bébert in a sack . . . He can't move a muscle! . . . total immobil-
ity . . . the guard's watching . . ."

He wrote frequent pleading letters to his lawyer, Thorvald Mikkelsen. Although he was allowed to write his lawyer, he was not allowed to write to his wife. To solve this problem, Céline often began

letters to his lawyer, then with no break and right in the middle of the letter, slipped in a message to his wife. Dutifully, Mikkelsen took these messages to Lucette. Speaking of France, Céline told Lucette, "That country, that justice are no longer anything but devices for vengeance in the hands of clans. It is only a question of killing, just as they killed Denoël, that's all." Lucette and Céline were in absolute misery. According to Lucette, at one time or another, both seriously considered suicide. As Céline said, "They told me three weeks, it has been three months. Will it be three years? . . . 30 years? It doesn't make sense." Lucette refused to leave Céline in spite of the fact that she was living alone in dire poverty in a land whose language she did not understand, staying in a room in the frigid north with almost no heat. Neither one dared to think of tomorrow—while French and Danish officials wrangled.

In prison Céline's health rapidly deteriorated. Often he was so weak he could not walk. His vision blurred. He was constantly constipated, enduring countless enemas. Everything seemed to be falling apart. In describing the prisoners (and himself) on death row, he said, "They are not all killed! Allow me to tell you for your edification that at the bottom of the pit the body is overtaken by mold, I mean the limbs, the trunk, the skin, and even the eyes!" Céline continued to proclaim himself to be totally innocent on all counts. According to him, he had never collaborated, never attended any of Abetz's parties, and never gone to the German embassy. He even claimed that he had not written one single anti-Semitic word since 1937. But even his lies seemed lost on officials. His status remained unchanged. He continued to be imprisoned on unknown charges while France sought to extradite him for trial. He felt particularly guilty for Lucette's situation, saying, "And it is especially you, the victim of this torture in many acts. Me, at my age, life is already escaping, but at your age, this is a vivisection—where have I taken you? I hold myself responsible. I suspected it, too. I felt myself led toward an ignoble and stupid fatality. They have already killed us. No one then can separate us. We are dead to the world together."

Finally, on 24 June 1947 Céline was officially released from incarceration. But he was not free to leave Denmark. It would be four more years before he could return to his own country. He spent most of that time living in poverty, with no bathroom or running water, in houses or rooms that had inadequate heat, so vital in those long Nordic winters. They adopted a dog and other cats. They lived and ate simply. But it was too cold for a garden, vegetables were nearly nonexistent, and meat was rare and often less than desirable. There was fish, even a concoction of smoked herring and oatmeal. With little money, poor food, and such a cold climate, Lucette and Céline knew hardship. It was while he was in Denmark that Céline began to correspond with his new publisher, Jeanne Loviton.

He did not like her right from the start. But Céline had never liked publishers. Then in April of 1948 Jeanne Loviton did something absolutely wonderful for Céline. That trial of Les Editions Denoël on charges of collaboration, which had been scheduled to begin six days after Denoël's murder in 1945, was not canceled. It was merely postponed until the spring of 1948. And in 1948 it was Jeanne Loviton who would defend this company—Jeanne Loviton, with all of her influential friends and knowledge of the courts and of how to fix trials. At the original trial set for 8 December 1945 Robert Denoël intended to admit that his company had collaborated. His defense was that all other publishers had also collaborated and that, given the circumstances of Nazi rule, they really had no other choice.

Jeanne Loviton's defense was much simpler. She claimed that Les Editions Denoël had never collaborated at all, not once. And, of course, she won. "The house of Denoël had been found not guilty of publishing in time of war 'brochures and books in favor of the enemy, of collaboration with the enemy, racism or totalitarian doctrines.' " That was not all. She received total compensation for all of her court costs. I remembered some of the anti-Semitic and collaborative books Denoël had published: *How to Recognize the Jew?* (*Comment reconnaître le Juif?*); *Medicine and the Jews* (*La Médecine and les Juifs*), and *The Press and the Jews* (*La Presse et les Juifs*). Even worse, Denoël had published the pamphlets of Rebatet and Céline, which provided virulent anti-Semitism and collaborationist ideas in their most readable and enjoyable forms. Countless thousands of readers had bought and read these works. As Céline's biographer, Frédéric Vitoux, said, "It was unbelievable. . . . What influence, what support had Jean Voilier [Jeanne Loviton] relied upon?" The implications of this verdict for Céline were enormous. If Les Editions Denoël had never published any collaborationist works and was totally exonerated, then Céline, who had published all of his works at Les Editions Denoël, should be exonerated, too. He wrote a Paris friend, "Denoël's acquittal and its terms seem to me so amazing that I would be obliged to you if you would immediately send me a hundred copies duplicated at my expense."

Jeanne Loviton's trial fixing (there can logically be no other name for it) helped Céline in his own attempt to return to France a free man. His lawyers cited the verdict in this case at every opportunity. But if Céline appreciated Loviton's tactics in this trial, it was the only aspect of Jeanne Loviton that met with his approval. Perhaps his suspicions were aroused because he had so long been associated with Robert Denoël and knew how much his company meant to him. He knew Robert would never sell his publishing business. While other employees of Les Editions Denoël kept quiet, Céline began to accuse the new owner of Denoël's publishing house—sometimes publicly. He called Jeanne Loviton "Denoël's mystifying/stupendous/amazing heiress."

Just as Robert Denoël once was, in Céline's eyes, an incompetent pimp and half-grocer, Jeanne Loviton became a swindler, a phony inheritor, and worse. Céline had always linked his own death with that of his publisher. Now he stated that "they desired my death so they could inherit from me! As she inherits from R. Denoël! She is an unbridled heiress! A farce." For him, she was the biggest swindler of all, the biggest scoundrel, "a bitch who dreams only of lawsuits." It was only a few steps from "unbridled heiress" to murderess. Céline made that jump easily. And in his contempt and derision, he implicated another man in all of this. He accused Pierre Roland-Lévy of receiving a payoff from Jeanne Loviton. "Of course, Madame Loviton-Lévy must have given huge pledges to the Lévy clan in order to get herself out of the trouble, and in particular to swear to have me and my books killed off. Not likely! That will require perfect undercover work, that's all, and at a very high price. It's a lot of goat shit."

In one of Céline's more thoughtful moments, he summed up his feelings for Jeanne Loviton in just two sentences: "Old Lady Loviton belongs to the race of victorious nobility and finds it absolutely unheard of for anyone to even think of daring to challenge her and all her rights of life and death over everything within her grasp. The absolute power of a lord." I looked at some of the other activities of Jeanne Loviton during her long and wealthy life. I discovered that she had boasted to many people that because of her influential friends and connections, she had become "untouchable." She also owned properties and rented them out. She was allegedly accused of illegal rent increases and was sued. Apparently, another "magic" intervention occurred, causing the entire case to be dropped. It was also claimed that the "tenants in the building out of which the publishing house of the Editions DOMAT-MONTCHRESTIEN operates are in open revolt against her without ever being able to reach her." Was she an absentee slum landlord?

Then I looked at what Jeanne Loviton had done with all those letters, poems, manuscripts, original drawings, and autographed first editions that Paul Valéry had given her throughout their long liaison. I remembered that during his lifetime Valéry had made no secret of his belief that his private letters and papers, along with those of other celebrities, should never be published or sold. In fact, I recalled that his former mistress, Catherine Pozzi, had burned all of his letters when their affair ended. But Jeanne Loviton had no intention of burning Valéry's letters and mementos.

At first, Jeanne gave some indications to several scholars that she might decide to give much of her invaluable Valéry materials to the elite, prestigious, highly restrictive Jacques Doucet Library, noted for its vast holdings of Valéry materials. But such a generous gift was really not her intention. Her second thought was to find someone to buy all of Valéry's letters and poetry, along with her house at 11, rue de l'Assomption and turn the whole thing into a museum. After all, Valéry had spent a great deal of time at that house and considered that private garden to be his favorite spot for writing. But Loviton decided that any prospective buyer would have to agree to two points: First, he would have to pay well over market price for everything. And second, after paying for the property, he would have to allow Jeanne Loviton to live in that house, totally undisturbed, until her death. Needless to say, no such buyer was found. Then she decided simply to find a private buyer who would pay her a greatly inflated price for the entire lot of her Valéry letters and poetry. In that way, at least the entire collection would be kept together, possibly providing invaluable information to the researcher and scholar. Unfortunately, no such buyer or collector could be found who was willing to pay the astronomical prices she was asking. And Jeanne Loviton was not willing to lower her price.

She then decided to divide her Valéry letters and poetry into more than one hundred small lots. Using questionable appraisers, all of her considerable influence, and blatant manipulation to raise the prices as high as possible, she sold her collection at auction in Monte Carlo in October 1982. Carlton Lake, who had at one time expressed interest in buying some of her treasures, summed up the auction: "One dealer quoted the old saying, *'Ça sent la macaque'*—it smells to high heaven." The collection of Paul Valéry's letters and poetry once owned by Jeanne Loviton is now scattered across the world, from Japan to America, and will probably never be completely available to any scholar, no matter how wealthy or assiduous.

At some point prior to 1982, Jeanne Loviton sold her home at 11, rue de l'Assomption to a real-estate developer for $1,400,000. She then moved into a sumptuous Parisian apartment. While he was inspecting some of her Valéry material, Carlton Lake was invited to dine with her there. The repast was served by a butler in white gloves while she discussed her own poverty and "how well off the French working class really was." Lake also described "her standard monologue: her health, money problems, loss of jewelry [resulting from a boating accident], lawsuits in profusion, treachery on all sides." Lake wrote about her in two of his books dealing with his attempted acquisition of some Valéry material. He described at length her manipulations and her use of contacts and influence in her later years. He didn't realize, of course, how long she had used such tactics—and how effectively. And deeply aware of her far-reaching influence and highly litigious nature, he carefully concealed her real name, always referring to her in his book by her pseudonym, Jean Voilier, or by one of Valéry's pet names for her, Héra.

I looked at some of the men she had left in her wake. I thought of Pierre Frondaie, that tempestuous, talented romantic who had married Jeanne and who had written so many long-running plays and successful novels. He had all but vanished from any history or literature book. Now, at least, I knew why his name was so forgotten. First, he was a man fighting against the times, one who preferred romantic, action-packed plays at a time when surrealism was in vogue. Some of his criticisms of surrealism had proven to be accurate. A great play does need to tell a great story, whether it is through plot or character development. But Frondaie had three other strikes against him. First, he spurned the concept of the importance of contacts and influence. As he grew older, he became even more solitary, spending most of his time in the south of France. Second, he admired many of the ideas of those Fascists, their concept of strength and purity, their stated ideals, and their revolt against decadence. And following the Liberation, most Fascist writers and even those who admired them, became very unpopular. And finally, he once was married to Jeanne Loviton, who later attained great power within Parisian circles—and who openly disparaged him, even in her own writings. No, it was better simply to ignore the existence of the dashing man who wore capes, captivated audiences, and sometimes walked like a jaguar. It made the history books so much simpler. Still writing, still producing plays, Pierre Frondaie died of a heart attack at the age of sixty-four, in 1948. Few took notice.

And then, of course, there was Paul Valéry. What more could be said about him? He died a fool in his own eyes. At least he never knew that Jeanne would sell off to the highest bidder all of the intimate thoughts and messages that he had sent to her for so many years. How he would have loathed her auction! She was no longer interested in his thoughts and feelings. Had she ever been? The surviving members of Paul Valéry's family have gone to great lengths to keep his liaison with Jeanne Loviton out of print, and out of the reach of scholarly investigation. To an amazing degree they have succeeded in their attempt. Many of the materials concerning the relationship between Paul Valéry and Jeanne Loviton are still locked away.

As for Robert Denoël, leaving him with a bullet in his back and stealing his company wasn't enough. There were two more insults yet to come. The first insult also involved his widow. It turned out that Robert Denoël, who had often been hounded by creditors during his career, was hounded by bills right into the grave. Two women had, for several years after his murder, professed their love and devotion for Robert Denoël—in court. Both sought his estate, although Cécile sought it in the name of their son. And apparently both women wanted to pay for his funeral. But once buried, neither woman paid his cemetery bill. Nor did anyone else. Therefore, on 10 April 1973 Robert Denoël's body was exhumed from its grave in Montparnasse cemetery and transferred to the Thiais cemetery, where it was placed in a common grave. Then in 1980 his bones were moved once again. His remains were placed anonymously in the Thiais ossuary, joining countless other remains in a bone bin.

I have looked at dozens of reactions to the murder of Robert Denoël, recorded mainly in journals and police dossiers of the time. Many, particularly Denoël's friends and associates, were gravely shocked by his death. Some of the reactions of his wife and those of his mistress, too, are recorded. Interestingly, I could find no record that proves that either Jeanne Loviton or Cécile Denoël actually shed tears over Denoël's death. If they did, history has left no account of their grief. But history did record the tears of one woman. As a fitting tribute to the death of this man of contradiction, this publisher of the anti-Semitic works of Céline and Rebatet, the one woman who openly wept after hearing of the death of her friend and publisher was the Russian Jew, Elsa Triolet.

Robert Denoël, murdered, his company stolen, his cemetery bill unpaid, had one other profound insult to endure at the hands of Jeanne Loviton. Had he known, it might have been worse than that bullet:

In 1951, only ten months after she became its undisputed legal owner, Jeanne Loviton sold 90 percent of Les Editions Denoël to Robert Denoël's arch enemy and publishing rival, Gaston Gallimard.

Gaston Gallimard, the wily fox, had won. His company, Les Editions Gallimard, is even today one of the foremost publishing houses in France. I decided to use the Internet and surf the Web, giving as the key word for my search, "Les Editions Denoël." And there it was! By merely pressing a button, I could have a complete description and catalogue in either French or English of this "important division of Les Editions Gallimard." I decided to press English. Then I read, "Ever since 1930, Denoël, a publishing house with a prestigious past—Louis-Ferdinand Céline, Blaise Cendrars, Jean Rhys, Ray Bradbury—has from the start contributed to the discovery of new talents, both in French and foreign literature, and continues to publish first novels." The entire slick advertising package for Les Editions Denoël implied that it had always been a part of Les Editions Gallimard, even in the 1930s. Now the Gallimard house gave the impression that it had discovered all of Denoël's writers, even Céline. There was, of course, no mention of Robert Denoël himself, and certainly no hint of the decades of enmity between Gallimard and Denoël. I sat silently for several minutes staring at the screen.

The problem with research is that it never really answers all the questions. And now with the research nearly done, I still had some big questions. Was Gaston Gallimard involved in the murder of Robert Denoël? Did he hire the people who killed Denoël in order to get his hands on Denoël's defense dossier, which implicated Gallimard in collaboration? Had he joined forces with Jeanne Loviton?

I knew one thing for certain. Robert Denoël had been right to assume that he was the designated scapegoat for publishing. Following his murder and even right up to today, scholars of the period tend to dismiss him as "that collaborationist publisher." If they say any more about him they cite his continual money problems and his occasional attempts at monetary trickery. Blatant errors are also common regarding the night of his murder. So many different and conflicting stories! In one account by a reputable author, Denoël is supposedly killed "by machine-gun fire in the street." Scholars tend to overlook what Denoël's friend, Robert Poulet, said of him: "Only take note, our brazen trickster would have given everything he had in order to publish the unsalable work of a genius. Stealing everything from everyone and robbing even himself for the love of literature, he gave the example of disinterested dishonesty." That fundamental and accurate part of Robert Denoël has generally been dropped from the history books.

Yet Gaston Gallimard and other publishers escaped collaborationist epithets. Their collaboration has generally been forgotten. As for Denoël's murder, Jeanne Loviton's version of events is now accepted as truth in all of the books I found (more than twenty describing his murder in almost exactly the same way): "He was murdered under mysterious circumstances the night of 2 December 1945 while fixing a flat tire."

I knew about some of the collaborationist activities of Gaston Gallimard, particularly his pro-Nazi and anti-Semitic publications in the *New French Review (N.R.F.)* I decided to visit the graduate library to see if I could find any more about this now-golden publisher. I didn't having much luck. I found snippets of information about Gallimard here and there, but nothing substantial. I realized that three men knew a great deal about Gallimard's collaboration: Pierre Drieu La Rochelle, Robert Denoël, and Otto Abetz. The pro-Nazi and anti-Semitic Drieu La Rochelle, who headed Gallimard's *N.R.F* during the Occupation, committed suicide shortly after the Liberation. Some believed he killed himself in order to spare others. Robert Denoël was murdered shortly after the Liberation. The dossier implicating Gallimard vanished forever following Denoël's murder, as did the only other copy of his dossier. That left Otto Abetz, the Nazi who placed Drieu La Rochelle at the head of Gallimard's *N.R.F.* In

1949 Abetz was sentenced to twenty years hard labor for his activities during the Occupation. He was released after serving five years. Then in 1958 he was killed in an automobile accident. I had written to a scholar in the field, requesting information on Abetz. His response astonished me. He stated that Abetz's auto accident was probably no accident at all. There was allegedly considerable evidence to suggest that Otto Abetz had been murdered. Three men knew the exact nature of Gaston Gallimard's collaboration, and all three died of unnatural causes: suicide, murder, probable murder.

I would have given just about anything for one small peek at Robert Denoël's court defense dossier. What had he found? And why did it take him so long to find it? Denoël and Loviton had spent months working day and night on that defense. If they were just looking for collaborationist books and their publishers in that giant *Bibliographie de France*, along with the publishers' collaborationist advertisements, why had it taken them so long? I had already looked at that huge bibliography. Most books listed there gave away their political leaning just from their titles, as in *The Ancient Aryans*, published by Gallimard. Researching those books just shouldn't have required so much time, I reasoned. What was he looking for? And why couldn't someone else just do the same thing with that bibliography of works published during the Occupation? For example, why couldn't I do it? No, there had to be more.

I repeated over and over in my head what Robert Denoël had said about Gaston Gallimard and other French publishers of the Occupation. "They all did exactly the same things that I did." Slowly, finally, it began to dawn on me. What did Robert Denoël do? He created fictitious companies and funneled his pro-Nazi and anti-Semitic works through them, leaving his main catalogue relatively free from collaborationist works. Of course! Now I knew. Finally I realized why it had taken Robert Denoël so long to ferret out all the collaborationist works of Gaston Gallimard and others. In all likelihood, they too had created fictitious companies for their more compromising books. False names, phony publishing companies, wrong addresses, straw men as titular heads, Denoël had probably traced them, located the true sources of those fictitious publishing establishments and found the true collaborationist publishers behind the façades. It would require someone with the knowledge and connections of a French publisher of the times to follow those leads to their true sources. I couldn't replicate Denoël's research today, and neither (I believe) could anyone else.

I already knew that Gallimard had *filiales* (subsidiaries). In fact, Jeanne Loviton sold most of Les Editions Denoël to just such a Gallimard *filiale* called ZED. Subsidiaries (with totally different names), fictitious companies, straw men, all seemed to be part of French publishing, practiced by some publishers, at least during the Occupation. Tracking down the owners of such subsidiaries and possibly fictitious companies would have been quite a task.

Then Denoël made a serious mistake. He told others that he had proof that Gaston Gallimard had collaborated just as much as he had, if not more. And furthermore, he intended to implicate Gallimard in court. He would make public what he had learned. And in all probability, what he learned cost him his life.

But I had no proof. It was all just conjecture. There was nothing to tie Gallimard to the murder as long as the three who were present at the scene of the crime were totally exonerated. It was almost the same as Céline's case. If Denoël's company was found totally innocent of all charges of collaboration, then logic said that Céline had to be found innocent, too. And if Jeanne Loviton, Guillaume Hanoteau, and Pierre Roland-Lévy were all found to be innocent bystanders at Denoël's murder, no one could ask them that all-important question: Did someone pay them to dispose of Denoël's defense dossier? So in addition to all of Jeanne Loviton's important contacts, she might also have added Gaston Gallimard and all of his influence as a powerful ally to her court case.

But I had only circumstantial evidence against Gaston Gallimard. All that I really had was a missing defense dossier and Robert Denoël's statements about what that dossier contained. Plus that ever-nagging question: Who would want to have that defense dossier at all costs? I looked endlessly at books, diaries, and newspapers in the graduate library. I wrote letters, asked questions. Sometimes I received chilling responses: "*Qui êtes-vous?* Who are you? What are your credentials and how dare you ask such questions?" I found almost nothing. If Gaston Gallimard was guilty of paying anyone to get that dossier, he had totally covered his tracks.

Gaston Gallimard had one more star to put into his crown, and everything would be complete. Céline. He wanted Céline, had always wanted him, ever since he had let him slip right through his hands back in 1932. Céline, in a registered letter, had officially attempted to quit the literary stable of Jeanne Loviton in December 1947. But nothing was simple with Héra. Squabbles ensued between Céline and Loviton; she threatened lawsuits, even initiated one, then dropped it. Jeanne Loviton simply wasn't interested in reprinting the old Céline works or investing in his new ones. And as long as Céline was in Denmark, he sought non-French publishers so that his earnings and royalties would not be impounded by the French government. But he was not very successful in his quest. What non-French publisher truly wanted a notoriously difficult, outdated, exiled anti-Semitic writer who had collaborationist charges hanging over his head? Thanks primarily to the passage of time, a new French amnesty law, and Jeanne Loviton's astonishing innocent verdict for Les Editions Denoël, Céline's period of exile was coming to a close.

Finally, France tried Céline in absentia. He was sentenced in 1950 to one year in prison (he had already served eighteen months in Denmark), fined fifty thousand francs, and declared to be in "national disgrace." A sum not to exceed 50 percent of all of his future earnings would be taken from him by the state. But even that decree was soon overturned. In 1951 France finally granted him amnesty, and, along with his wife, his very old cat, Bébert, and his other animals, Céline returned to France. He settled in the village of Meudon, where he would complete possibly his best works ever, his trilogy about his exile from France and the devastation he witnessed following World War II. He chose a new publisher—who else?—Gaston Gallimard.

Céline's friend Pierre Monnier approached Gallimard on the writer's behalf in the summer of 1951. Monnier described his meeting with Gaston Gallimard in his office at the rue Sébastien-Bottin:

> Of medium height, dressed in black with a bow tie, he reminded me of a high-ranking chef at Prunier's. After asking me to sit down, he stared at me and smiled. A good 10 seconds passed without anything between us but that smile. And then he spoke. With marvelous cunning and genial false humility, 'I would be glad for the chance to publish Céline. I've had all the great names of literature here, Gide, Claudel, Faulkner, Valéry. All of them! And the only one I missed was Céline. Yes, I missed Céline. It was a mistake, a slip-up. So you can understand that now I'll do whatever I have to to get him.'

And he did. Céline would castigate his new publisher in his future works in much the same way that he had castigated Denoël. As for Robert Denoël, he sometimes spoke more gently about his murdered publisher. As he said in *Castle to Castle*:

> While we're on the subject of literature, let me tell you about Denoël . . . Denoël, who was assassinated . . . oh, he had his nasty ways . . . ! There's no denying it, he sold you down the river when necessary . . . given the right time and circumstances, he tied you hand and foot, and sold you out . . . after which he was perfectly capable of changing his mind and apologizing . . . like . . . like (a hundred names) . . . but he had one saving grace . . . his passion for literature . . . he really recognized good work, he had respect for writers . . . Brottin [Céline's name for Gallimard] is a horse of a different color . . . Achille Brottin is your sordid grocer, an implacable idiot . . . the only thing he can think about is his dough! More dough! Still more! The complete millionaire! More and more flunkeys around him . . . with their tongues hanging out and their pants down . . .
>
> Denoël the assassinated read everything . . . Brottin is like

Claudel, all he reads is the financial page . . . his reading is done
by the "Pin-brain-Trust" . . .

The first day of July 1961, only one day after he completed his second
draft of the third book in his trilogy, *Rigadoon*, Céline died in his
home at Meudon. Death, which had always haunted his works, which
had been a topic between Denoël and Céline at their very first meeting, which accompanied this writer wherever he went, now embraced
him. Céline, the doctor, knew he was dying. He faced his death
alone, naked, refusing the intervention of other doctors, not even
allowing his wife to be with him that long sweltering day. She came
to him only after giving her dance lessons. She was with him only at
the moment of his death. Perhaps he had already described his view
of the world and its reaction to his death: "The whole world's riled
at us! Nothing left to do. Everything we do is taken the wrong way.
On our deathbeds they'll say we rattle wrong." No, there was no
grand Valéry-type funeral for Louis-Ferdinand Céline, Dr. Destouches. He was entombed quite simply, without fanfare. It was a new
era in France, a time when most people wanted to forget the past,
forget Céline. But his words did not die with him. In spite of his
anti-Semitism, in spite of his vast hatreds (once he said, "I live more
on hatred than on noodles . . . but genuine hatred . . . no cheap
imitation . . ."), few can deny that he is one of the most important,
most innovative novelists of this century, influencing countless future
writers with his verve and style.

Unlike his publisher, Céline had his own permanent vault. His
wife inscribed his name and hers on it, then had a cross engraved,
along with the image of a sailing ship, a three-master. Céline loved
sailing ships, the sea. No, this corpse had no surprises awaiting it, as
had Robert Denoël—except perhaps for one. I wonder what Céline
would have thought if he knew. A few years after Céline's death,
Frédéric Vitoux wrote an astonishing and beautiful biography of him.
In his book Vitoux carefully, painstakingly sifted out Céline's lies and
exaggerations, revealing an infinitely complex and contradictory, always ailing, dour genius almost constantly at work—living in and wit-

nessing the most confusing and serious of times. And for his biography, Vitoux won that prize most coveted by Céline: the Goncourt. Although Céline's writing never won the Goncourt, the story of his life did.

Gaston Gallimard lived a long, wealthy, and influential life—almost totally unblemished. He managed to escape the pitfalls of the Occupation and the purges of the Liberation unscathed—even making significant profits during both periods. As for the notion that he had ever collaborated, Gallimard took great pains to see that the full story of his role as publisher during the Occupation was never printed. Publishers and what they did, and what he himself had done during and after the Occupation, were forbidden topics for Gallimard. He died on Christmas day in 1975 at the age of ninety-four. According to his specific wishes, only his surviving family members and his longtime intimate female friend were present at his funeral. The press, his associates, and his friends were not even notified of his death until the day after his burial. The innumerable eulogies that followed were unanimous in their praise. His publishing house, now encompassing Denoël's former publishing house, continues to thrive.

As for Jeanne Loviton, she outlived them all. I knew that she was still alive, quite rich, and litigating in the 1980s. I knew she was still alive in 1995. For some time I diligently searched French newspapers for her obituary, finding none. Then suddenly I stopped my search, feeling a certain satisfaction in this final missing piece. I began to think of her seated at a lavish table playing cards with Death and cheating. Perhaps, I reasoned, it's better to think of her eternally alive, still manipulating and influencing events her way—for if anyone could find a way to outmaneuver Death, it would be Jeanne Loviton.*

---

*After most of this research had been completed. I discovered that Jeanne Loviton died at her luxurious Paris domicile on 20 July 1996. She was ninety-three. A very private funeral was held for her at Notre-Dame-de-la-Consolation in Paris. Interestingly, her death announcement did not carry her real name, listing rather her pseudonym, Jean Voilier.

Acknowledgments

Many people have provided invaluable assistance in the research and writing of this book. I would particularly like to thank Dr. John Harwood and Karen Louise Staman for their ideas, suggestions, and encouragement, as well as for their careful editing. I am also indebted to Carolyn Chu and Peter Wolverton of St. Martin's Press, for their fine critiques and enthusiasm, and to my agents, the late Sam Hughes and Bob Solinger, for believing in me. Several of the subscribers to H-France provided many suggestions and leads for some of my most difficult problems. Without the amazing staff and resources of the libraries of the University of Michigan, I could not have completed this book. I wrote many letters to French bureaucrats seeking information about marriages, deaths, burials, and divorces. Often, I received courteous informative responses, for which I am most grateful. Others who have given me considerable assistance with this project include Dr. Bryan Skib, who tackled some of my thorniest research questions; Dr. Adele King, who found some important sources in Belgium and sent them to me; Matthew Peable of Great Britain and Dr. Bertram Gordon, both of whom provided me with important information regarding the Nazi Otto Abetz; Roger Wiesenbach, who helped me with French law and lawyers; Bob and Nancy Parker, Joan Scott, Laura Staman, Jeanette Staman, and my husband, Mike Staman, who provided encouragement at every turn (and who put up with me); and a large black cat, Rupert, who has been my constant companion throughout the writing of this book, either busily knocking paper clips and pens onto the floor or sleeping comfortably on my research.

Appendix A

SOME IMPORTANT AUTHORS WHOM ROBERT DENOËL LAUNCHED IN FRANCE

Eugène Dabit	Louis-Ferdinand Céline	Nathalie Sarraute
Jean Genet	Luc Dietrich	René Barjavel
Gilbert Dupré	Dominique Rollin	Elsa Triolet
Blaise Cendrars	Jean Rhys	

OTHER WRITERS WHO GOT A SIGNIFICANT BOOST IN THEIR CAREERS BECAUSE OF DENOËL

Antonin Artaud	Louis Aragon	René Laporte
Paul Vialar	Lucien Rebatet	

Appendix B

SOME LITERARY PRIZES (*PRIX*) AWARDED TO THE
PUBLISHING HOUSES OF GASTON GALLIMARD AND
ROBERT DENOËL

Prix Goncourt

1932 Guy Mazeline, for *Les Loups* (Gallimard's NRF)

1933 André Malraux, for *La Condition humaine* (Gallimard's NRF)

1939 Philippe Hériat, for *Les Enfants gâtés* (Gallimard's NRF)

1941 Henri Pourrat, for *Vent de mars* (Gallimard's NRF)

1942 Marc Bernard, for *Pareils à des enfants* (Gallimard's NRF)

1943 Marius Grout, for *Passage de l'homme* (Gallimard's NRF)

1944 Elsa Triolet, for *Le Premier Accroc coûte deux cents francs* (Denoël)

Prix Théophraste Renaudot

1931 Philippe Hériat, for *L'Innocent* (Denoël)

1932 Louis-Ferdinand Céline, for *Voyage au bout de la nuit* (Denoël)

1933 Charles Braibant, for *Le Roi dort* (Denoël)

1935 François de Roux, for *Jours sans gloire* (Gallimard's NRF)

1936 Louis Aragon, for *Les Beaux Quartiers* (Denoël)

1937 Jean Rogissart, for *Mervale* (Denoël)
1938 Pierre-Jean Launay, for *Léonie la bienheureuse* (Denoël)
1939 Jean Malaquais, for *Les Javanais* (Denoël)

Prix Cazes
(started in 1935)
1936 Pierre Albert-Birot, for *Grabinoulor* (Denoël)
1942 Albert Paraz, for *Le Roi tout nu* (Denoël)
1943 Jean Proal, for *Où souffle la Lombarde* (Denoël)

Prix des Deux-Magots
1933 Raymond Queneau, for *Le Chiendent* (Gallimard's NRF)
1935 Jacques Baron, for *Charbon de mer* (Gallimard's NRF)
1936 Michael Matveev, for *Etrange famille* (Gallimard's NRF)
1938–40 No awards
1943 Jean Milo, for *L'Esprit de famille* (Denoël)
1944 No award

Prix Fémina
1931 Antoine de Saint-Exupéry, for *Vol de nuit* (Gallimard's NRF)
1932 Ramon Fernandez, for *Le Pari* (Gallimard's NRF)
1934 Robert Francis, for *La Chute de la maison de verre* (Rieder: Gallimard's NRF)
1936 Louise Hervieu, for *Sangs* (Denoël)
1938 Félix de Chazournes, for *Caroline* (Gallimard's NRF)
1939 Paul Vialar, for *La Rose de la mer* (Denoël)
1940–43 No awards

Prix Interallié
1931 Pierre Bost, for *La Scandale* (Gallimard's NRF)
1933 Robert Bourget-Pailleron, for *L'Homme du Brésil* (Gallimard's NRF)
1934 Marc Bernard, for *Anny* (Gallimard's NRF)
1935 Jacques Debû-Bridel, for *Jeunes ménages* (Gallimard's NRF)
1936 René Laporte, for *Les Chasses de novembre* (Denoël)
1938 Paul Nizan, for *La Conspiration* (Gallimard's NRF)
1940–44 No awards

Prix du Roman Populiste
1931 Eugène Dabit, for *L'Hôtel du Nord* (Denoël)
1933 Henri Pollès, for *Sophie de Tréguier* (Gallimard's NRF)

1936 Tristan Rémy, for *Faubourg Saint-Antoine* (Gallimard's NRF)
1937–39 No awards
1940 Jean-Paul Sartre, for *La Nausée* (Gallimard's NRF)
1941 Jean Rogissart, for *Le Fer et la forêt* (Denoël)
1942 Louis Guilloux, for *Le Pain des rêves* (Gallimard's NRF)
1944 Jean Merrien, for *Bord à bord* (Gallimard's NRF)

Prix Courteline
(given every other year)
1932 Marcel Sauvage, for *La Fin de Paris* (Denoël)
1936 André Sévry, for *Cavalerie* (Gallimard's NRF)

Appendix C

RECOMMENDED READING IN ENGLISH FOR THOSE
INTERESTED IN CERTAIN TOPICS IN THIS BOOK

Louis-Ferdinand Céline

Although many biographies of this writer exist in English, the best and most readable is Frédéric Vitoux's *Céline: A Biography*, ably translated by Jesse Browner (New York: Marlowe & Company, 1994). A more recent work written originally in English is Nicholas Hewitt's *The Life of Céline: A Critical Biography* (Oxford: Blackwell Publishers, 1999).

Céline's Novels

With the exception of his anti-Semitic writings, nearly all of his works are readily available in English. I would particularly recommend his trilogy *Castle to Castle*, *North*, and *Rigadoon* (although the last work is not as polished as the first two—Céline died after completing the second draft of *Rigadoon*). *Journey to the End of the Night* is excellent; *Death on the Installment Plan* is also excellent, but very dark; and *Conversations with Professor Y* provides a different look at this writer and his style.

Paul Valéry's Poetry and Life

I know of no true English biography of this famous poet. His poetry can be found in various English anthologies, for example, *Paul Valéry: An Anthology* (London: Routledge & Kegan Paul, 1977).

Antonin Artaud

Most of the significant works by Antonin Artaud are readily available in English. There are also several English biographies of this man. One of the most interesting is Stephen Barber's *Antonin Artaud: Blows and Bombs* (London: Faber and Faber, 1993).

Gaston Gallimard

A very interesting and informative biography on this publisher is *Gaston Gallimard: A Half-Century of French Publishing*, by Pierre Assouline, translated by Harold J. Salemson (New York: Harcourt Brace Jovanovich, 1988).

Jean Voilier

Two books by Carlton Lake demonstrate Voilier's manipulations and use of influence regarding the papers of Paul Valéry: *Confessions of a Literary Archaeologist* (New York: New Directions Books, 1990); and *Baudelaire to Beckett: A Century of French Art and Literature* (Austin: Humanities Research Center, University of Texas, 1976).

France (1925–1948)

One of the best works on France in this amazing and confusing period is Milton Dank's *The French Against the French: Collaboration and Resistance* (Philadelphia and New York: J.B. Lippincott Co., 1974). Other interesting works include *The Purge* by Herbert R. Lottman (New York: William Morrow, 1986); *The Crazy Years: Paris in the Twenties* by William Wiser (New York: Atheneum, 1983); and *Paris After the Liberation: 1944–1949* by Antony Beevor and Artemis Cooper (New York: Doubleday, 1994).

French Anti-Semitism

One of the best works dealing specifically with French anti-Semitism is Pierre Birnbaum's *Anti-Semitism in France: A Political History from Léon Blum to the Present*, translated by Miriam Kochan (Oxford: Blackwell Publishers, 1992).

Notes

1 "about 6:45 P.M.": All of the times and actions in this book are based upon witness depositions in the court and police dossier of Robert Denoël, located at the Paris Archives (cited below).

1 "shiny black Peugeot": Although the numbers of the Peugeot vary considerably (301, 203, 302, 201) in different accounts of this murder, the first police investigation (25 January 1946) and the third police investigation (25 May 1950) use the number 302.

1: LOCATING THE VICTIM

5 "Bonnat-Montechrétien": *Le Monde*, 4 December 1945, 8.

5 "avoided giving her name": *Ce Soir*, 4 December 1945, 1.

5 "more forthcoming": *La Libération*, 4 December 1945, 1.

6 "called Domat-Montchrestien": Also spelled Domat-Montchrétien.

6 "France in the 1930s": D'Amat et Limouzin-Lamothe, *Dictionnaire de Biographie française*, p. 1066.

7 "Histories of the town": Descriptions and history of Liège taken from Mon-

marché's *Belgique* (1920); Fodor's *Belgium and Luxembourg: 1963*; and Gibson's *Belgium* (1939).

8   "one volume per day": *Le Bulletin célinien*. March 1989, 5.

11   "more established *Sélection*": Robert, *Céline et les Editions Denoël*, 8.

12   "kisses and consolations": Marin, "Une Forte Tête," 29. Other humorous stories by Denoël include "Si François usait . . ." and "Un homme de circonstances." See bibliography for details.

12   "to see myself annihilated": Marin, "Une Forte tête," 31.

13   "death of my grandmother": Marin, "Une Forte tête," 32.

14   "the forces of love": Denoël, *Brouillon* (a long letter in the dossier written by Denoël to his wife), 1.

14   "that vast wild land": Fouché, "Robert Denoël: Le Découvreur." *Livres hebdo.*, 66.

15   "my name and my destiny": Marin, "Vers Louis Aragon," *Sélection*, 184.

18   "old, rare, and luxury editions": Robert, *Céline et les Editions Denoël*, 8.

21   "entered Georges's bookstore": Denoël met Irène Champigny on that date. Denoël would publish her songs of the sea in 1930 (at her expense) under the title *The Great Wind (Le Grand vent)*. *Le Bulletin célinien*, 16.

24   "St. Gervais Meadow": Champigny's art gallery generally presented the works of a loosely organized group of artists known as l'Ecole du Pré St. Gervais, who were inspired and/or influenced by little-known artist Maurice Loutreuil. One of these artists would later become Denoël's first real publishing success: Eugène Dabit.

2 : FINDING THAT WOMAN

30   "Frondaie's leading lady": Beauplan, introduction to Frondaie's *La Menace* (no page numbers).

31   "the celebrated Cora Laparcerie": Beauplan, introduction.

31   "without a strong plot": Frondaie's manifesto against surrealism appears in the preface to *La Menace*.

34   "comparing her 'eloquence' ": This poem, by Paul Valéry, appeared in *Le Figaro*, 15 October 1971, 32.

36   "woman was not amused": *Les Nouvelles littéraires*. 20 August 1927, p. 2.

36   "simply ignored me": The story is related by Joseph in *Catherine Pozzi*, 225.

37   "Muhlfield's hip deformity": Joseph, *Catherine Pozzi*, 149.

37   "secrets of the gods": Billy, *L'Epoque contemporain*, 226.

37   "he courageously submits": Joseph, *Catherine Pozzi*, 155.

37 "passions of an assembly": Trarieux, "De la scène au roman," *Les Nouvelles littéraires.* 23 May 1925, 1.

38 "one of the witnesses": The Mairie of the Commune de Saint Raphaël 8th arrondissement in Paris, 24 May 1927, cites Maurice Garçon as a witness to the Frondaie/Loviton marriage.

3: STARTING OUT . . . STARTING UP

39 "Goethe or Citroën": Artaud, *Oeuvres complètes.* vol. 2, of book 1 (1971), 285.

40 "physical portrait of that person" Artaud, *Oeuvres complètes,* 285.

41 "part art gallery": Moremans, *La Meuse* (Liège). 6 March 1973, 7F.

43 "caressing their bindings": Putnam, *The World of Jean de Bosschère,* 146.

45 "illustrate his own works": Putnam, *The World of Jean de Bosschère,* 146–47.

45 "the artist Christian Caillard": *Le Bulletin célinien,* 9.

45 "famed book collector": *Le Bulletin célinien,* 6.

48 "Gaston is the first man": Actually, a critic first coined this phrase about Gallimard. Assouline, *Gaston Gallimard,* 128.

48 "corpse of Marcel Proust": Assouline, *Gaston Gallimard,* 106.

49 "enjoy a great comedy": Assouline, *Gaston Gallimard,* 115–16.

50 "means only 250": Bourdet, *Vient de paraître,* 15.

51 "about women drivers": Based upon the story appearing in *Les Nouvelles littéraires,* entitled "Femme de sport," 12 November 1927, 2.

52 "writings of his friends": One recent source has stated that Maurice Garçon and Jeanne Loviton did indeed have an affair at the time, but that source would prefer to remain anonymous, and I was unable to locate any total confirmation, except for highly circumstantial evidence.

52 "with the number three": Joseph, *Catherine Pozzi,* 258.

53 "too many faults of character": Joseph, *Catherine Pozzi,* 157.

55 "knack for literary discovery": Most notably, Denoël's early publications at the author's expense include *l'Art et la mort,* by Antonin Artaud, and *Victor ou les enfants au pouvoir,* by Roger Vitrac.

56 "most of the financing": Robert, *D'un Hôtel du Nord l'autre: Eugène Dabit 1898– 1936,* 82.

57 "look out for myself": The story of Gallimard and Denoël regarding the writer Eugène Dabit can be found in Eugène Dabit and Roger Martin du Gard, *Correspondance I (1927–1929),* 430–35.

59 "I am the only one.": Dabit, *Correspondance I (1927–1929),* 432.

60 "some bigger company": Assouline, *Gaston Gallimard,* 46.

4: WHEN LOSING IS WINNING

63 "as principal manager": Although the exact date of the establishment of Les Edition Denoël et Steele varies, the first police investigation of 25 January 1946 places it at 10 April 1930.

67 "unparalleled work under contract": Céline, *Lettres à la N.R.F.*, 15.

67 "time to read it": Céline, *Lettres à la N.R.F.*, 17.

67 "proposal of another publisher": Céline, *Lettres à la N.R.F.*, 18.

67 "Denoël's new publishing house": Many biographies of Céline relate his struggles to get *Journey to the End of the Night* published. Two particularly good accounts in English can be found in the biographies by Nicholas Hewett, (108–11) and Frédéric Vitoux (166–69 and 194–205).

68 "an unparalleled masterpiece": Denoël, "Comment j'ai connu et lancé Louis-Ferdinand Céline," first unnumbered page.

69 "to publish her novel": Denoël, "Comment j'ai connu et lancé Louis-Ferdinand Céline," first unnumbered page.

69 "an empty formality": Poulet, *Entretiens*, 22.

70 "hearing from him soon": This story is related in its entirety in Denoël's "Comment j'ai connu et lancé Louis-Ferdinand Céline" (5½ unnumbered pages). Poetic license has been taken with some of the quotations.

72 "his gaze seemed burning": Denoël, "Louis-Ferdinand Céline: Le Contemporain capital," 7.

74 "enough impressionism": Vitoux, *Céline*, 201.

74 "Keep this title in mind": For example, this advertisement appeared in *Les Nouvelles littéraires*. 15 October 1932, p. 2.

75 "never grovel enough": Vitoux, *Céline*, 210.

77 "Grands-Echézeaux 1915": Gibault, *Céline*, book 2, 24.

77 "picked it up and kept it": Gibault, *Céline*, book 2, 25.

78 "5000 newspaper articles": Denoël, "Comment j'ai connu et lancé Louis-Ferdinand Céline," 4.

5: DIFFICULTIES

81 "an affair between publishers": Gibault. *Céline*, book 2, p. 26

81 "table was always set": Denoël, Céline. *La Meuse*, 6 March 1973, p. 7.

82 "nothing more, nothing less": Robert, *Céline et les Editions Denoël*, 25.

83 "best works by young writers": For example, in *Les Nouvelles littéraires*, 18 October 1930, 7.

84 "gluttonous parasite": Robert, *Céline et les Editions Denoël*, 54.

84 "letters to Monsieur Steel": In Robert's *Céline et les Editions Denoël*, Céline deliberately misspells Steele's name as "Steel" throughout, as, for example, on page 54.

85 "a riot, isn't it": Céline, *Conversations with Professor Y*, 5.

85 "leapt with enthusiasm": Céline, *Journey to the End of the Night*, 20.

85 "armed to the eyeballs": Céline, *Journey to the End of the Night*, 9.

85 "hot summer air": Céline, *Journey to the End of the Night*, 8.

86 "the apocalypse": Céline, *Journey to the End of the Night*, 9.

86 "pissing blood": Céline, *Journey to the End of the Night*, 34.

86 "Swallowed up tirelessly": Vitoux, *Céline*, 71.

86 "friendly and polite": Céline, *Journey to the End of the Night*, 7.

86 "The rest is blarney": Céline, *Journey to the End of the Night*, 10.

87 "heads or tails of the war": Céline, *Journey to the End of the Night*, 52.

87 "ingenuous, and gullible": Rim, *Le Grenier d' Arlequin*, 164–65.

87 "right in the head": Céline, *Journey to the End of the Night*, 86.

87 "by a shell fragment": Céline, *Journey to the End of the Night*, 14.

88 "you go crazy": Vitoux, *Céline*, 77.

88 "scrambled for good": Céline, *Journey to the End of the Night*, 94.

88 "sneering bottom lip": Poulet, *Entretiens familiers avec L.-F. Céline*, 31.

6 : Affairs, Psychology, Games, and Madness

90 "Dr. Daudel introduced his patient": Barber, *Antonin Artaud*, 15.

91 "surrealists threw me out": The story of Artaud's expulsion from the surrealist movement is related by Barber, *Antonin Artaud*, 29.

91 "My best works": Artaud's strong identification with ideas or the heroes of his writings is discussed in Brau, *Antonin Artaud*, 61. At times Artaud really believed himself to be surrealism, or the terrible Count Cenci, for example.

92 "utterly hopeless": Cassou, "Poésie." *Les Nouvelles littéraires*, 27 July 1929, 12.

92 "claimed our couch": Denoël calls Artaud "our parasite" in *Brouillon*, 4.

93 "Antonin's lessons on theater": Artaud, *Selected Writings*, 209.

95 "masks and disguises": Nin, *The Diary of Anaïs Nin*, vol. 1, 22.

95 "decidedly not masculine": Nin, *The Diary of Anaïs Nin*, Vol. 1, 215.

95 "behind it was Allendy's office": Barillé, *Anaïs Nin*, 111.

96 "sometimes violet": Barillé, *Anaïs Nin*, 120.

96 "shoulders like a bull": Nin, *Incest*, 107.

96 "full, heavy-featured": Nin, *Incest*, 133.

96 "frail, nervous, potent": Nin, *Incest*, 118.

97   "tyranny of a household mechanism": Nin, *Incest*, 107.

98   "play Artaud": Barillé, *Anaïs Nin*, 121.

98   "exhale oxygen": Barillé, *Anaïs Nin*. 121.

99   "nice hotel in the south of France": Barber, *Antonin Artaud*, 65.

101   "*Chroniques italiennes*": Hayman, *Artaud and After*, 96.

101   "other impressive notables": Barber, *Antonin Artaud*, 70.

101   "Jean-Marie Conty": Esslin, *Artaud*, 123.

102   "Abdy purchased the role": Plunka, *Antonin Artaud and the Modern Theater*, 33.

102   "Artaud reserved the Folies-Wagram": Barber, *Antonin Artaud*, 71.

104   "loves attained their paroxysm": Denoël, *Brouillon*, 4.

104   "as important as the text": Gouhier, *Antonin Artaud et l'essence du théâtre*, 119.

106   "The costumes, the scenery": Plunka, *Antonin Artaud and the Modern Theater*, 13.

106   "I am suffocating": Artaud, *The Cenci*, 33.

107   "cover the bruises": Rim, *Le Grenier d' Arlequin*, 239.

107   "rushed into the establishment": Brau, *Antonin Artaud*, 163.

107   "Artaud mocks us": Gouhier, *Antonin Artaud et l'essence du théâtre*, 123.

107   "each passing day": Denoël, *Brouillon*, 4.

7 : CÉLINE, FRANCE, AND THE JEWS

110   "entirely mad": Hindus, *The Crippled Giant*, 57.

112   "rift never closed": This story is related in Robert's *D'un Hôtel du Nord l'autre*, 193.

112   "the worst possible terms": Céline, *Lettres à des amies*, 171.

112   "offer less surface": Céline, *Death on the Installment Plan*, 271.

113   "calamity personified": Céline, *Death on the Installment Plan*, 314.

113   "cackle that seized him": Vitoux, *Céline*, 2.

113   "Let's not alienate them": Poulet, *Entretiens familiers avec L.-F. Céline*, 53.

114   "collectors of rare editions": Robert, *Céline et les Editions Denoël*, 76.

114   "a product of sewers": Some of the critics' reactions to *Death on the Installment Plan* can be found in Vitoux, *Céline*, 290–93.

115   "Flaubert, Balzac, and Zola": Denoël, *Les Cahiers de l'Herne*, 234–36.

118   "of Jewish origin": Dorian, *Les Cahiers de l'Herne*, 26–27.

119   "temporary residency in France": Kingston, *Anti-Semitism in France During the 1930's*, 130.

119   "Editions Denoël into bankruptcy": Robert, *Céline et les Editions Denoël*, 17–18. Poetic license taken with quote.

119   "no one had yet realized it": Boisdeffre, "Sur la Posterité de Céline," 214.

121   "failures, hicks, outrages": Céline, *Bagatelles pour un massacre*, 15.

122 "carried that same statement":*Les Nouvelles littéraires,* 25 December 1937, 2.

122 "shitty publisher": Quote taken from a letter written by Céline to Milton Hindus in 1947 and published by Hindus in *The Crippled Giant,* 94.

122 "boil is with puss": Hindus, *The Crippled Giant,* 28.

123 "real and fictional": Lefevre, "Une Heure avec Pierre Frondaie," 6.

123 "like Pierre Benoit": Frondaie quote found in Lefevre, "Une Heure avec Pierre Frondaie," 4.

125 "to get her novel published": Lagarde, "Les Mille visages de Pierre Frondaie," 8.

126 "exulting in their love together": Peeters, *Paul Valéry,* 226.

127 "something like God": Valéry, in Florenne's "Amour fou de M. Teste," 3.

128 "appealed to them both": Peeters, *Paul Valéry,* 226–27.

128 "a private intimacy": Lanoux, *Paris 1925,* 25.

128 "les femmes (the women)": Joseph, *Catherine Pozzi,* 147.

128 "its own secret meaning": Chalon, "La Gardienne du trésor," 1.

129 "It's a fact": Florenne, "Amour fou de M. Teste," 2.

129 "my vigil and corrections": Valéry, *Paul Valéry secret,* no. 6.

130 "turned it over to the New York Public Library": Voilier, *Jours de lumière.* Inside page of the edition still in the New York Public Library.

8 : War and Occupation

133 "became nearly impossible": Kingston, *Anti-Semitism in France During the 1930's,* 130.

133 "catechisms until 1942": Chélini, "L'Église sous Pius XII," 204.

134 "subversive of German ideals": Shirer, *The Rise and Fall of the Third Reich,* 333.

134 "Week of the Broken Glass": For a more detailed account of this event, see Shirer, *The Rise and Fall of the Third Reich,* 580–89.

134 "escape burning to death": Shirer, *The Rise and Fall of the Third Reich,* 581.

135 "20,000 Jews were arrested": Shirer, *The Rise and Fall of the Third Reich,* 581–82.

135 "ebb and flow of his fears": Vitoux, *Céline,* 327.

135 "unequivocal dementia": Vitoux, *Céline,* 329.

135 "stock pens for Jewish killings": Céline, *L'Ecole des cadavres,* 287.

135 "Pencil-necked shitslingers": Vitoux, *Céline,* 327.

136 "Léon Daudet as well as Léon Blum": Assouline, *Gaston Gallimard,* 201.

136 "let's bleed the Jews": Céline, *Bagatelles pour un massacre,* 15.

137 "his German Céline": *Le Bulletin célinien,* 19.

139   "suppression of the remark": An account of this lawsuit can be found in Hewitt's *The Life of Céline*, 181–182,

140   "Kraut tanks": Céline, *Castle to Castle*, 158.

141   "I could never catch up": Vitoux, *Céline*, 339.

141   "15 million of us who saw it": Vitoux, *Céline*, 339–40.

142   "due to old age": Dank, *The French Against the French*, 71.

143   "totals forty-one": The losses Denoël sustained at the hands of the Germans are outlined in Fouché, *L'Edition française sous l'Occupation*, book I, p. 33.

144   "the secret passageway": The story of Denoël's secret entrances into and exits from his own publishing house is recounted in *Le Bulletin célenien*, 20.

146   "confidence in the German soldier": Dank, *The French Against the French*, 175–76.

148   "the path of collaboration": Galtier-Boissière, *Journal: 1940–1950*, 17.

148   "France is Pétain": Dank, *The French Against the French*, 89.

149   "the Otto List": Gordon, *Historical Dictionary of World War II France*, 269–70.

149   "Nazis expect him to publish": *Le Bulletin célinien*, 20.

152   "sunk by their allies the French": Vitoux, *Céline*, 336.

152   "no Christmas this year": Dank, *The French Against the French*, 82.

9: EARLY OCCUPATION YEARS

154   "the Dental Institute": Céline. *North*, 63, and glossary, 445.

155   "burned them in his furnace": Dank, *The French Against the French*, 216.

156   "four patriotic collections": Fouché, *L'Édition française sous l'Occupation*, book I, p. 216.

157   "pride of my winter": Valéry, *Poèmes secrets inédits*, 26.

159   "attracts and terrifies me": Valéry, *Paul Valéry secret*, no. 60.

159   "he was worn out": Gregh, *L'Age de fer*, 234.

160   "countless hundreds of deaths": Voilier, *Ville ouverte*, first printed page.

10: LOVE AND WORK

166   "extraordinary eloquence": Galtier-Boissière, *Journal: 1940–1950*, 109.

168   "no longer be friends": Marcou, *Elsa Triolet*, 257.

169   "a man to be trusted": Marcou, *Elsa Triolet*, 258.

170   "Denoël paid for everyone": Fouché, *L'Edition française sous l'Occupation*, book I, p. 109.

171   "expense of this new luxury": Rebatet, *Les Mémoires d'un fasciste*, 99.

171   "sold out in a week": Fouché, *L'Édition française sous l'Occupation*, vol. 2, p. 113.

172   "forbidden mail there": Marcou, *Elsa Triolet*, 257–258. (In addition to the quote, these pages relate Denoël's dilemma in publishing *The White Charger*. According to Marcou, by publishing this work with only one cut, Denoël actually did "the impossible.")

173   "Cat Eaters!": Dank, *The French Against the French*, 164–67. The general privation of the French populace is described in these pages.

174   "most successful movies": Dank, *The French Against the French*, 183.

174   "her publishing house, Domat-Montchrestien": Loviton's publishing house, Domat-Montchrestien, is also often known simply as Domat.

174   "Madame Tardieu": Picq, Sworn statement, 25 May 1950, 14–15.

175   "1.9 million French prisoners of war": Dank, *The French Against the French*, 97.

175   "cost of the Occupation": Dank, *The French Against the French*, 27.

175   "the whole jaw": Dank, *The French Against the French*, 255.

176   "vit dees French": Vitoux, *Céline*, 375.

177   "so long": Vitoux, *Céline*, 381.

178   "escorted Céline out": Vitoux, *Céline*, 386–87.

178   "not a likable man": Denoël, "L-F. Céline," *Marianne*. 10 May 1939, 7.

179   "vestige of mythology": Valéry, Letter of 6 August 1943, *Poèmes secrets inédits*, 47.

179   "tail of the Devil": Valéry, Letter of 16 July 1942, *Poèmes secrets inédits*, 46.

179   "mystical wind appears": Valéry, letter to Loviton in lot no. 53 in *Paul Valéry secret*.

179   "perfect hours of my life": Valéry, letter to Loviton in lot no. 48 in *Paul Valéry secret*.

179   "your astonishing faculties": Valéry, letter to Loviton in lot no. 74 in *Paul Valéry secret*.

179   "one calls 'life' ": Valéry, undated letter to Loviton in *Poèmes secrets inédits*, 49.

180   "gravely ill": Bruyneel, sworn statement of 20 September 1946, 1–2.

181   "Denoël? You? Me?": McCarthy, *Céline*, 219.

182   "obituary in *The Literary News*": "*Pressentiments*," *Les Nouvelles littéraires*, 6 December 1945, 4.

182   "coffin—with his name on it": Drawings of coffins were sent to Robert Denoël on more than one occasion, according to the police testimony of Cécile Denoël, 3 December 1945.

183   "cry for death": The written and phone threats against Denoël are outlined in *Le Bulletin célinien*, 21.

186   "see this farce": Dank, *The French Against the French*, 278.

186   "writers of genius": Lottman, *The Purge*, 158. Writers and entertainers were,

in fact, singled out for collaboration more even than the French who helped build the "Atlantic Wall" and those who provided munitions and tanks for Germany.

188   "Every publisher collaborated": Maurice Bruyneel, sworn statement 2.

188   "I won't be the only one": René Barjavel, statement made to Pierre Assouline, cited in Assouline's *Gaston Gallimard*, 322.

191   "your memory is king": Valéry, *Poèmes secrets inédits*, 23.

191   "Ha . . . I thought": Valéry, *Poèmes secrets inédits*, 20.

191   "live as paupers": Valéry, undated letter to Loviton in *Poèmes secrets inédits*, 51.

192   "I close my eyes": Valéry, letter to Loviton in lot no. 36 of *Paul Valéry secret*.

192   "where no lies are told": Valéry, *Poèmes secrets inédits* [1944?], 19.

192   "creations of mind and spirit": Valéry, undated letter to Loviton in *Poèmes secrets inédits*, 50.

11: LOVE LOST

194   "riddled from the air": Céline, *Rigadoon*, 34–35.

194   "end in a smash": Céline, *Rigadoon*, 70.

194   "phosphorus": Céline, *Rigadoon*, 71.

196   "I was speechless myself": Vitoux, *Céline*, 416.

196   "plunging into the Danube": Céline, *Castle to Castle*, 132.

196   "the Circus of Europe": Céline, *Castle to Castle*, 43.

196   "written in black and white": Céline, *Castle to Castle*, 63.

197   "stinking good-for-nothings": Céline, *Castle to Castle*, 316.

197   "sell you for stew meat": Céline, *Castle to Castle*, 5.

198   "exclusion from the profession": Durand-Auzias, sworn statement 8 October 1946, 1.

198   "pleasing to the Nazis": Assouline, *L'Epuration des intellectuals*, 32.

200   "every respect but legal title": second police investigation, 15 November 1946, 13.

200   "run by Monod": sworn statement, 15 November 1946, 3.

201   "the one I so love": Valéry, *Poèmes secrets inédits*, 28.

202   "ending of that relationship": Peeters, *Paul Valéry*, 229.

202   "immobile and despairing": Bertholet, *Paul Valéry: 1871–1945*, 410.

203   "We must try to live": Valéry, *Poésies*, 105.

203   "have pity on me in distress": Valéry, letter to Loviton, lot no. 112 in *Paul Valéry secret*.

203   "simply wasted time": Peeters, *Paul Valéry*, 231.

203 "between life and you": Valéry, letter to Loviton, lot no. 110 in *Paul Valéry secret.*

203 "They are for you": Valéry, letter to Loviton, lot no. 113 in *Paul Valéry secret.*

204 "flown into the tempest": Bertholet, *Paul Valéry: 1871–1945*, 410.

205 "justly acquired": Lake, *From Baudelaire to Beckett*, 180.

206 "personal danger to himself": Fouché, *L'Edition française sous l'Occupation*, book 2, p. 204.

207 "Russian, Jewish, and Communist": Galtier-Boissière, *Journal: 1940–1950*, 466.

212 "no need to hurry": Mengelle, sworn statement, 2.

12: 2 DECEMBER 1945

218 "he pardoned M. Maurice Thorez": Galtier-Boissière, *Journal: 1940–1950*, 861.

220 "a social leper": Assouline, *Gaston Gallimard*, 317.

221 "playing the piano, out of tune": Céline, *North*, 59–60.

222 "put my trust in France": This quote and the Pétain quotes above can be found in Dank, *The French Against the French*, 289–90.

223 "Most of the time, he dozed": Dank, *The French Against the French*, 295.

223 "confiscation of his goods": Dank, *The French Against the French*, 312.

223 "hasn't changed a bit": Dank, *The French Against the French*, 312.

223 "rubbed with onion": Céline, *Castle to Castle*, 150.

224 "then age twelve": The best and most complete account of the events leading up to the murder of Robert Denoël on 2 December 1945 can be found in the third police investigation (*Rapport*, 25 May 1950), collected by Chief Inspector Voges and head Inspector Colletta.

224 "our relationship more distant": Third police investigation (25 May 1950), 55.

225 "to the Agnès Capri Theater": Third police report (25 May 1950), 60.

225 "theater as an excuse": Third police investigation (25 May 1950), 55.

229 "*histoire de bonne femme*": Armand Rozelaar, letter to Judge Gollety, 26 April 1950, 4.

229 "recorded their exit": Armand Rozelaar, letter to Judge Gollety, 26 April 1950, 4.

229 "127, rue de Grenelle": Armand Rozelaar, letter to Judge Gollety, 26 April 1950, 11.

230 "taxi at 9:30 P.M.": Armand Rozelaar, letter to Deputy Attorney General Bertrand, 21 December 1949, 7.

230 "attitude seemed suspicious": Third police investigation (25 May 1950), 59.

230 "always looking behind her": Third police investigation (25 May 1950), 59.

231 "My darling, it's my fault": Third police investigation (25 May 1950), 59.

232 "That was all": Testimony of Jeanne Loviton to police, 3 December 1945.

232 "*Crime crapuleux*": *Crime crapuleux* was the conclusion of the first police investigation (26 January 1946). The entire report was only six sheets of paper, typed front and back.

13: NOT ONLY MURDER BUT THEFT

237 "in the private war": The Hermès notebook incident is recounted in a letter written by Armand Rozelaar to Judge Gollety (21 May 1946), 5, and elsewhere in the court documents. Jeanne Loviton confirmed this story in her sworn statement of 10 October 1946, fourth unnumbered page. She states there that she had a "sentimental" feeling for this notebook which was otherwise "without value."

238 "he recognized the car": This incident is recounted in a letter from Armand Rozelaar to Judge Gollety (21 May 1946), 5.

239 "*Komm mit*": Céline, *North*, 117.

239 "And so powerless": Vitoux, *Céline*, 442.

240 "with all my heart": Artaud, *Oeuvres complètes*, book 9, 1971, p. 237. Interestingly, there is no footnote or explanation regarding Artaud's topic of 2 December. One could therefore assume that Artaud is simply ranting, rather than truly referring to the murder of his publisher.

241 "lived there for eight days": Jeanne Loviton, sworn statement to the police (3 December 1945), 1.

243 "never picked up the tire": Although unanswered questions about that supposed flat tire occur throughout the entire dossier, the best summation of the total lack of information concerning the tire occurs in the third police investigation (25 May 1950), 66.

243 "car jack near one hand": Third police investigation (25 May 1950), 1.

243 "more of his attackers": Rozelaar, letter to Gollety, 3 February 1950, 11.

243 "his keys were missing": Rozelaar, letter to Gollety, 26 April 1950, 2.

244 "only remainder of Denoël's money": Third police investigation (25 May 1950), 3.

244 "money found on his body": As stated in third police investigation (25 May 1950), 11, and elsewhere.

245 "dossier which never existed": Sworn statement by Jeanne Loviton before Judge Gollety (28 April 1950), fourth unnumbered page.

245 "intention to implicate other publishers": Sworn statement given to the court by Jeanne Loviton, 10 October 1946, 5.

246 "discussed with Pierre Assouline": Assouline, *Gaston Gallimard*, 322.

247 "more than $4,500,000": *Aux Ecoutes*, 7 May 1948, 12.

247 "two days before his murder": Jeanne Loviton, sworn testimony (10 October 1946), second unnumbered page.

248 "no more than I myself": Roland-Lévy, letter to police, dated 4 December 1945.

252 "important things to tell you": Cécile Denoël, letter to Judge Gollety, dated 2 May 1946, 1.

252 "become a *partie civile*": Cécile Denoël, letter to Judge Gollety, dated 2 May 1946, 2.

253 "contrary to Jeanne Loviton's claims": Rozelaar, letter to Judge Gollety, dated 21 May 1946, 4.

253 "object of diverse maneuvers": Rozelaar, letter to Judge Gollety, dated 21, May 1946, 8.

14: CLOSING IN ON THE TRUTH

257 "help him if he needs it": Denoël, "Brouillon," 5–6.

257 " '*familiers*' of the publishing house": Denoël, "Brouillon," 4.

257 "taking my wife with the other": Denoël, "Brouillon," 5.

257 "people who admire you": Denoël, "Brouillon," 6.

260 "come upon that draft": For example, see page 7 of Rozelaar's letter of 21 May 1946 to Judge Gollety.

262 "no tools at all": Discussions of the various versions of the last time Loviton saw Denoël before the shooting, and her multiple versions of his overcoat occur in several places in the dossier, for example, in the second police investigation (15 November 1946), 23.

263 "night of the murder": Second police investigation (15 November 1946), 5. Madame Loviton could not even say at what date the maid had supposedly left her employ.

264 "did what they were told": This incident is discussed in the third police investigation (25 May 1950), 56.

264 "at least twenty minutes": Robert Beckers, sworn statement (7 October 1946), 1.

265 "fifteen million [francs]": Auguste Picq, sworn statement (18 September 1946), 2.

265 "vulgarizations of scientific works": Auguste Picq, sworn statement (1 February 1950), 1.

265 "Seventy-five thousand francs": Third police investigation (25 May 1950), 42.

266 "in gold and currency": Auguste Picq, sworn statement (1 February 1950), 1.

266 "the hands of Madame Loviton": Auguste Picq, sworn statement (18 September 1946), p. 2 verso.

266 "rue Petitot in Geneva": Third police investigation (25 May 1950), 16.

267 "that of obstructing justice": *Combat.* 3–4 December 1949, p. 2.

269 "a woman involved": The discrepancies in the stories of Hanoteau, Roland-Lévy, and the written record of Ré are discussed at length in the third police investigation (25 May 1950), 71–75.

269 "another version of events": *Express-Dimanche*, 4 June 1950, p. 1.

270 "not even legal": Second police investigation (15 November 1946), 7.

273 *"un rassemblement"*: Third police investigation (25 May 1950), 66.

273 "for a moment thoughtful": Rozelaar, letter to Judge Golléty, 26 April 1950, 4.

273 "composed of three people": Rozelaar, letter to Judge Golléty, 26 April 1950, 5.

275 "that exalted post": Rozelaar, letter to Judge Golléty, 16 April 1950, 9.

277 "meeting that went badly": Third police investigation (25 May 1950), 52.

278 "crime of interest": *France-Soir,* 13 January 1950, 1.

15: THE VERDICT

282 "Denoël nor I are taxi drivers": court testimony of Jeanne Loviton, 25 March 1950, 3.

282 "a living stopwatch": court testimony of Jeanne Loviton, 25 March, 1950, 4.

282 "strange, unhelpful answer": court testimony of Jeanne Loviton, 25 March, 1950, 5.

284 "written record of that night watchman": Definitive judgment by the Attorney General, 1 July 1950.

285 "I swear fidelity": Besson, *Le Mythe de la justice,* 259.

287 "maintenance of public order": Besson, *Le Mythe de la justice,* 364.

288 "the path of duty": Besson, *Le Mythe de la justice,* 181.

288   "to lie to himself": Besson, *Le Mythe de la justice*, 139.

288   "he alone would be the judge": Besson, *Le Mythe de la justice*, 141.

289   "a sovereign uniquely committed": Besson, *Le Mythe de la justice*, 360–61.

289   "impotence that is manifest": Besson, *Le Mythe de la justice*, 361.

289   "young and somewhat overcome": Beevor and Cooper, *Paris After the Liberation*, 110.

289   "he doesn't like Frenchmen": Beevor and Cooper, *Paris After the Liberation*, 116.

289   "In Bido Veritas": Beevor and Cooper, *Paris After the Liberation*, 116.

290   "only witness of Katyn": Pellissier, *Brasillach . . . le Maudit*, 388–89.

291   "engaged in clandestine activities": Pellissier, *Brasillach . . . le Maudit*, 330.

291   "accused Georges Bidault": For example, "interventions of all sorts to falsify the course of Justice" are cited in Cécile's Denoël's undated letter (probably written in July 1950) following the Definitive Judgment.

16: THE WINNERS TAKE ALL

293   "the guard's watching": Vitoux, *Céline*, 454.

294   "just as they killed Denoël": Céline, *Lettres de prison*, 21 March 1946, 75.

294   "it doesn't make sense": Céline, *Lettres de prison*, 30 March 1946, 87.

294   "even the eyes": Vitoux, *Céline*, 453.

294   "dead to the world": Céline, *Lettres de prison*, 7 April 1946, 101.

296   "What influence, what support": Vitoux, *Céline*, 478.

296   "duplicated at my expense": Céline, *Ferdinand furieux*, 90.

296   "mystifying/stupendous/amazing": Céline, *Ferdinand furieux*, 19.

296   "A farce": Céline, *Ferdinand furieux*, 135.

296   "dreams only of lawsuits": Céline, *Ferdinand furieux*, 24.

297   "a lot of goat shit": Céline, *Ferdinand furieux*, 134.

297   "power of a lord": Céline, *Ferdinand furieux*, 135.

297   "in open revolt": Cécile Denoël, letter to appellate court (July? 1950), 2.

298   "smells to high heaven": Lake, *Confessions of a Literary Archaeologist*, 178.

298   "treachery on all sides": Lake, *Confessions of a Literary Archaeologist*, 168.

302   "machine-gun fire": Ostrovsky, *Voyeur Voyant*, 199.

302   "disinterested dishonesty": Poulet, *Entretiens*, 22.

306   "a slipup": Vitoux, *Céline*, 571–18.

307   "Pin-brain-Trust": Céline, *Castle to Castle*, 10.

307   "we rattle wrong": Vitoux, *Céline*, 492.

307   "no cheap imitation": Céline, *Castle to Castle*, 111.

308   "her pseudonym, Jean Voilier": "le carnet du jour,"*Le Figaro*, 26 July 1996.

Bibliography

Allard, Paul. *Les Favorites de la IIIe République*. Paris: Les Editions de France, 1942.

Alméras, Philippe. *Céline: Entre haines et passions*. Paris: Editions Robert Laffont, 1994.

Archives de Paris (Villemoisson), Les. "Le Dossier de non-lieu du 28 juillet 1950," no. 1019W, carton 26.

Aron, Robert. *Histoire de l'Epuration: Des prisons clandestines aux tribunaux d'exception Septembre 1944–Juin 1949 (L'épuration politique)*. Paris: Fayard, 1969.

Artaud, Antonin. *The Cenci*. Translated by Simon Watson-Taylor. London: Calder and Boyars, 1969.

———. *Oeuvres complètes*. Paris: Editions Gallimard, 1971.

———. *Selected Writings*. Translated by Helen Weaver. New York. Farrar, Straus and Giroux, 1976.

Assouline, Pierre. *L'Epuration des intellectuals: 1944–1945*. Brussels: Editions complexe, 1985.

———. *Gaston Gallimard: A Half-Century of French Publishing*. Translated by Harold J. Salemson. New York: Harcourt Brace Jovanovich, 1988.

L'Aurore (Paris), "L'Assassinat de l'éditeur Denoël," 18 January 1950,8.

Bachelier, Christian, and Denis Peschanski. "L'Epuration de la magistrature sous Vichy." *L'Epuration de la magistrature de la Révolution à la Libération*. Paris: Editions Loysel, 1994.

Badinter, Robert. "Conclusion." *L'Epuration de la magistrature de la Révolution à la Libération*. Paris: Editions Loysel, 1994.

Bancaud, Alain, and Henry Rousso. "L'Epuration des magistrats à la Libération (1944–1945)." *L'Epuration de la magistrature de la Révolution à la Libération*. Paris: Editions Loysel, 1994.

Barber, Stephen. *Antonin Artaud: Blows and Bombs*. London: Faber and Faber, 1993.

Barillé, Elisabeth. *Anais Nin: Naked Under the Mask*. Translated by Elfreda Powell. London: Lime Tree, 1992.

Beauplan, Robert de. "La Menace au théâtre de la Renaissance," introduction to *La Menace* by Pierre Frondaie. Paris: La Petite Illustration, 1925.

Beckers, Robert. Sworn statement, 7 October 1946.

Beevor, Antony, and Artemis Cooper. *Paris After the Liberation: 1944–1949*. New York: Doubleday, 1994.

Bertholet, Denis. *Paul Valéry: 1871–1945*. Paris: Plon, 1995.

Besson, Antonin. Definitive Judgment 1 July 1950.

———. *Le Mythe de la justice*. Paris: Librairie Plon, 1973.

Bidault, Georges. *Resistance: The Political Autobiography of Georges Bidault*. Translated by Marianne Sinclair. New York: F. A. Praeger, 1967.

Bidault, Suzanne. *Je n'ai pas oublié* . . . Paris: La Table Ronde, 1971.

———. *Par une porte entrebaillée*. Paris: La Table Ronde, 1972.

———. *Souvenirs de guerre et d'occupation*. Paris: La Table Ronde, 1973.

Billy, André. *L'Epoque contemporain, 1905–1930*. Paris: Tallandier, 1956.

Birnbaum, Pierre. *Anti-Semitism in France: A Political History from Léon Blum to the Present*. Translated by Miriam Kochan. Oxford: Blackwell Publishers, 1992.

Blondiaux, Isabelle. "Louis-Ferdinand Céline et le diagnostic de paranoia." *Actes du Colloque international de Paris*. Paris: Du Lérot & Société des études céliniennes, 1992.

Blumenkranz, Bernard. *Histoire des Juifs en France*. Toulouse: Edouard Privat, 1972.

Bodin, Paul. "Commis voici plus de quatre ans le mystérieux assassinat de l'éditeur Robert Denoël revient à l'ordre du jour: Crime passionnel? Crime d'un rôdeur? Crime politique?" *Le Carrefour*, 17 January 1950, 3.

Boisdeffre, Pierre de. "Sur la postérité de Céline," *Les Cahiers de l'Herne* 2 (n.d.): 214.

Bosschère, Jean de. *Portraits d'Amis*. Paris: Editions Sagesse, 1935.

Bourdet, Edouard. *Vient de paraître*. Paris: La Petite Illustration, 1928.

Brassie, Anne. *Robert Brasillach ou Encore un instant de bonheur*. Paris: Editions Robert Laffont, 1987.

Brau, Jean-Louis. *Antonin Artaud*. Paris: La Table Ronde, 1971.

Braunschweig, André. "Les Fonctions de l'Epuration." *L'Epuration de la magistrature de la Révolution à la Libération*. Paris: Editions Loysel, 1994.

Brogan, D. W. *The Development of Modern France: 1870–1939*. Vol. 2. New York: Harper & Row, 1966.

Bruyneel, Maurice. Sworn statement, 20 September 1946.

Buckley, William K. *Critical Essays on Louis-Ferdinand Céline*. Boston: G. K. Hall, 1986.

Bulletin célinien, Le (monthly journal), year 8, no. 79, March 1989.

Cabanis, José. *Le Diable à la NRF: 1911–1951*. Paris: Editions Gallimard, 1996.

Cassou, Jean, "Poésie." *Les Nouvelles littéraires*. 27 July 1929, 12.

Ce Soir. "L'Éditeur Denoël assassiné hier soir rue de Grenelle," 4 December 1945, 1.

Céline, Louis-Ferdinand. *Bagatelles pour un massacre*. Paris: Editions Denoël, 1937.

———. *Castle to Castle*. Translated by Ralph Manheim. Normal, Ill.: Dalkey Archive Press, 1997.

———. *Conversations with Professor Y*. Translated by Stanford Luce. Bilingual edition. Hanover: University Press of New England (for Brandeis University Press), 1986.

———. *Death on the Installment Plan*. Translated by Ralph Manheim. New York: New Directions, 1966.

———. *L'Ecole des cadavres*. Paris: Editions Denoël, 1938.

———. *Ferdinand furieux: Avec trois cent treize lettres de Louis-Ferdinand Céline*. Edited by Pierre Monnier. Lausanne: Editions l'Age d'Homme, 1979.

———. *Journey to the End of the Night*. Translated by Ralph Manheim. New York: New Directions Publishing, 1983.

———. *Lettres à des amies*. Edited by Colin W. Nettelbeck. Paris: Editions Gallimard, 1979.

———. *Lettres des années noires*. Edited by Philippe Alméras. Paris: Berg International, 1994.

———. *Lettres à la N.R.F.: 1931–1961*. Edited by Pascal Fouché. Paris: Editions Gallimard, 1991.

———. *Lettres à son avocat: 118 Lettres inédites à Maître Albert Naud*. Edited by Frédéric Monnier. Paris: La Flute de Pan, 1984.

———. *Lettres de prison à Lucette Destouches & à Maître Mikkelsen: 1945–1947*. Edited by François Gibault. Paris: Editions Gallimard, 1998.

———. *North*. Translated by Ralph Manheim. Normal, Ill.: Dalkey Archive Press, 1996.

———. *Rigadoon*. Translated by Ralph Manheim. Normal, Ill.: Dalkey Archive Press, 1997.

Chalon, Jean. "La Gardienne du trésor." *Paul Valéry secret: Correspondance inédite adressée à Madame Jean Voilier*. Paris: Shiffer, 1982.

Charpier, Jacques. *Paul Valéry*. Paris: Editions Seghers, 1975.

Chélini, Jean. *"L'Eglise sous Pie XII: La Tourmente 1939–1945*. Paris: Fayard, 1983.

Combat. "Tout se sait. Un secret bien gardé," 3–4 December 1949, 2.

Dabit, Eugène, and Roger Martin du Gard. *Correspondance I (1927–1929).* Edited by Pierre Bardel. Paris: Editions du Centre National de la Recherche scientifique, 1986.

———. *L'Hôtel du Nord.* Paris: Editions Denoël, 1953.

———. *Journal intime: 1928–1936.* Edited by Pierre-Edmond Robert. Saint-Amand: Editions Gallimard, 1989.

D'Amat, Roman, *Dictionnaire de Biographie française.* Vol. 49. Paris: Librairie Letouzey et Ané, 1960.

D'Amat, Roman, and R. Limouzin-Lamothe. *Dictionnaire de Biographie française.* Paris: Librairie Letouzey et Ané, 1960.

Dank, Milton. *The French Against the French: Collaboration and Resistance.* Philadelphia and New York: J. B. Lippincott Company, 1974.

Denoël, Cécile. Sworn statement, 3 December 1945.

———. "Celui qui devait bouleverser la littérature entra chez nous un soir, presque clandestinement," *La Meuse* (Liège), 6 March 1973, 7.

———. Letter to appellate court, July? 1950.

———. Letter to Judge Ferdinand Gollety, 8 January 1950.

Denoël, Robert. Advertisement for *Bagatelles pour un massacre. Les Nouvelles littéraires,* 25 December 1937, 2.

———. "Apologie de 'Mort à crédit,' " *Les Cahiers de l'Herne,* no. 2, 234–236.

———. *Brouillon* (handwritten document in police dossier, submitted by Jeanne Loviton, 2 December 1946).

———. *Les Cahiers de l'Herne* 3 (1963): 26–27.

———. *Comment j'ai connu et lancé Louis-Ferdinand Céline.* N.p.: [1941]. Reprint. Paris: Van Bagaden, 1989.

———. Interview by Pierre Langers in 1936. *Les Critiques de notre temps et Céline.* Edited by Jean-Pierre Dauphin. Paris: Editions Garnier Frères, 1976.

———. Interview by André Roubaud, published under the title "L.-F. Céline." *Marianne,* 10 May 1939, 7.

———. "Louis-Ferdinand Céline: Le Contemporain capital." *Le Cahier jaune* I (November 1941): 4–5.

———. See also MARIN, ROBERT (pseudonym).

Dinar, André. *Fortune des livres.* Paris: Editions Nantal, 1939.

Domino, M. "Le 'poète maudit' chez lui." *l'Ordre de Paris,* 15–16 February 1948, 2.

Dorian, Max. "Céline rue Amélie." *Les Cahiers de l'Herne* 3 (1963): 25–27.

Dufay, Philippe. *Jean Giraudoux: Biographie.* Paris: Editions Julliard, 1993.

Durand-Auzias, Raymond. Sworn statement, 8 October 1946.

Aux Ecoutes. "Les Dessous d'une affaire retentissante," 20 January 1950, 6–7.

———. "La Succession Denoël," 7 May 1948, 12.

Ennetières, Elisabeth d'. *Nous, et les autres: Souvenirs d'un tiers de siècle avec Jean de Bosschère.* Aurillac: Editions du Centre, 1967.

Esslin, Martin. *Artaud.* London: John Calder, 1976.

Express-Dimanche. "Le Dossier secret de l'affaire Denoël," 30 April 1950, 1, 3.

———. "Le Scandale Denoël," 2 May 1950, 1.

———. "L'Affaire Denoël," 4 June 1950, 1.

Le Figaro. "le carnet du jour," 26 July 1996, 14.

———. "Non-lieu definitive dans l'affaire Denoël," 29 July 1950, 26.

———. "La Société d'éditions Denoël est acquittée," 2–3 May 1948, 4e.

First police investigation, 26 January 1946. In "le dossier de non-lieu du 28 juillet 1950," no. 1019W, carton 26.

Florenne, Yves. "Amour fou de M. Teste." *Paul Valéry secret: Correspondance inédite adressée de 1937 à 1945 à Madame Jean Voilier.* Paris: Shiffer, 1982.

Fodor, Eugene, ed. *Belgium and Luxembourg 1963* (Fodor's Modern Guides). New York: David McKay Company, 1963.

Fouché, Pascal. *L'Edition française sous l'Occupation: 1940–1944.* 2 vols. Mayenne: Bibliothèque de Littérature française contemporaine de l'Université de Paris 7, 1987.

———. *L'Histoire de l'édition française.* "L'Edition littéraire, 1914–1950." Vol 4: *Le livre concurrencé 1900–1950,* edited by Henri-Jean Martin, Rober Chartier, and Jean-Pierre Vivet. Paris: Promodis, 1986.

———. "Robert Denoël le Découvreur," *Livres hebdo* 355 (29 October 1999). 66–69.

Foyer, Jean. "Les Fonctions de L'Epuration." *L'Epuration de la magistrature de la Révolution à la Libération.* Paris: Éditions Loysel, 1994.

France-Soir. "Mme Denoël à *France-Soir*: 'J'ai la conviction que mon mari n'a pas été victime d'un rodeur,' " 14 January 1950, 3.

Frondaie, Pierre. *La Menace.* Introduction by Robert de Beauplan. Paris: La Petite Illustration, 1925.

Galtier-Boissière, Jean. *Journal: 1940–1950.* Paris: Quai Voltaire, 1992.

Gherra, Georges. "La justice a rouvert le dossier du meurtre de l'éditeur Denoël." *France-Soir.* 13 January 1950, 1, 3.

Gibault, François. *Céline.* Part 1: *Le Temps des espérances, (1894–1932);* Part 2: *Délires et persécutions (1932–1944);* Part 3: *Cavalier de l'Apocalypse (1944–1961).* Paris: Mercure de France, 1977, 1985, 1981.

Gibson, Hugh. *Belgium.* Doubleday, Doran & Company, 1939.

Gordon, Bertram M., ed. *Historical Dictionary of World War II France: The Occupation, Vichy, and the Resistance, 1938–1946.* Westport, Conn.: Greenwood Press, 1998.

Gouhier, Henri. *Antonin Artaud et l'essence du théâtre*. Paris: Librairie philosophique, 1974.

Greene, Naomi. *Antonin Artaud: Poet Without Words*. New York: Simon and Schuster, 1970.

Gregh, Fernand. *L'Age de fer*. Paris: Bernard Grasset, 1956.

Hayman, Ronald. *Artaud and After*. London: Oxford University Press, 1977.

Hewitt, Nicholas. *The Life of Céline: A Critical Biography*. Oxford: Blackwell Publishers, 1999.

Hindus, Milton. *The Crippled Giant: A Literary Relationship with Louis-Ferdinand Céline*. Hanover: University Press of New England (for Brandeis University Press), 1986.

Jaloux, Edmond. "L'Esprit des Livres." *Les Nouvelles littéraires*, 10 December 1932: 3.

Joseph, Lawrence. *Catherine Pozzi: Une Robe couleur du temps*. Paris: Editions de la Différence, 1988.

Kaplan, Alice Yaeger. *Reproductions of Banality: Fascism, Literature, and French Intellectual Life*. Minneapolis: University of Minnesota Press, 1986.

Kessel, Joseph. "Romans." *Les Nouvelles littéraires*, 15 May 1936, 5.

Kingston, Paul J. *Anti-Semitism in France During the 1930's: Organisations, Personalities and Propaganda*. Hull, England: University of Hull Press, 1983.

Knapp, Bettina L. *Antonin Artaud: Man of Vision*. New York: David Lewis, 1969.

——. *Céline: Man of Hate*. University, Alabama: University of Alabama Press, 1974.

Knowles, Dorothy. *French Drama of the Inter-War Years: 1913–1939*. London: Harrap, 1967.

Lagarde, Pierre. "Les Mille Visages de Pierre Frondaie." *Les Nouvelles littéraires*, 12 December 1936, 8.

Lake, Carlton. *Baudelaire to Beckett: A Century of French Art and Literature*. Austin: Humanities Research Center, University of Texas, 1976.

——. *Confessions of a Literary Archaeologist*. New York: New Directions Books, 1990.

Lanoux, Armand. *Paris 1925*. Paris: Bernard Grasset, 1975.

Lefèvre, Frédéric. "La Littérature et le peuple: Une heure avec Eugène Dabit romancier." *Les Nouvelles littéraires*. 27 December 1930, 1, 7.

——. "Une heure avec Pierre Frondaie." *Les Nouvelles littéraires*, 29 June 1935, 4, 6.

La Libération. "L'assassinat de l'éditeur Robert Denoël serait un crime crapuleux," 4 December 1945, 1.

Lottman, Herbert R. *The Left Bank: Writers, Artists, and Politics from the Popular Front to the Cold War*. Boston: Houghton Mifflin, 1982.

——. *The Purge*. New York: William Morrow and Company, 1986.

Loviton, Jeanne. Police and court testimony. In "le dossier de non-lieu du 28 juillet 1950," no. 1019W, carton 26. (See also VOILIER, JEAN.)

McCarthy, Patrick. *Céline*. New York: Viking, 1975.

Manouvriez, Abel. "La Volonté du mort: Querelle autour de l'épisode dramatique et balzacien de la cession des parts de la Société Denoël," 18 November 1949, 7.

Marcou, Lilly. *Elsa Triolet: Les Yeux et la Mémoire*. Paris: Librairie Plon, 1994.

Marin, Robert [Robert Denoël]. "Une Forte tête." *Le Disque vert*. Third year, fourth series. Paris/Brussels 1924 [or 1925?], 25–26.

———. "Si François usait . . ." *Sélection* 6 (March 1925): 360–78.

———. "Un homme de circonstances." *Sélection* 6 (March 1926): 275–92.

———. "Vers Louis Aragon." *Sélection* 6 (October 1926): 182–84.

Marriage certificate of Pierre Frondaie and Jeanne Loviton. Mairie of the Commune of Saint Raphaël, 8th arrondissement, Paris, 24 May 1927.

Mengelle, Catherine. Sworn statement, 16 January 1950.

Le Monde. "Assassinat de l'éditeur Robert Denoël," 4 December 1945: 8.

Monmarché, Marcel. *Belgique. (Les Guides bleus)*. Paris: Hachette, 1920.

Moremans, Victor. *La Meuse* (Liège) 6 March 1973, 7F.

Nadaud, François. "Louis-Ferdinand Céline ne rentrera pas en France." *L'Ordre de Paris*. 8–9 February 1948, 1, 3.

National Personnel Records Center, military personnel records for Bernard Steele.

Nin, Anaïs. *The Diary of Anaïs Nin: Volume One: 1931–1934*. ed. and intro. by Gunther Stuhlmann. New York: The Swallow Press and Harcourt, Brace & World, Inc. (A Harvest Book), 1966.

———. *Incest: From a Journal of Love: The Unexpurgated Diary of Anaïs Nin, 1931–1934*. New York: Harcourt Brace Jovanovich, 1992.

Nordmann, [no first name cited]. "Intervention de Maître Nordmann, Membre de la Commission d'Épuration en 1944–1946." *L' Epuration de la magistrature de la Révolution à la Libération*. Paris: Editions Loysel, 1994.

Les Nouvelles littéraires. 20 August 1927, 2.

———. 18 October 1930, 7.

———. 15 October 1932, 2.

———. 25 December 1937, 2.

———. "Femme de sport," 12 November 1927, 2.

O'Connell, David. *Louis-Ferdinand Céline*. Amherst: Twayne Publishers, 1976.

Ostrovsky, Erika. *Voyeur Voyant: A Portrait of Louis-Ferdinand Céline*. New York: Random House, 1971.

Paicheler, Geneviève. *L'Invention de la psychologie moderne*. Paris, L'Harmattan, 1992.

Peeters, Benoît. *Paul Valéry: Une Vie d'écrivain?* Paris: Les Impressions nouvelles, 1989.

Pellissier, Pierre. *Brasillach . . . le maudit*. Paris: Editions Denoël, 1989.

Peloux, Jean. "Quand Paul Valéry l'Assomptionniste imitait Pétrarque." *Le Figaro*, 15 October 1971, 32.

Picq, Auguste. Sworn statement, 18 September 1946.

———. Sworn statement, 1 February 1950.

———. Sworn statement 3. In *Rapport de 25 mai 1950*, 14–15.

Piédelièvre, Dr. *Rapport medico-legal (le corps de Robert Denoël)*, 7 December 1945.

Plunka, Gene A., ed. *Antonin Artaud and the Modern Theater*. Rutherford: Fairleigh Dickinson University Press, 1994.

Poulet, Robert. *Le Caleidoscope: Trente-neuf portraits d'écrivains suivi de Flèches du Parthe*. Lausanne: Editions l'Age d'homme, 1982.

———. *Ce n'est pas une vie*. Paris: Editions Denoël, 1976.

———. *Entretiens familiers avec L.-F. Céline suivis d'un chapitre inédit de* casse-pipe. Paris: Librairie Plon, 1958.

———. *Louis Ferdinand Céline: Robert Denoël ou l'édition à qui perd gagne toujours*. Edited by Pierre Aelberts. Liège: Editions nationales, 1981.

———. *Partis Pris*. Brussels/Paris: Les Ecrits, 1943.

"Pressentiments." *Les Nouvelles littéraires*, 6 December 1945, 4.

Prévost, M., Roman D'Amat, and H. Tribout de Morembert. *Dictionnaire de Biographie française*. Vol. 15. Paris: Librairie Letouzey et Ané, 1980.

Putnam, Samuel. *The World of Jean de Bosschère*. N.p.: The Fortune Press, [1931?].

Rebatet, Lucien. *Les Mémoires d'un fasciste I, Les Décombres/Les Mémoires d'un fasciste II, 1941–1947*. 2 vols. in one. Paris: Pauvert, 1976.

Rim, Carlo. *Le Grenier d'Arlequin: journal, 1916–1940*. Paris: Editions Denoël, 1981.

Robert, Pierre-Edmond. *Céline et les éditions Denoël: 1932–1948*. Epinal: IMEC Editions, 1991.

———. *D'un Hôtel du Nord l'autre: Eugène Dabit 1898–1936*. Paris: Bibliothèque de Littérature française contemporaine de l'Université, 1967.

Roland-Lévy, Pierre. Letter to *Express-Dimanche* on 27 May 1950, and printed in *Express-Dimanche*. 4 June 1950, 1.

———. Letter to police, 3 December 1945.

Rozelaar, Armand. Letters to the court. In "le dossier de non-lieu du 28 juillet 1950," no. 1019W, carton 26.

Second police investigation, 15 November 1946. In "le dossier de non-lieu du 28 juillet 1950," no. 1919W, carton 26.

Shirer, William L. *The Rise and Fall of the Third Reich*. New York: Crest Books, 1960.

Talvart, Hector, and Joseph Peace. *Bibliographie des Auteurs modernes de langue française: 1801–1927*. Paris: Editions de la Chronique des lettres française, 1933.

Third police investigation, 25 May 1950. In "le dossier de non-lieu du 28 juillet 1950," no. 1019W, carton 26.

Trarieux, Gabriel. "De la Scène au roman: Pierre Frondaie." *Les Nouvelles littéraires.* 23 May 1925: 1.

Tréolleyre, Jean Marc. "La Succession de M Pierre Roland-Lévy." *Le Monde,* 20 October 1951, 6.

Valéry, Paul. *Cahiers.* vols. 19–29. Paris: Centre national de la recherche scientifique, 1957.

———. *Paul Valéry secret: Correspondance inédite adressée de 1937 à 1945 à Madame Voilier.* Paris: Shiffer, 1982.

———. *Poèmes secrets inédits: suivis de fragments de lettres inédites.* Paris: Chez Monsieur Teste, n.d.

———. *Poésies.* Paris: Editions Gallimard (NRF), 1958.

Vialar, Paul. *L'Enfant parmi les hommes: Souvenirs.* Paris: Editions Albin Michel, 1990.

Virmaux, Alain, and Odette Virmaux. *Artaud: un bilan critique.* Paris: Pierre Belfond, 1979.

Vitoux, Frédéric. *Céline.* Paris: Pierre Belfond, 1987.

———. *Céline: A Biography.* Translated by Jesse Browner. New York: Paragon House, 1992.

Voilier, Jean [Jeanne Loviton]. *Jours de lumière.* Paris: Émile-Paul Frères, 1938.

———. *Ville ouverte.* Paris: Émile-Paul Frères, 1942.

Walzer, Pierre-Olivier. "Valéry secret." *Paul Valéry poèmes secrets (1937–1945): Lettres intimes, poèmes inédits.* Paris: Schiffer, 1982.

Wiser, William. *The Crazy Years: Paris in the Twenties.* New York: Atheneum, 1983.

Index